Woeful Afflictions

Woeful Afflictions

Disability and Sentimentality in Victorian America

Mary Klages

PENN

University of Pennsylvania Press

Philadelphia

Copyright © 1999 University of Pennsylvania Press
All rights reserved
Printed in the United States of America on acid-free paper

10 9 8 7 6 5 4 3 2 1

Published by
University of Pennsylvania Press
Philadelphia, Pennsylvania 19104–4011

Library of Congress Cataloging-in-Publication Data

Klages, Mary.
   Woeful afflictions : disability and sentimentality in Victorian
America / Mary Klages.
      p.   cm.
   Includes bibliographical references (p.   ) and index.
   ISBN 0-8122-3499-5 (acid-free paper)
   1. Handicapped — United States — History — 19th century.
2. Handicapped — United States — Public Opinion.   3. Handicapped in
mass media — History.   4. Handicapped in literature — History and
criticism.   5. Public opinion — United States.   I. Title.
HV1553.K53   1999
362.4'0973'09034 — dc21   99-19317
                                                                   CIP

For my mother,
who didn't live to see this finished
and for Tasha, who did

Contents

Illustrations

Introduction: Disability and Sentimentality

I am not disabled, at least, not in the way that word is currently understood. "Disability," in legal, medical, and educational discourses in late twentieth-century American culture, designates a socially-constructed category that groups together people with a wide variety of physical and mental differences, including limb deficiencies, neuromuscular and orthopedic dysfunctions, sensory impairment, mental impairment (including both mental illness and mental retardation), and chronic or terminal illness. I fall into none of these categories.

There is, however, a personal component to my scholarly interest in disability. My younger sister Sally was born with Down Syndrome, and thus I grew up experiencing first-hand the various ways our culture conceives of the social meanings of disability. Because Down Syndrome, in addition to causing mental retardation, creates a distinctive set of physical characteristics, I learned early on that people with visibly different bodies are treated as alien, as "other." I learned too that nondisabled people react to that otherness with combinations of wonder, fear, disgust, horror, curiosity, and even sexual interest.

My sister, now an adult, works in a college cafeteria, and also serves as an associate board member for the National Down Syndrome Congress as well as a spokesperson for local Down Syndrome associations. She talks to large and small groups about "self-advocacy." She exemplifies the ability of disabled people to speak for themselves, and to be represented and respected as knowledgeable adults who can articulate their own needs, feelings, and complaints without the intervention or interpretation of nondisabled people, whether parents, guardians, or professionals. The strength of organizations like the National Down Syndrome Congress lies in their insistence on bringing together people with disabilities, people who work with disabilities — doctors, psychologists, teachers — and families affected by disabilities, creating networks in which the disabled person becomes a participant in working to solve his or her own problems, rather than the passive recipient of custodial care.

According to disability rights activists, including Sally, one of the main difficulties faced by disabled people has been their inability to speak for themselves, and be listened to, about their condition. Rather, since the first efforts to integrate disabled people into mainstream culture in the late eighteenth century, disabled people have existed largely as "poster children." They have served as silent spectacles, images to be viewed by the non-disabled, whose importance has been in their ability to appear pathetic and to produce a sympathetic or sentimental response in nondisabled people. They have, as a result, been relegated to the status of permanent children, defined by their perceived dependence on the nondisabled. Like children, they are assumed to need protection, whether in the form of individual guardianship or of special laws governing their educational and economic existence. Until the efforts to integrate disabled people into mainstream schools and jobs gained widespread legislative and popular support in the 1970s, the education of the handicapped in segregated schools and their employment in segregated "sheltered workshops" created what disability rights activists have called a system of "apartheid." "Special" education and treatment perpetuated the cultural conception of disabled people as "other," as pathetic spectacles, as dependent children — not as adults, and certainly not as sexual beings.[1]

As disability rights activist Laura Hershey has commented, representations of disabled people as perpetual "poster children" work to reinforce the cultural conception of them as passive and wretched. Reducing disabled people to "the status of tragic figures," these images "posit compassion and generosity as the 'remedy' for our supposed suffering."[2] In constructing a public conception of disabled people as necessarily dependent sufferers, these images preclude any alternative understandings of the meanings of disability and of the psychological effects of disability on an adult sense of self. Confined within images that present them always as childlike or feminized in their dependence on others' compassion, disabled people have found it difficult to establish themselves as effective social actors.

One of the goals of the disability rights movement, modeled after the campaigns for equality and civil rights for women and for people of color, is to break the associations between disability, dependence, and sympathy by advocating and creating new images that present disabled people as capable of autonomy and self-determination, as people who are neither confined nor defined by their bodies. Drawing on theories of the social construction of race and gender, disability rights theorists specify a distinction between "disability," a bodily configuration, and "handicap," a set of social relations or meanings assigned to a particular bodily configuration. The predominant meanings of disability in contemporary U.S. culture center around the notion of disabilities as limitations, things that bodies cannot do, constructing disability as abnormality and as dysfunction. The identities or forms of selfhood available to "handicapped" people are thus entirely circumscribed by the limitations of their disabled bodies; "handicapped" individuals are defined, in dominant cultural representations, as the product of their defective physicality, hence as dependent, helpless, pitiful, and deserving of charity and compassion.

When the disabled body and the handicapped self are inscribed as deficient and dependent, disabled people are aligned with other social groups perceived as needing supervision, assistance, and guardianship. The idea of autonomy and independence, central to most psychological definitions of healthy adult selfhood, is premised on the presumption of physical independence, of a self that embodies its own freedom in its very movements. In the absence of such bodily autonomy there is little basis for assuming any other forms of autonomy; hence disabled people who have limited independence of movement are also often subject to limited independence of decision-making and self-governance. Disability rights activists point to several important areas where the ideas of bodily-based autonomy have infringed on the basic civil rights of disabled people, including the right to make one's own decisions about sexuality and reproduction, the right to equal access to education and employment, and the right to vote.[3]

Laura Hershey insists in her analysis of the fund-rasing images of disabled people that the "liberation" of disabled people from their status as "poster children" depends on changing both practices and ideas about disability. Disabled people are discriminated against by both physical and attitudinal barriers. Material practices can be changed by legislation (such as laws requiring wheelchair accessibility and the availability of telecommunications devices for deaf people and blind people), but attitudinal barriers require the revision of cultural images and meanings. "Images of misfortune reinforce our dependency," Hershey concludes; "the idea of powerlessness contributes to the fact of powerlessness."[4] What limits disabled people is not the physical conditions of their bodies but the social interpretations or meanings of those bodies and the confinement of definitions and assumptions of selfhood to those interpretations.

This study examines the ways various sets of social meanings and interpretations have been assigned to disabled bodies, which then serve as "signs" or signifiers of particular cultural values. It begins by looking at efforts for the education of the deaf and blind in the middle of the eighteenth century, and concentrates on the meanings associated particularly with blind bodies through the nineteenth century in the United States. The first efforts to educate (and hence redeem) disabled people, to fit them into existing models of independent adult selfhood, focused on problems of educating blind and deaf people; the "crippled" and "spastic" did not attract attention as an identifiable group, and hence did not have special schools designed for their particular needs, until the end of the nineteenth century. These efforts, occurring at the same time, with the same motives, and often involving the same people as the more widely recognized efforts directed at slavery, women's rights, prison and asylum reform, and educational reform, labeled disabled people specifically as "afflicted," as people who suffered from different configurations of the bodies that defined and delimited their social roles.[5] By mid-century, the scientization and professionalization of institutional care for the disabled began to produce images of disabled people as defective, as failed humans, and thus as a class distinct from, and inferior to, nondisabled people; these depictions marked a separation between the professional and the popular cultural sentimental views of disabled people, which continued to portray them as "afflicted."

By the end of the century, disabled people were classified in professional representations with social deviants of all sorts, and labeled as part of the "defective, dependent, and delinquent" classes. By the early twentieth century, with the first efforts to mainstream disabled children in special classes in public schools, disabled people became "the handicapped." The increased efforts beginning in the mid-1970s to integrate disabled people fully into all areas of American cultures shifted the designation of this group of people to "the disabled"; with the campaigns of the disability rights movement and the increased attention given since then to the power of popular cultural labeling, disability became embroiled in what some call the "political correctness" battles, and labels such as "differently abled" and "physically challenged" appeared as attempts to erase pejorative connotations from the language describing disability.[6]

These names, from "afflicted" to "differently abled," reflect the history of attitudinal barriers — the ideologies of disability that set parameters for the cultural meanings ascribed to disabled bodies, and hence set limits on efforts to integrate disabled people into the mainstream population. The history of disabled people in the United States in the nineteenth century shows a continual struggle to understand the meaning of disabled bodies and their differences from "normal" bodies. That history has striking parallels to the Victorian histories of other people defined by their "abnormal" bodies, including women, people of color, and invalids. As Diane Price Herndl argues in her study of feminine illness in American culture, the status of the body defines the status of the person; a body defined as "invalid," as weak and dysfunctional, creates a certain mode of selfhood, and thus a certain set of cultural roles, expectations, and images, for the person so designated.[7] Other recent studies of the relation between bodily configurations and forms of selfhood have focused on the ways identity is framed as either a product of or a transcendence of the body. Scholars investigating the cultural constructions of racialized and gendered bodies, including Karen Sánchez-Eppler, Laura Wexler, Shirley Samuels, and Joy Kasson, have argued that various nineteenth-century discourses attempted to relocate identity outside the body in order to escape the physical configuration's determination of identity and selfhood; thus both abolitionist and feminist discourses countered the inscription of the black and the female body as an incontrovertible signifier of otherness and inferiority by attempting to define selfhood as a product of something other than physical being.[8]

The primary arena for such nineteenth-century attempts at reshaping the cultural meanings of different bodies, these scholars note, is sentimental forms of representation, both fictional and nonfictional. As Samuels argues, "body" and "identity" appear "as objects of struggle, not fixed terms" in sentimental texts. Sentimental representations actively debate the question of where "identity gets located, in the heart or on the skin, in the interior or on the exterior?"[9] For disabled people, as for women, invalids, and people of color, the main vehicle for representing the relationship between body and self or identity has been the sentimental mode. Race and gender, like disability, were represented in sentimental conventions for particular political purposes in nineteenth-century American discourse, but the sentimentality associated with disability did not work directly to "liberate" disabled people. Rather, sentimental representations of disabled people provided a particular model of selfhood within which a disabled body could become something more than just a "poster" arousing the compassion of able-bodied others. This model, however, also created strict limits to the cultural meanings and functions of disabled bodies. Sentimental representations persisted into the twentieth century and have served to confine representations of disabled people within narrow parameters.

This study expands the ideas offered by recent scholars on embodiment, identity, and sentimentality by locating disability as sets of cultural meanings defined and articulated in two main public areas in nineteenth-century American culture: the reports of professional institutions founded

for the protective care and education of the disabled, focusing on the segregated schools formed in the antebellum period for the education of the deaf
and the blind, and the pages of domestic and popular cultural representations, in fiction, biography, and autobiography, of people with disabilities.

The first attempts to fit the deaf and the blind into ablebodied norms
focused on normalizing, erasing, transcending, or marginalizing the differences between disabled and nondisabled bodies. These efforts hoped to
assert the equality of the subjectivity of disabled people by erasing the
sources of their difference from the nondisabled. When these efforts failed,
representations of disability, like those of race and gender, relied on sentimental forms to reinscribe the cultural meanings of different bodies. Both
public reports and popular cultural representations placed disabled people
in what Gillian Brown has described as the female subculture of "self-denial
and collectivity," which fostered the "ethos of sympathy" characteristic of
sentimentality.[10] This subculture, which Brown argues is coterminous with
the domestic sphere, creates a mode of subjectivity defined by something
other than the self-interest prominent in the self, conceived as masculine,
that operates with the economic and political spheres.

Within this domestic female subculture arises an empathic sensibility, a
form of selfhood oriented toward emotionality and toward a recognition of
weakness, dependence, and physical differences, as a means not of denying
but of marking adult human status. This empathic selfhood was first articulated by the eighteenth-century moral philosophers, including Hume and
Adam Smith, and the Scottish Common Sense philosophers, particularly
Thomas Reid; their delineations of the genesis and development of the
capacity for "fellow-feeling" became an integral part of the ideologies of
domesticity and True Womanhood in the nineteenth century. Within the
domestic sphere that creates the empathic self, humans are recognized as
fundamentally embodied, but the significance of those bodies is inscribed
through their ability to feel for (and act on behalf of) the weak or dependent or suffering, rather than through their genitalia, skin color, sensory
apparatus, or capacity for rationality. Empathic subjectivity is defined as a
fundamentally embodied and also universal form of self, one that considers
bodies similar on the basis of their capacity to feel and express emotions.
The body is framed as a site not of sexuality, productive labor, or rationality,
but of feeling for others and acting to help others.

While other definitions of adult selfhood placed disabled people, defined by their ineradicable bodily differences, inevitably in the position of
"other," as abnormal, the empathic model produced new possibilities of

selfhood for the disabled. Disabled people continued to function as images to encourage and strengthen the empathic capacities of the ablebodied. In addition, however, they were increasingly depicted as fully able to transcend their own "woeful afflictions" in order to feel for, and act to relieve, the suffering of others, and hence able to be included in definitions of empathic adulthood.

My study examines how sentimental forms of representation in Victorian America framed conceptions of disability in attempting to create new meanings for disabled bodies and new ideas about disabled selfhood. Starting with the premise that disabled people have always functioned as "posters" that generate a particular response in ablebodied viewers, I argue that Victorian portrayals of disability worked to expand and rewrite that function, insisting that disabled people could be more than just bearers of cultural meaning. Examining the ways fictional and institutional discourses constructed notions of disability, I show that both employ sentimental conventions to represent disabled people as "posters," as empathic actors, and eventually as selves who can speak and write about their own experiences. The movement from sign to writing subject offers disabled people new models for adulthood in the framework of sentimentality, even while that framework bars them from acceding to other forms of adulthood, including economic and sexual independence.

My investigation of the sentimentality of representations of disability in nineteenth-century American culture focuses primarily on depictions of blindness. Deafness and blindness were the two most recognizable forms of disability, the only forms that generated special institutional concern until the latter half of the nineteenth century; as such, they are the most widely represented forms of disability in Victorian culture. Blindness is more prevalent than deafness. It was considered the more "pathetic" form of disability; it also generated more popular cultural representations because of the obstacles lack of vision posed in an industrializing and consumer-based culture increasingly oriented toward visual perceptions as defining adult subjectivity. While scholars have done a magnificent job in recovering the history of the deaf in America, through studies focusing on the institutions formed for deaf education, the communities formed by deaf people themselves, and the debates about sign language versus oral speech in the nineteenth century, there has been comparatively little attention paid to nineteenth-century writings about blindness. By examining the Annual Reports of the first school for the blind in the United States, the Perkins Institution, as well as popular cultural depictions of blindness, I show how institutional and popular/fictional discourses constructed the social meanings of blindness which determined public attitudes toward blind people.

Chapter 1 examines the attitudes toward blindness, and toward disability in general, in the middle of the eighteenth century, focusing on how philosophical questions concerning the relation between sensory perception and mental functioning spurred the first attempts of educators to discover methods for teaching blind and deaf students. The materialist philosophies that follow Descartes in positing a necessary connection between sensory perception and consciousness prompted educators to experiment with alternate methods to teach blind people to read and write, but also concluded that those lacking a sense could never achieve an intellectual state equal to that of a full-facultied person. These materialist philosophies stand in contrast to the moral philosophers, such as Hume, who investigated the workings of the heart and the emotions rather than the intellect. I argue that these moral philosophers, in articulating the fundamental premises of sentimentalism, offered a new conception of selfhood that did not depend on sensory perception, and thus offered a new means to represent blind and deaf people as fully human.

Chapter 2 turns to the Annual Reports of the Perkins Institution for the Blind and the first attempts in the United States to educate blind people to become productive citizens. Finding that the specifics of their embodiment barred them from full participation in industrialized market relations, Samuel Gridley Howe — the first Director of the Perkins Institution and a pioneer in the education of the blind, deaf, deaf-blind, and mentally retarded — constructed the blind as entirely abnormal, as unsuited for economic production or sexual reproduction. He argued that the blind should be relegated to the domestic sphere, where the dependence created by their disability would always find a compassionate response.

Chapter 3 shows how fictional representations of disability use some of Howe's logic about the incompatibility of blindness and market relations, and agree in placing blind people within the domestic sphere; these fictions, however, using sentimental conventions about the power of weakness and suffering to generate an empathic response, refuse to confine disabled people to the home. Rather, they show disabled people functioning in the public realm, working to reform the hardhearted values of the marketplace by prompting the ablebodied to respond with sympathetic concern to the sign of suffering and misery the disabled body bears. Chapter 4 continues to investigate how sentimental popular fiction rewrites the institutionally constructed meanings of blindness by focusing on the question of whether a blind character can function as anything more than such a "poster" to arouse the empathic emotions of others. A detailed examination of Maria Cummins's novel *The Lamplighter* discusses how sentimental fictions in general operate to create empathic feelings in readers, and how the blind heroine of the novel specifically provides a model of empathic agency for readers to emulate.

Chapter 5 returns to the institutional discourse on the blind, showing how Howe uses sentimental conventions to construct a new definition of the social utility of his blind students. Having found them, by virtue of their defective bodies, unfit for economic production or sexual reproduction, Howe places them in a domestic context and discovers their capacity to arouse sympathy in others and to be empathic agents in their own right. Using sentimental strategies to represent the blind students, Howe discovers ways to normalize them, to create identifications between his students and the sighted people who read his Annual Reports. Chapter 6 looks at Howe's representations of the most famous disabled person in Victorian America, deaf-blind Laura Bridgman, as he attempts to use sentimental conventions to frame Bridgman both as a "poster" and as an empathic agent. His efforts to claim a sentimental or empathic form of adulthood for Bridgman, however, falter on his own doubts about the limitations of her deafness and blindness, particularly in regard to her ability to use language adequately.

The question of language usage, and whether disabled people can become adequate speaking and writing subjects, is the topic of Chapter 7, which examines two autobiographies by blind women. Both use sentimental conventions to present their authors as "posters," as empathic agents, and as writing selves. One also uses the devices of slave narratives to present blindness as a form of social oppression and autobiographical representation as a means of resistance; the other insists that the significance of writing is to create an idealized sentimental world as a reality, rather than to protest against an existing reality. These themes arise again in Chapter 8's discussion of sentimental representations of Helen Keller, which summarize, at the end of the nineteenth century, the existing meanings for, and debates about, disabled selfhood. The final chapter examines the attempts in the 1950s to discard the sentimental representation of disability through a reading of *The Miracle Worker*, William Gibson's play about Helen Keller which was made into an Academy-award-winning film. This chapter returns to questions concerning embodiment, language use, and sentimentality in representing the possibilities for disabled selfhood.

I

The Semiotics of Disability

Disability in various forms has always existed both as a particular physical condition for individuals and as a cultural sign or signifier, a condition operating within a semiotic system and having reference or meaning to ideas beyond the existence of the individual. Notions of disability have traditionally been part of a system of "marking," a way of distinguishing individuals based on bodily configuration or capacity; blindness or a crippled limb, in pre-Enlightenment Europe as in many non-Western civilizations, was considered a mark or sign placed on an individual by a deity.[1] Cultures differed widely as to whether they interpreted the sign as a mark of favor or of punishment. The meanings of various types of disability differed from culture to culture and age to age, but disability remained (and perhaps still remains) a signifying system, a semiotic as well as a physical condition.

The cultural meanings of disability depend largely on the framework or contextual system in which disabilities appear. In Greek and Roman societies they were explained and given significance in reference to the gods: a disability was usually a mark of punishment for some transgression against a deity, but often the disabled person was also compensated for the handicap with some extra skill or power. Hephaestus, for example, after being crippled by Zeus, was given the ability to forge beautiful objects. The graver the disability the greater the compensation, and blindness, considered the most miserable affliction because of the physical helplessness it inflicted on the bearer, was likely to be balanced by the most impressive gifts, the ones most resembling the powers of the gods, such as Tiresias's gift of prophecy. While blindness in literature was figured as a fate worse than death, evoking pity from the sighted audience, it also became associated with a mysterious otherworldly power, beyond mortal ken.[2]

The Old Testament attitude toward disability also figured blindness as the most grievous affliction and therefore deserving of special care and consideration.[3] The four types of disabilities mentioned in the Talmud and

Midrash — deafness, dumbness, lameness, and blindness — are all considered unclean, but blindness is the most severe affliction. The New Testament singles out disabled people, especially the blind, as particularly wretched outcasts who thus gain Christ's attention; he repeatedly urges his followers to include these "unclean" people in their worship and makes special effort to cure their conditions.[4] The value of the blind in the Christian framework was twofold: the restoration of their sight provided an opportunity to demonstrate God's power to perform miracles, and the contrast between blindness and sight served as an analogy between disbelief and faith. The uncured blind meanwhile retained their status as miserable creatures, and their inclusion in Christ's sympathies symbolized the Christian focus on care and concern for "the least of these."

In the Middle Ages, the significance of disability retained many of its classical features: disabled people were often regarded as being punished for some sin and as having some supernatural powers (whence the idea of touching a hunchback's hump for luck, for example). To the religious, disabled people represented particular opportunities to practice the charity enjoined by Christ, as well as souls to be saved. To the aristocracy, however, disability had an additional significance: as a source of amusement, dwarves, cripples, idiots, and deaf and blind people were often features of court life.[5]

These various meanings of disability — as punishment, as supernatural, as pitiable, and as amusement — persisted into the modern period. During the European Enlightenment, however, disability began to take on new significance. Philosophers' interest in the relations between sensory perception and mental functioning provided a new context within which deafness and blindness became anomalies that had scientific value. The attention to the mental condition of those with sensory anomalies, and the information they could provide about those with normal senses, attracted the notice of educational and social reformers, who used the philosophers' speculations to formulate plans for the education of the deaf and the blind. The combination of the Christian ethos of charity and sympathy and the Enlightenment interest in education and improvement resulted in yet another new context and cultural meaning for disability, that of suffering humans trapped within defective bodies and needing to be rescued by the earnest efforts of educators. This last would become the dominant mode of representation of disability throughout the nineteenth and well into the twentieth century.

In 1771, Valentin Haüy, passing by the Café St. Ovide in Paris, heard a caterwauling of badly-played musical instruments accompanied by raucous laughter. Curious, Haüy discovered that the café's "orchestra" consisted of ten blind men, wearing outsized leather glasses, dunce caps with pasteboard asses' ears, and ridiculous costumes, with roughly-made musical "scores" propped on stands before them. As Haüy watched, the mocking crowd in the café threw money to the blind performers, who scrambled eagerly after the sound of the coins, knocking down the music stands, chairs, and one another in their frantic efforts. This scene, according to Haüy's reminiscences, first inspired him to do something to help save blind people from humiliating beggary; in 1784 in Paris he opened the first organized school for the blind, L'Institution Nationale des Jeunes Aveugles.[6]

The blind men whose plight moved Haüy were performing more than bad music: they were performing a set of existing cultural meanings of disability. The asses' ears pointed to their status as inhuman, as animalistic, while the dunce caps further labeled them as subhuman, as idiotic. The outsized leather eyeglasses framed and exaggerated their blindness, making their disability into a spectacle (in both senses of the word). Their inability to produce recognizable music from their instruments provided a display of incompetence, and their wild scrabbling for coins they could not see highlighted their poverty and their need to beg for subsistence. The laughter of the crowd and the money they threw marked their enjoyment of this performance of disability and their eagerness to participate as an audience for the spectacle of disability presented by the blind men.

This performance of disability as a spectacle of mockery and derision summarizes the idea that disability served as a sign labeling the bearer as outcast and an object of ridicule. The absurdly costumed beggars received payment for displaying themselves as freaks, and their antics were as much a source of amusement as those of the insane inmates of Bedlam. The blind beggars were aligned with the class of bodily exotics—including dwarves, people with acute physical deformities, and people from different ethnicities, including Africans and Asians—who were frequently displayed for the amusement and amazement of the aristocratic classes.[7]

These displays of bodily exoticism (whether innate, as for dwarves, or self-inflicted, as for people with tattoos) would continue to be a profitable source of public amusement well into the twentieth century, in various forms from P. T. Barnum's "museum" to carnival sideshows, but by the middle of the nineteenth century the blind, deaf, and simply crippled were no longer included in such displays.

In part as a result of Valentin Haüy's efforts, certain categories of disability became "normalized," or normalizable. As the description of the blind beggars shows, by the latter half of the eighteenth century the mere fact of blindness was not sufficient to label blind people as freaks and allow them to earn money for the simple display of their disabilities; the costumes and devices worn by the beggars are needed to exacerbate their status as freaks. As educational facilities became more available for blind and for deaf people, and as orthopedic medicine turned more attention to the alleviation of various neuromuscular conditions, these forms of disability became normalizable. The inhabitants (or prisoners) of the sideshow, whom we would now recognize as disabled, included the less- or non-normalizable forms of bodily configuration, such as dwarfism, giantism, severe obesity, excess bodily hair, microcephaly and hydrocephaly, sex ambiguities, and forms of twinism.[8] (Non-normalizable forms of ethnicity were also commonly displayed as "freaks," including "pygmies," "cannibals," and "Aztecs.") The difference between being a freak and being disabled lay almost entirely in the meanings assigned to the person rather than in any physical or mental quality per se. "A freak was defined not by the possession of any particular quality but by a set of practices, a way of thinking about and presenting people with major, minor, and fabricated physical, mental, and behavioral differences."[9]

The formation of schools to educate blind people and deaf people, first founded in the late eighteenth century, provided the means to begin the transformation of the practices that had defined disabled people as freaks. Hoping to substitute skills in manufacturing and music for the mere exhibition of blindness as a means to generate income, Haüy consulted the works of philosophers who had studied the effects of blindness on mental functioning in order to understand the best methods to use in educating blind people. He found a wealth of material available, as blindness had had particular fascination for Western philosophers since Descartes's studies of optics and the mechanics of vision in the sixteenth century.

The transformation of the cultural meaning, or discursive construction, of blindness begins with John Locke's speculations about the ways blindness as an anomaly might illuminate the relation between sensory perception and cognition. His insistence that the mind was essentially the product of sensory perception became central to virtually all conceptions of how the human mind operated. His postulation of what became known as "Molyneux's problem," after Irish philosopher William Molyneux, provided the foundation for ideas about sight and cognition articulated by Berkeley, Leibniz, Condillac, Voltaire, and Diderot, all of whose works on the mechanisms of vision informed the founders of the first schools for the blind. "Molyneux's problem," as stated in Locke's *Essay Concerning Human Understanding* (c. 1690), asked whether a person born blind, whose vision was restored, could recognize by sight objects previously known only by touch. Locke answered "no," as did his successors Berkeley, Condillac, and Voltaire, arguing that each sense provided some specific form of knowledge to the mind, and that the newly-sighted person would have no frame of reference within which to understand the information provided by sight in relation to the information provided by touch.

Locke and Berkeley settled for armchair speculations about the mental operations of blind people; they did not consult blind people themselves, nor did they attempt to incorporate advances in ophthalmology and surgery into their conceptions. In the early eighteenth century, however, ophthalmic surgeons were experimenting with methods of cataract removal that would provide empirical evidence to answer Molyneux's problem. British surgeon William Cheselden successfully removed the congenital cataracts of a thirteen-year-old boy in 1728, and published his account of his techniques, *The Theory of Vision Vindicated and Explained*, in 1733. Voltaire, familiar with Locke and Berkeley's analyses, reported on Cheselden's experiments in his *Elements of Newton's Philosophy* (1738), noting that they confirmed Locke's and Berkeley's conclusions: the boy could not recognize by sight objects, such as his cat, which he had known by touch.[10]

This discussion prompted Denis Diderot to seek out a similar surgery in France, in order to witness for himself the effects of the restoration of sight on one born blind. Unable to find such a surgery, however, Diderot resolved to answer his questions about blindness by a radically new method: he interviewed a blind man about his own experiences and ideas. Diderot presented the results of his interview with Msr. Lenotre, known as "the blind man of Puiseaux," in his *Lettre sur les aveugles* in 1749.[11]

The philosophical investigations of the relation between sensory perception and mental functioning framed sensory disability, particularly blindness, as a kind of laboratory, a place where empirical investigations and experimentation could provide useful knowledge about the condition of the nondisabled. This philosophical construction of the social meaning of blindness removed blind people from the status of "freaks," whose infirmity provided only a spectacle, but relegated them still to the status of anomalous objects—of investigation rather than of ridicule. Because these studies formulated disability in relation to how it affected consciousness, they framed disabled people only as objects, not as subjects in their own right. They emphasized the centrality of rationality and abstract thought as the highest forms of human cognition, and so concerned themselves solely with the intellectual functions of the disabled people they studied, without regard to any of their other human capacities.

Most strikingly, the philosophers' reports on their observations of blind people leave out any reference to their subjects as miserable, as suffering, or as wretched — a surprising absence, since those feelings had constituted the primary cultural meanings of disability from the classical era. In treating their informants as objects of information about intellectual functioning, the rationalist and sensationalist philosophers take care to omit any descriptions of them as emotional beings. This is most evident to the contemporary reader in descriptions of cataract surgeries; the operations were performed without anesthetic, but the accounts of them make little or no mention of the obvious agony the blind person must have felt. Scottish Common Sense philosopher Dugald Stewart's account of an operation performed on deaf-blind James Mitchell in 1809, for example, focuses on how a Dr. Saunderson, attempting to couch a cataract in Mitchell's left eye, "used every effort which the violent struggles of the boy would permit, to depress the cataract; but not the least advantage resulted from the operation."[12] The boy's "violent struggles," embedded in the middle of the passage, have significance only as the cause of the operation's failure, not as a sign of his experience of pain. In a similar passage, Stewart describes another cataract operation performed on Mitchell in 1810, in which the doctor "endeavoured, by means of powerful machinery, as well as the aid of numerous assistants, to fix the boy's head in a position sufficiently steady for so delicate an operation" in order to succeed where his predecessor had failed; again, Mitchell's "struggles were so violent as to render every effort for this purpose ineffectual."[13] Stewart's final hope about Mitchell was that some means could be discovered to teach him a language of arbitrary signs, so that he could be made to understand the benefit to himself of such surgeries and could therefore be persuaded to be more cooperative in the future.[14]

The experiments performed on blind people (all boys or men, in the accounts I have read) succeeded in recasting blindness as something understandable and curable, rather than something mysterious and inflicted by supernatural or divine powers. In so doing, they gave a radically new meaning to blindness, and to disability in general, which potentially removed the disabled from their age-old status as outcasts and freaks and provided them with the possibility of being cured, hence normalized. In so doing, however, the philosophical, medical, and scientific accounts of blindness made the blind person into an anomaly, whose humanness was secondary to his importance as an experimental object. "The curable blind man exist[ed] as a fortuitous accident, an object lying in the road of progress, to be used and discarded."[15] Within this framework, there was no room for any consideration of the blind person as miserable, or as deserving sympathy or charity, because the blind person had value only as an informant; he gives his testimony, whether consciously, as in Diderot's direct interviews, or unconsciously, as in James Mitchell being observed and reported on second-hand, and disappears.[16] Most often his name is not even recorded; one must search many sources to find Diderot's informant named as anything other than simply "the blind man of Puiseaux."

*   *   *

In his sequel to the *Lettre sur les aveugles*, written in 1782 to correct some misconceptions in the original letter, Diderot presented the results of his interview with Mademoiselle Mélanie de Salignac, the first blind woman to become the object of philosophical inquiry. Because Mlle. de Salignac was of the aristocracy, the daughter of an educated and cultivated woman, and herself well-educated, though she had lost her sight in infancy, Diderot records her name, and refers to her by it rather than solely by disability and location, as he referred to the blind man of Puiseaux in his original *Lettre*. The questions he asks her, and her responses, also differ from those posed in the original work, as Diderot investigates some of the emotional dimensions of blindness in his female informant.

Having found that she was "not anxious to see," Diderot asked her why, and she responded that

then I should only have my own eyes, whereas now I have the use of everybody's; by this loss I am always an object of interest and pity, at every instant people do me kindness, and at every instant I am grateful. Alas! If I could see, no one would trouble about me.[17]

The combination of others' kindness to her and her own gratitude stemmed directly from her "infirmities," she concluded. "What would become of me if I were to lose the interest that I inspire?"[18]

Mlle. de Salignac's statements, as reported by Diderot, point to what the majority of philosophical investigations of the relation between sensory perception and consciousness leave out: the association between blindness or other forms of disability and the sympathy, compassion, and care these generate in nondisabled others. Mlle. de Salignac's insistence that she is

only of "interest" to others because of her disability points to the most prevalent modern framework in which disability comes to have social meaning.
This framework, which blossomed in the late eighteenth century and came
to fruition in the nineteenth century, was first articulated in terms of Christian ethics, which enjoined charity toward the disabled, and elaborated
on by the Enlightenment moral philosophers. David Hume and Scottish
Common Sense philosopher Thomas Reid, in particular, emphasized the
importance of benevolence and sympathy in forming the bonds of human
relationship that provided the necessary basis for all forms of social organization, from the family to the state. This combination of charity, benevolence, and sympathy found its expression in a new mode of representation,
sentimentalism, which came to dominate popular literature and drama well
into the nineteenth century. Disability as mark or sign operated within a
system of sentimental semiotics, in which physical signs produced emotional meanings. Sentimental representation, focusing on providing scenes
of suffering and woe to which characters and audience members responded
with sympathy and care, proved an ideal mode for representations of disability, recasting disabled people as necessarily suffering, and thus deserving
of others' compassion. Mlle. de Salignac states that her loss inspires kindness and pity in others and gratitude in herself; this is the basis of the notion
of the "poster child," whose meaning is fixed as object of sympathy and
whose status as subject is also fixed as grateful recipient of others' care.

While rearticulating an age-old meaning of disability, sentimental representation in the context of moral philosophy also provided a reaccentuation, a new meaning for the disabled person. Moral philosophers, emphasizing the importance of emotions in forming social organizations, placed
the capacity to feel at the heart of their definition of human subjectivity; the
marker of humanness was no longer the capacity for rational thought, as
with Descartes and Locke, but the capacity for benevolence and sympathy,
the capacity to respond to the signs of others' woes. This model offered disabled people an alternate conception of selfhood. In the rationalist model
the blind or deaf person could only be an anomaly, someone whose mental
functioning illuminated the functioning of normals but whose own capacity for rational thought was limited by sensory deprivation (which meant
that some forms of knowledge were inaccessible). In the moral philosophers' model, however, the blind or deaf person, while producing the emotions of sympathy in others, also had the potential to feel those emotions in
his or her own right and could thus be both sign and subject, both the
signifier and the perceiver of signification.

Recasting the cultural meaning of disability in this context raised questions about how the semiotics of suffering signified. How, for example, did one learn to respond to the suffering of others with benevolence? David Hume, in his *Treatise of Human Nature* (1739–40), stressed that knowledge of another's feelings came not from any kind of rational assessment, but from the ability to perceive a relation between others and ourselves, and thence to sympathize with them. The chief foundation for shaping such relations, according to Hume, lay in the resemblance that each person has to others. Just as we perceive others' bodies to be similar in general formation to our own, Hume argued, so we may assume others' minds and feelings similar to our own; once we can identify with others who are like ourselves, Hume concludes, we can readily sympathize with them and understand their feelings. When we observe the moral actions of others, we then assume, on the basis of this sympathetic similarity, that their actions spring from the same pleasurable moral sensations as our own actions would and do. Insisting that the basis for sympathetic identification came from a perceived similarity between people, Hume recast the disabled as similar to, rather than as unlike, the nondisabled — a similarity marked by the nondisabled person's ability to feel pity for the disabled.

Scottish Common Sense philosopher Thomas Reid argued that the capacities for relationship, sympathy, and fellow-feeling anatomized by Hume were innate in all humans, but that such faculties needed proper training and exercise to develop fully. Such training usually occurred within the family circle, where parents who cared selflessly for their dependent children, motivated solely by love and by the pleasurable feeling of exercising their organs of benevolence, provided a model which, Reid hoped, would serve as the basis for all forms of human relations, including compassion for all weak or helpless persons, no matter what their relation (or lack thereof) to oneself. Reid noted that the capacity for selfless care of the weak resulted from the organization of the family, whether that family were human or animal:

How pleasant it is to see the family economy of a pair of little birds in rearing their tender offspring; the conjugal affection and fidelity of the parents; their cheerful toil and industry in providing food for their family; their sagacity in concealing their habitation; the arts they use, often at the peril of their own lives, to decoy hawks, and other enemies, from their dwelling place, and the affliction they feel when some unlucky boy has robbed them of the dear pledges of their affection, and frustrated all their hopes of their rising family.[19]

In this analogy, Reid moves from the positive model of the parents, who show their disinterested benevolence in all forms of care for their "rising family," to the negative model of the "unlucky boy" who steals "the dear pledges of their affection." Presumably the boy who plunders the nest of the happy bird family is "unlucky" because he did not learn the benevolent affections properly in his own "nest"; if he had, he surely would have felt protective rather than predatory toward the weak and helpless fledglings, if only because he remembered his own experiences as a dependent infant and would have identified so much with both the fledglings' and the parent birds' feelings as to be unable to cause such "affliction." Such affections were crucial to the formation of harmonious family relations and harmonious social relations of any kind, according to Reid. "The security, the happiness, and the strength of human society," he concluded, "spring solely from the reciprocal benevolent affections of its members" — affections learned, ideally, by proper training within the family circle.[20]

More specifically, Reid argued that the exercise of the innate capacities for benevolence relied on teaching children to understand the emotional expressions of others, in order to identify with what they were feeling. The "unlucky boy" who plundered the nest needed lessons in how to read the parent birds' feelings. Without human facial expressions, the birds' emotional cues were doubtless different from human ones. Reid describes these cues, whether of countenance or of fluttering wings, specifically as a form of language, the language of "natural signs" of emotions. In Reid's view (and that of many of his followers, including Dugald Stewart and the phrenologists who popularized the Scottish Common Sense views), emotional expressions such as tears or laughter served as universal signs, which God had enabled every creature to understand.[21] "These natural signs are more eloquent than [arbitrary] language," Reid insisted; "they move our hearts, and produce a sympathy, and a desire to give relief. There are few hearts so hard, but great distress will conquer their anger, their indignation, and every malevolent affection."[22]

The ability to comprehend the emotional language of natural signs came from what Reid named "the law of sympathetic imitation," a characteristic innate in all humans. An individual's feelings become knowable to others only when expressed in outward signs, in the natural language of emotions. Such signs are inseparable from the feelings they represent: sadness is signified by tears, happiness by a smile, and so on, without any ambiguity or room for interpretation. Unless one has worked at using one's rational faculties to suppress the natural signs of emotions, they will inevitably and unequivocally signal to others what one is feeling. Because these natural signs are more reliable than arbitrary signs (such as words), as their meanings are fixed and universal, Reid argues that manifesting the signs of emotions will produce the signified feeling: cry and you will feel sad; laugh and you will feel happy. The law of sympathetic imitation held that individuals learn, in their earliest family relations, to imitate the bodily manifestations of other people's emotions, hence arousing similar feelings in themselves. This capacity, strongest in children, becomes habitual in most adults if nothing occurs to alter the relation between the natural sign and the emotion, such as an acquired or artificial meaning or the interposition of rationality to suppress emotional expression.[23]

Reid's "law of sympathetic imitation" takes one step farther the idea of resemblance and relationship posited by Hume as the source of the ability to feel compassion or pity for others. What Reid and Hume name "sympathy" is what twentieth-century psychological theorists call "empathy": the capacity to feel the emotions of another as if they were one's own.[24] As psychologist Judith V. Jordan explains,

empathy begins with the basic capacity and motivation for human relatedness that allows perception of the other's affective cues, verbal and non-verbal. This is followed by a surrender to affective arousal in oneself — as if the perceived affective cues were one's own — thus producing a temporary identification with the other's emotional state.[25]

What produces this empathy, in Reid's view, is the innate response every individual has to the natural signs of emotions; when we see tears, according to the law of sympathetic imitation, we feel sad, and thus we identify in ourselves the emotions we see signified in another's natural signs.

For both Hume and Reid, the similarities and resemblances between individuals prompted observers to read the natural signs of emotions, and to allow the power of imitation to produce those emotions in themselves. While this process worked in general for any emotion, it was by far the most powerful in the context of feelings of affliction and sorrow. Suffering of any sort, signified in a variety of natural signs, from tears and sighs to expressions of resignation and despair, would produce, immediately and strongly, a similar emotion in an observer, and would immediately prompt the observer to do something to alleviate or lessen the pain of the sufferer — and, by extension, the observer's imitative pain.

It is in this context of the automatic response to the natural signs of suffering that the cultural meanings of disability began to be reaccentuated or redefined at the end of the eighteenth century. Disability itself, as sign or marker, was taken as an indication of inevitable suffering and misery; blindness as well as other visible forms of disability became a natural sign, the equivalent of tears or sighs, signifying the emotional state of the bearer and prompting an echoing emotion in the nondisabled observer. The work of reformers and educators such as Valentin Haüy, coupled with the efforts of surgeons to cure, hence to normalize, blindness, had stressed the resemblance between disabled and nondisabled people. In order to create the bond of similarity on which the law of sympathetic imitation depended, they tried to erase the distinctions exaggerated by the ridiculous costumes that had made the blind beggars into freaks and spectacles. Doing so, however, also framed disability as necessarily associated with grief and affliction, feelings that would inspire the sympathy and affections of the nondisabled. In rejecting disability as a sign of inhuman difference, such reformers had to embrace disability as a sign of weakness, suffering, and pathos, deserving of compassion and benevolence. The reaccentuation of blindness as a sign of misery guaranteed compassionate care from the nondisabled; as Mlle. de Salignac stated, blindness made her the object of everyone's concern and kindness.

The framework laid out by moral philosophy placed the human capacity to feel emotions, and to identify empathically with the emotions of others, at the center of definitions of individual subjectivity and of social interactions at all levels. In this framework, which formed the basis of sentimental representation, there was a physical language of natural signs, a language based specifically in the body, whose proper objects of expression were the vast range of human emotions, conceived similarly as products of a physical body. This natural language of emotions stood in sharp contrast to the arbitrary language of words, whose proper objects of expression were rational and abstract thoughts, and which was itself conceived of as the product of abstraction, rather than as emerging innately from bodily processes.[26]

As the source and locus of these natural signs, the body and its capacity to feel and to show emotion took primacy over the intellect and its rational abstractions. The disabled body was still framed as different from the nondisabled body, but the difference was recoded. Blind people and deaf people were different from the nondisabled, not because of a deficiency, such as the absence of a sense, but because of an *excess* — in this case, an excess of sentimental signification. Not only could they signify the usual emotions, through the usual signs of tears or laughter, but their bodily condition, their disability, was itself a natural sign, one that was interpreted as meaning suffering and misery.

In this sentimental semiotic system, however, the excess of signification possible through the disabled body raises questions about the ability of the disabled person accurately to read the signs of others' bodies, and hence to become a reading subject, a perceiver of signification. Disabled people could exist fully — even more fully than nondisabled people — as the locus of emotional signs, as "poster children," but could they assume positions as subjects? The question arose specifically in relation to blind people. If the natural signs of emotions were facial expressions, how could the blind "read" what they could not see? Hume had posited that to produce a feeling of relationship between people, pity and sympathy depended not only on contiguity and resemblance but more specifically on the *sight* of the suffering object. Because women and children, according to Hume, were "most guided by that faculty" of sight, they were "the most subject to pity. . . . The same infirmity, which makes them faint at the sight of a naked sword, tho' in the hands of their best friend, makes them pity extremely those, whom they find in any grief or affliction."[27]

By this logic, the more visible the disability, the more pitiable the sufferer; since blindness, limiting physical mobility, produced a more visible form of disability than deafness, blindness became the form of disability producing the most sympathy and compassion. By the same logic, however, the blind, while most pitiable, would be least able to see others' sufferings, least able to feel sympathy for them, and thus least eligible for inclusion in definitions of humanity dependent on the capacity for benevolent fellow-feeling.

This logic informed Diderot's conclusions, in his *Lettre sur les aveugles*, that a blind person, lacking the ability to see the natural signs of another's suffering, feels less pity for that suffering than would a sighted person. Arguing that "the state of our organs and our senses has a great influence on our metaphysics and our morality, and that those ideas which seem purely intellectual are closely dependent on the conformation of our bodies," Diderot concluded that, for a blind man, there is no difference "between a man making water and one bleeding in silence," since the blind man cannot perceive the difference between the two fluids.[28] Blindness, in this formulation, acts as a distancing mechanism: "Do not we ourselves cease to be compassionate when distance or the smallness of the object produces on us the same effect as deprivation of sight upon the blind?"[29] It is less disagreeable, Diderot noted, to kill an ox at a distance than to do so up close, so the blind, with not perception of contiguity or resemblance based on sight, must feel less pity than the sighted, and hence must be excluded from definitions of humanity based on the capacity for empathy.[30] Indeed, Diderot concluded, so reliant are all our moral sensibilities on our physical perceptions that blind people must be more atheistic than sighted people, if only because they cannot behold the wonders of nature and hence cannot understand the evidence for the divine Creator.[31]

Diderot's conclusions about the abilities of the blind to feel sympathy were based on his interviews with Msr. Lenotre, the blind man of Puiseaux. His interviews with Mlle. de Salignac, however, forced him to retract these conclusions, prompting him to publish the sequel to his *Lettre* in 1782. Mlle. de Salignac stated that she "would not forgive [him] for [the] statement that the blind, to whom the symptoms of suffering are invisible, must be cruel," and insisted that her compassion had nothing to do with her sensory abilities or disabilities. The suffering she herself had experienced as a result of her blindness, she argued, would make her all the more attuned to the afflictions of others, however silently they might endure their trials.[32] Coupled with the heightened sense of pity and tenderness that Diderot as well as Hume attributed to the female gender, Mlle. de Salignac's own blindness strengthened rather than weakened her feelings of benevolence and compassion for others. Indeed, it was precisely her own suffering — her own status as a sign producing compassion in others — that enabled her to be a subject, one who responded to the signs of others' suffering. In this interview, she articulated to Diderot the two responses required of disabled people to make the transition from sign to subject within the framework of sentimental moral philosophy: they must understand their own suffering as developing and reinforcing their capacity for empathic identification with the suffering of others, and they must respond with gratitude to the kindness that their disability, as sign, prompts in others.

Mlle. de Salignac's explanation of how she is able to perceive the signs of others' sufferings focuses on two factors: her gender, her tender womanly heart that predisposes her to be sensitive to others' feelings, and her blindness, which because it has caused her own pain and misery has similarly heightened her responsiveness to others. In these statements she agrees with attitudes prevalent from the eighteenth through the late twentieth century about the social meanings of womanhood and blindness. As Dugald Stewart pointed out in his study of "The Sexes,"

From the greater delicacy of their frame, and from the numerous ailments connected with their sexual temperament, combined with their constant familiarity with distresses which are not their own, the sympathy of women with the sufferings of others is much more lively, and their promptitude to administer relief, wherever it is possible, is much more eager than the generality of men.[33]

So universal is this capacity for sympathy, being both physiologically produced and socially reinforced, Stewart concluded, that women of even the most savage tribes will extend their care to enemies and strangers in distress. Mlle. de Salignac's insistence that her blindness, as a form of suffering, heightened her ability to sense and respond to others' woes is also upheld by twentieth-century sociological studies of attitudes of sighted people toward blindness, which note that respondents frequently think blind people have "a greater ability to understand other people's suffering," and tend to be more sympathetic in general, than sighted people.[34]

Mlle. de Salignac's answer, that her gender and her blindness overdetermine her ability to know others' sufferings, bypasses the specific question of how she reads the signs of others' emotions by positing a general sensitivity to feeling, based on her own experiences and her knowledge of her own emotions and their expression. In so doing, she implies that her ability to read comes, not from a specific sensory perception of others' tears or visible emotional signs, but rather from her own position as a generator of signs. The distinction she makes is one Diderot also made in his earlier *Lettre*, in discussing with Msr. Lenotre how he understood the meaning of the word "mirror." Lenotre uses the word correctly in several different contexts, but his definition of the term ("une machine . . . qui met les choses en relief, loin d'elles-mêmes") replaces visual qualities with tactile ones. Lenotre shows that, when asked for a precise definition of visually based objects or concepts, he must translate them into the terms of his own experience; when using words evocative of sight without having to tie them directly to visual objects, however, his language usage is no different from that of a sighted person.

In a fascinating discussion of the reaccentuation of the meanings of blindness in eighteenth- and nineteenth-century France, historian William Paulson points to Diderot's interview with Msr. Lenotre as highlighting two conflicting notions of how language operates. In asking Lenotre to define "mirror," Diderot insists on a denominational portrait of language, one in which words have meaning because language users know (via direct sensory experience) the things that words represent. In contrast, Lenotre's correct use of the word "mirror" in context offers an alternate portrait, one in which the operation of language depends on the internal coherence of an entire system of signification, rather than on the specific links between an individual word and a thing. Put in semiotic terms, the denominational view of language stresses the centrality of the relation between sign and referent; the systemic view of language stresses the centrality of the relation between signifier and signifier in a chain of signification, wherein the presence of one element calls into play all the other terms in the system. The former is the view stressed by Ferdinand de Saussure's structuralism; the latter is articulated in the poststructuralist visions of the operations of language. As Paulson argues, "the blind man [of Puiseaux] calls into question what Foucault has called the *épistéme* of representation," the centrality of the thing represented to the knowledge of the meaning of the word.

While Diderot hopes to expose Lenotre's linguistic lack, his inability accurately to define the meaning of a word denoting an object related to visual experience, Lenotre's response insists that he functions within the system of language with no lack, as if he were sighted—or as if language makes meaning without reference to sensory perceptions of objects and their qualities. He insists that, as an inhabitant of the structure of language itself, he is equal to all other language users in his ability to employ words in context. As Paulson concluded, "the sign systems of the blind are poor in signs only, and rich (by necessity) in the abstractions and combinations that make up the formal structure of the system."[35] This formulation provides an answer to Molyneux's problem by reformulating the question of "knowing" or "recognizing" as one of contexts of meaning, rather than one of sensory perception, and also provides an answer to the question of how blind people can become subjects within the sentimental semiotics of natural language. Rather than being barred from subject positions because they cannot "read" the visible signs of others' sufferings, blind people can inhabit a position within the structure of natural language, just as Lenotre does in arbitrary language: knowing one part of the system of signification, they have access to the entire system and all its signs and meanings, regardless whether they can verify the relation between a particular sign and what it denominates. In other words, so long as a blind person can feel and express emotions, can be a generator of signs that she or he understands, she or he is a subject within the system of signification; the ability to feel one's own emotions becomes sufficient to explain the ability to read the emotions of others. Thus, in the system of natural language, disabled people—including the blind—could become signs and readers, both objects and subjects of the signifying practices constituting sentimental semiotics.

The subject position posited in sentimental moral philosophy rests on the ability to read and respond to the signs of others' suffering with compassion and care, rather than on the ability to speak for oneself as an autonomous agent, as in rationalist philosophy. In nineteenth-century depictions of blind people the question would arise whether the disabled could also speak for themselves, and in what terms they understood and articulated their own experience. Mlle. de Salignac begins to answer this question by speaking for herself, through the medium of Diderot's reporting; disabled writers in the nineteenth century would do so more directly in penning their autobiographies.

The question of the distinctions between language as a denominational system depending on the direct perception of objects represented by words and language as a structure of linked elements referring only to each other would also become central in nineteenth-century writings about deaf-blind people and their ability to become language-using subjects. Both Laura Bridgman and Helen Keller would encounter the prevalence of the former attitude as a barrier to their claims for linguistic equality, an important part of their claim to full human status. Most important, however, the debates about the place of the disabled, particularly the blind, in a model of subjectivity that stressed the importance of reading the natural emotional language of others and responding sympathetically to signs of suffering led specifically to questions about the proper arena in which natural signs and sympathy could effectively be utilized. The moral philosophers posited the family and the domestic sphere as the place where all first learned the sentimental semiotics of emotions, and they argued that the family was, and should be, the model for all forms of social relations, including economic and political ones. Sentimental representations, particularly in literature and drama, upheld the moral philosophers' hopes that the close-knit family was the predominating social unit, and familially-based affections the most powerful social force in operation. But these hopes were challenged increasingly in the nineteenth century by the demands of an industrial capitalist economy (and a democratic political organization) which insisted that the heart and the emotions must be relegated to the home and had no place in the public sphere.

For the reformers and educators who were trying to redefine the cultural meanings of disability, the debates about the proper sphere of influence for sympathy and benevolence provided particular obstacles. As they relied increasingly on framing disability as a physical sign of suffering to which others must respond with kindness, they seemed increasingly to relegate their disabled charges to domestic circles. At the same time, they worked to prepare the disabled to become self-supporting and independent economic producers.

As the founders of schools for the blind throughout Europe and the United States began to formulate, in their institutional reports, the characteristics of blindness and the capacities of the blind, they found themselves caught between a rhetoric of charity and compassion that invoked sentimental sympathy and a rhetoric of independence that assured the public that the blind were not going to remain the recipients of alms. Their reform efforts took two major directions. The first was an attempt to reform the physical conditions of blindness and the mental and psychological states resulting from those physical conformations, insisting that blindness had little or no social significance and that the blind could be easily trained to be as self-supporting as the sighted. The second focused on working, not with the disabled themselves or the conformation of disability or its cure, but with the public meanings of disability. Such reform efforts worked to show the importance of having disabled people on view to remind nondisabled people of their social and moral responsibilities. The two efforts, though often mutually contradictory, were carried out by the same people and organizations, as reformers found that, no matter how successful their efforts at education and training might be, their students still could not function as full members of their society until the nondisabled members learned to think and respond differently to the signs of disability.

Institutional Meanings for Blind Bodies

News of the successful education of blind people and deaf people in European schools began to reach the United States in the years after the War of 1812. Pointing to the pioneering efforts of the European schools, and to Rev. Thomas Hopkins Gallaudet's founding of the American Asylum for the Deaf in 1817, articles in newspapers and magazines began to urge the formation of a school for the blind.[1] In 1826 Dr. John D. Fisher of Boston visited Valentin Haüy's school in Paris to see his achievements first-hand, and returned to Boston determined to begin a school there. Assisted by other private citizens, including blind historian William Prescott, Fisher took a census of Massachusetts blind people and asked the legislature in 1829 to incorporate the New England Asylum for the Purpose of Instructing the Blind.[2]

Fisher's committee asked Dr. Samuel Gridley Howe to become the school's first director. A Harvard-trained physician, Howe had volunteered to fight in the Greek war against Turkey after his medical studies, and had returned to the U.S. to find himself a hero, noted for his fiery passion for fighting injustice and for aiding the weak and helpless.[3] On accepting Fisher's offer, Howe set off for Paris to study the methods used in Haüy's school.

He found conditions there sadly different from those he had read about in Haüy's *Essai sur l'éducation des aveugles* (1786). In the aftermath of Revolutionary upheavals, the school had been nationalized and combined with the Quinze-Vingts Asylum, an almshouse founded in the Middle Ages. The school combined the worst aspects of charity and custodial care, treating its students as helpless beings who would always be dependent on the asylum. Rather than concerning its curriculum with training blind students to become self-supporting, it taught them "to perform surprising but useless things" to impress the royal and government officials in charge of the school's budget.[4] The other schools Howe visited in Europe, in London, Edinburgh, Dresden, and Berlin, were no better than the Paris school; all treated the blind "as objects of charity" to be petted and caressed, not as potentially independent beings who needed to be trained in vocational skills and in literacy in order to become useful members of their society.[5]

Haüy and his fellow educators had done their work only too well, Howe found. They had succeeded in joining the Christian ethic of charity toward the unfortunate with the benevolence encouraged in moral philosophy to define the disabled as necessarily pitiable sufferers, people whose visible signs of misery could prompt ready sympathy and a desire to assist those who were presumed to be dependent. Haüy had found a café of blind men performing the age-old equation between blindness and beggary; his efforts at education changed the terms of that equation only slightly, by associating blindness with dependence and asylum care or institutionalized charity rather than with individual almsgiving. The essential significance of blindness — lifelong dependence on others — remained unchanged. The blind still remained a class apart from the sighted, marked by their status as objects of others' concern and barred from recognition as full adult subjects in their own right. Samuel Gridley Howe was determined to alter the equation between blindness and dependence to shift the status of blind people from dependent objects to independent subjects.

Howe was at the center of most reforming efforts in Boston before the Civil War, and a highly influential figure in New England and nationwide. His death in 1876 attracted notice in newspapers throughout the U.S. and across Europe, and he was memorialized in Boston and in Washington, in reminiscences by his wife, Julia Ward Howe, and in poems by John Greenleaf Whittier and Oliver Wendell Holmes.[6] In addition to founding the first school for the blind and the first school for the mentally retarded, he also established a school for the deaf, based on his own theories about the problems of using sign language in deaf education, and was active in prison reform, in insane asylum reform, in public school and normal school educational reform, and — of course — in abolition.[7] Howe's ideas proved widely influential, as his principles formed the basis for the operation of virtually all schools for the blind and the retarded, and for many of the schools for the deaf, until the last decades of the nineteenth century.

Howe's work with the blind drew on the same idealistic principles that informed other reform efforts of the time. Chief among these principles were the ideas that "every creature in human shape should command our respect," and that every person, no matter whether his or her defect was

Figure 1. Samuel Gridley Howe, circa 1874. From Julia Ward Howe, *Memoir of Dr. Howe.*

physical or moral, could be made perfect through a judicious mix of healthy habits, moral suasion, compassionate care, and discipline.[8] Public institutions, according to Howe and his fellow reformers, if modeled carefully after families, guided by rightminded individuals, and funded by an enlightened public, could transform unfortunates of any sort into useful and productive members of society.[9]

Howe's first efforts on behalf of the blind focused on ways to bring the blind into the realm of the human by insisting that there were no significant differences between blind and sighted people that education could not correct. With proper training, Howe insisted, blindness would be normalized, as a blind person could prove to be as independent and self-supporting as a sighted person. Howe hoped to redefine the social meanings of blindness and to prove that blindness did not automatically need to be linked to charity. This redefinition took two related forms. His school curriculum would attempt to teach manufacturing skills to his students, in order to provide them with the means of supporting themselves economically, thus breaking the association between blindness and charity in practice. Meanwhile, Howe's written accounts of his work, appearing in the Perkins Institution Annual Reports (which were often excerpted and reprinted in periodicals across New England), worked to disassociate blindness from the rhetoric of charity and sympathy, and to define it instead within a rhetoric of economic competition and self-sufficiency.

Like other New England reformers, Howe believed that all individuals had a right to develop their human potential to the fullest, and that it was the obligation of the state to provide the means for that development. Furthermore, he believed, such training would relieve the state, and the taxpayers, of the burden of having to provide care for dependent populations in almshouses and other relief programs. Though the motives for reform were thus rooted in economic and political concerns, the rhetoric most widely used to describe such reforms referred more often to feelings of charity and benevolence as the forces that moved individuals, and the nation as a whole, to alleviate social ills. Urging the formation of the first school for the blind, Howe insisted that benevolence was the reigning spirit of the age, the hallmark of humane civilization, which had

urged many to seek the maniac in his cell, and to break his whips and fetters; it has made men enter the dungeon of the criminal, and substitute mercy and reason for wrath and vengeance in his treatment; it has carried them into the haunts of corruption, and made them take the wretched and despised outcast by the hand, and try, by kindness, to win him back to the bosom of society; nay, it has taught the very dumb to speak, and given ears to those unfortunate beings, to whom perpetual silence made the world a moving sepulchre.[10]

Though Boston had its "Magdalen Societies, our Prison Discipline Societies, our Institutions for the Deaf and Dumb," Howe lamented, "the blind, with stronger claims on our sympathy than any class of the afflicted, and with greater capacity for improvement, have been entirely neglected."[11]

While Howe's description shows that he accepted the equation between blindness and sympathy in order to urge support for his school, he
also insisted that the attitude of charity was insufficient for the reforming
temper of Boston. Howe, like his fellow reformers in all fields, asserted that
"the character and honor of our age" lay in the fact that "society is not
content with administering charitable aid to the distressed, but that it seeks
to strike at the root of the evil, and prevent its recurrence." If certain unfortunate physical conditions were inevitable (and few reformers were willing
to admit that they were), the association of disability with economic dependence was not. Howe concluded, "it remains yet for our country to apply
this principle [of prevention] to the pauperism of the blind" (PR 1832, 5).

To break the equation between blindness and beggary, according to
Howe, was only a matter of education. Without such education,

the poor blind man [remained condemned] to stand at the corner of the street, and
ask for charity; or to remain cooped up within the walls of an alms-house, or to sit
and mope away his solitary existence among his happier friends, alike a burden to
them and to himself. (PR 1832, 4)

With the taxes and donations of a just and benevolent public, however,
"you may give to him the means of becoming an enlightened, happy, and
useful member of society; you may give him and his fellow-blind the means
of earning their own livelihood, or at least of doing much towards it"
(PR 1832, 4).

Howe's descriptions of the blind show his attempts simultaneously to
discard and reinforce the association of blindness with charity. The blind
man who is educated need not be a beggar, but Howe himself would beg on
his behalf. While urging the public not to view blind people as miserable
sufferers whose woes would move hearts and open pocketbooks for individual almsgiving, Howe still relied on portraying the pitiable state of the
uneducated blind in order to open those pocketbooks for his school. His
earliest reports illustrate this contradiction in another way, as he based his
insistence that the education of the blind was feasible and desirable on
opposite principles. As a good reformer, he believed and argued that the
blind were equal to the sighted in all important respects; like Mlle. de
Salignac, however, he also believed and argued the prevailing cultural view
that the blind were more afflicted, and more unfortunate, than any other
group, and hence had a special claim on the benevolent sentiments of the
public. While demanding that blind children had the same right as sighted
children to free public education, he also insisted that "no one can doubt or

deny the claim which the blind have on the charity of their more fortunate fellows" (PR 1832, 5).

At bottom, however, Howe insisted that the education of the blind was desirable, not as a matter of equal rights or of charity but because "the object is an economical one to the community." Money that might be given to individual blind people in the form of alms, which would encourage them to remain beggars, could be given to Howe's institution. Donors could thus satisfy their need to distribute charity, to placate their Christian consciences and exercise their faculties of benevolence, and at the same time soothe their economic worries. Donors could rest assured that, by giving to the Perkins Institution, they would "take from society, so many *dead weights* . . . and enable them to get their own livelihood: and society ought to consider any capital so invested as a *sinking fund* for the redemption of its *charitable debt*; as a provision for preventing the blind from becoming taxes to the community" (PR 1832, 5; emphasis original).

The tension between the languages of economic self-interest and charity characterized Howe's discussion of the project of the institution throughout his tenure as director from 1832 to 1876. The idea of producing, through education and training, blind people who could become self-supporting citizens, members of a republic of self-reliant autonomous individuals, was articulated in his Annual Reports alongside the idea of the blind as a necessarily dependent group who inspired sympathy and who deserved the benevolence a Christian community would unhesitatingly provide. These two ways of constructing the meaning of blindness often came into conflict, as Howe struggled to find appropriate models and rhetorical strategies in which to redefine the ways blindness signified.

Howe tried to redefine blindness by stressing that the blind were essentially no different from the sighted: they were merely people who could not see.

What is blindness? A mere bodily infirmity or imperfection, which deprives a man of the perception of light, and limits the freedom of his locomotion, but which touches not his life, which impairs not his health, which dwarfs not his mind, which affects not his soul, and which cuts him off from none of the high and essential sources of human happiness. (PR 1850, 34)

By naming blindness as solely a physical condition, Howe defined it as a consequence of "bodily infirmity" and attempted to separate bodily configurations from any other aspect of life or character. In his written description, the blind body was distinct from the mind and self of the person so afflicted. As such, that body could be minimized or erased, thus effacing any important distinctions between the blind and the sighted. As a merely physical accident, blindness, in Howe's most optimistic constructions, did not signify.

Howe first attempted to "normalize" the blind by insisting, in his written accounts, that blindness did not affect any important aspect of human existence, and by insisting, in his school curriculum and training programs, that the blind body could be a site of productive labor just like the sighted body. He based his original plan for the education of the blind on the premise that sight was not crucial to intellectual or manual forms of labor, and divided his students into three categories, corresponding "to the sphere [they are] destined to fill in life" (PR 1834, 13). The students who manifested "a disposition for intellectual acquirements, or whose relatives are in a situation to provide for them the means of subsistence," would pursue an academic course of study "where they may acquire a knowledge even in the higher departments of science, as well as be qualified to appear advantageously in society" (PR 1834, 13). The second rank would pursue a mixed curriculum of intellectual and manual training, preparing to join the middle classes of shopkeepers and artisans. While this group might need to rely on their vocational skills more than on their intellectual attainments, their education would open to them "a new world of intellectual enjoyment" (PR 1834, 11). The third class, "whose age or situation in life requires that they should devote their whole energies to the means of acquiring a livelihood, pass their time solely in learning handicraft work and music" (PR 1834, 8). Through such a curriculum, Howe anticipated "for many of our pupils a happy independence, and for some an honorable distinction" (PR 1834, 10).[12]

Some years of experience in working with the blind, however, forced Howe to alter his expectations and his curriculum. Rather than encouraging separate "tracks" for blind pupils based on social position, he required all students to pursue both intellectual and vocational training. When all students, regardless of rank, had the same opportunities for exposure to both kinds of skills, all would benefit. Working-class graduates would have the comfort and refinement of an enlightened intellect to enrich their existence, and the graduates from wealthy families would understand and appreciate "the dignity of labor" (PR 1843, 11) and strive to make themselves useful to those who supported them. Those who found their social positions not fixed by the circumstances of birth and family origin could also adjust to the vicissitudes of fortune: should a well-off graduate become impoverished, he would have the skills to earn his living.[13]

Part of Howe's reformation of the curriculum came from his reluctance to present any blind person, no matter how well-off, as willing to rely solely on the financial resources of others, since he constantly worked, throughout his tenure as director, to convince the sighted public that the blind could become self-supporting individuals. Another factor, however, was Howe's discovery that he had overestimated the abilities of his blind students in claiming that many of them would be able to earn their livings through intellectual pursuits. Though he pointed proudly to Perkins graduates who attended Harvard and Dartmouth, he continually lowered his expectations of the intellectual capacities of his blind students, finding that, contrary to his initial pronouncements, few of them had the mental or physical resources to become even adequate, much less outstanding, teachers, ministers, or philosophers. "It has been erroneously thought, and the early Reports of this institution may have contributed to the error, that many blind persons could be found who would make good teachers, even of seeing persons," Howe confessed (PR 1847, 10). The inability of the blind to use "mechanical aids" such as blackboards, diagrams, and experiments, coupled with the relative scarcity of books in raised print, all added to the unsuitability of the blind, however intellectually capable, to teaching. Similar handicaps, particularly in the availability of readable texts, prevented blind students from becoming ministers.

In addition to the intellectual handicaps he associated with blindness, Howe also discovered a linguistic one. The blind, Howe concluded, could never enter any profession, such as ministry or law, which depended on a precise mastery of language, because the absence of sight meant an absence of the knowledge of the objects which words represented. Referring back to the debates raised by Diderot, Howe noted that it had been a subject of philosophical inquiry whether a person born blind would encounter problems inherent in the nature of language "which would prevent his ever attaining the perfect use of it." Based on his observations of his blind students, Howe answered in the affirmative. While a deaf person only learned the arbitrary language of words with great difficulty, a blind person used language "like a native," but could never understand the meanings of certain words or phrases because the blind person

had never experienced the sensations which they are intended to express. The blind learn [such] words as figures of speech, and attach to them some kind of meaning, but not precisely such as other men do, certainly not as those do who have the rare power of associating clear and definite ideas with every word, and the habit of using them with propriety and precision — such men as compose the very small class of good speakers and writers. (PR 1847, 11)

Like many of his colleagues, Howe unfailingly held to the denominational view of language, in which sensory perception was necessary to verify the relation between a word and the object it represented.[14] Linking the capacity for language comprehension to physical sensation, Howe defined the body that was lacking a sense as incapable of full linguistic competence.[15]

Barred by the physical construction of their bodies from succeeding in any profession requiring the precise use of language, the blind, in Howe's estimation, would have to learn to support themselves through less intellectual means. Throughout the first fifteen years of his tenure Howe continually revised his curriculum to emphasize manual training, convinced that the majority of the blind, whatever their intellectual failings, could become self-supporting skilled artisans. "The object ever kept in view is to enable the pupil to gain his own livelihood in after life," Howe stressed. Though the blind worker would be competing with the sighted in this effort, Howe insisted that the sighted "have an advantage over him no greater than may be counterbalanced by superior industry and ingenuity, and by the application of powers to such pursuits as require the aid of but four senses" (PR 1834, 11).

One of the pursuits singled out by Howe as most appropriate to those lacking sight was music. Drawing on the assumption that the absence of one sense strengthens the acuity of the remaining senses, Howe insisted that "music is the field which seems to offer the blind the fairest opportunity for competition with *clairvoyans*; the post of church organist is one which a blind man can fill equally as well as a seeing person, and it should ever be an object to qualify as many of them for it as possible" (PR 1834, 9). The idea that the blind were natural musicians made this a logical choice for Howe's curriculum, and all students were required to pursue some type of musical studies. His mention of church organist again unites the notion of Christian charity with economic endeavor, implying that religious organizations might be more willing to hire a blind over a sighted organist. Howe also suggested that blind people, with their superior musical abilities, might make good music teachers, and that certainly the profession of piano-tuning would be lucrative one for them.

As with his expectations of their intellectual careers, however, Howe came to recant his views on the superiority of the blind as musicians. By 1843 he insisted that, while all blind students should be taught music, only a handful could expect to get their living that way; by 1858 he declared that a total lack of musical sense was more common among the blind than the sighted (PR 1843, 16; 1858, 11). The majority, with no special talent for music, might still study music as "a source of pleasure to themselves and a bond of sympathy with others" (PR 1858, 10). But while all blind students might benefit from musical training, they should not presume on the public by performing music and expecting money for it. For Howe, unqualified blind musicians were no different from the blind beggars who had inspired Valentin Haüy's original efforts to lift the blind from the misery of dependence and poverty. Those who played in public with little or no musical talent, Howe insisted, "take advantage of the ready sympathy which their infirmity excites, and get money for music which is so poor it would hardly be listened to, certainly not paid for, if perpetrated by ordinary persons" (PR 1857, 10–11). Blind musicians who would stoop to accepting this sort of alms were "persons of idle habits, who love to rove about and frequent taverns," Howe sermonized; they would soon "degenerate into mountebanks" and would eventually acquire "such habits of dissipation and depravity" as would unfit them for any regular labor (PR 1857, 10–11; 1843, 16).

As he realized that the majority of the blind attending the Perkins Institution would be poor, with no particular musical talents and no aptitude for teaching or intellectual pursuits, Howe increasingly insisted that the blind must rely on manual labor for their support, and that schools and workshops for the blind must focus on providing training in manufacturing handicrafts (PR 1848, 8). Initially, Howe concentrated on teaching students how to weave doormats, using Manila hemp and handlooms, how to do various types of basketwork, and how to make mattresses; later, he added broom- and brush-making, and eventually laundry and housecleaning, to the agenda of skills with which blind graduates might be able to earn their livings.

Having established a Work Department devoted to giving the older male students specific training in manual labor, Howe reported in 1838 that his students had "acquired considerable dexterity and skill in the trades which are taught," though he lamented that those trades were "of the simplest kinds" (PR 1838, 4). Blindness proved to be more of an obstacle to manual pursuits than he had initially estimated; while he announced confidently that "a blind person, having a natural inclination and aptitude for mechanics, may be taught to execute very intricate and ingenious work," he also admitted that work cost the blind student "a very great expense of time and labor" (PR 1838, 4).

In order to encourage his students, and to raise additional funds to offset the expenses of the Work Department, Howe opened a store to sell the goods made in the school. When the store opened in 1834, Howe hoped that the students' skills would soon be "render[ed] so perfect, that their work will command a market from its real value," and not because people would buy blind-made goods as a form of charity (PR 1834, 9). This theme recurs in virtually all Howe's Annual Reports, as he attempted to separate the rhetoric of economic self-interest from that of charity by assuring his readers that the goods sold in his shop were not inferior in any way to the goods sold in regular shops; that the prices were competitive; and that buyers should purchase them because they were good bargains, not because they could redeem their "charitable debt" by giving what would amount to a donation to the school. In 1836, he declared that the mattresses and chair cushions offered for sale were

warranted as good in material, and as strong in fabric, as any in the market. They are put at a low price, and the public are requested to call and examine them, without being expected to pay any more than their real value, on account of their being made by the blind. (PR 1836, 7)

In subsequent reports Howe similarly tried to convince the public that the sale of the blind-made goods would follow market laws, not the dictates of charity. Pointing out that the articles were sold at a low price in order to be competitive, Howe worried that the public still had the impression that "purchasers would be taxed for the support of the Institution." Again, Howe urged "purchasers to come to our shop, not with a view to being charitable, but to make a good bargain for themselves" (PR 1839, 5).

In 1840 Howe opened an experimental version of the Work Department for adult blind men, to provide manual training for those who might otherwise have become dependent on public or private charity. Though the adult workers initially used the same workshop and living facilities as the students, Howe insisted that the two operations were, and would remain, separate: he wanted to reassure the taxpaying public that the state funds provided under the rubric of free public education for all youths were not being spent to maintain adult blind people in any kind of asylum. The adult workshop, like the school, was open to any blind person "of good moral character," and was free to beneficiaries from the state of Massachusetts; blind people from other states had to pay an admission fee, which could come either from private funds or from their home state. Like the students, the blind workers trained in the Adult Work Department would attempt to sell their goods in the store; each worker would have an account that recorded the amount paid on his behalf (by the state or by friends), and the amount each earned beyond the cost of the materials, and would have deducted from that the cost of his board. After three years, "those who prove unable to earn their own livelihood will not be retained; as it is not desirable to convert the establishment into an almshouse, or to retain any but working bees in the hive" (PR 1841, 15–16).

Howe's central assumption in setting up the workshop for the adults was the same as that for his students: blind workers, properly trained in manual labor, could manufacture goods that would be competitive with those made by sighted workers, and the blind workers would operate on the same terms as sighted workers, making goods that could be sold for more than the cost of their materials, and generating a profit that would exceed the living expenses of the individual worker. His efforts to provide a facility where blind workers could achieve the financial — and hence moral, intellectual, and political — independence Howe deemed so important continually ended in frustration, however, as Howe found that his blind workers, adults or students, could not make goods that could be sold competitively in the market alongside sighted-made goods. Though "the articles manufactured will be warranted to be of the best materials and faithfully made up; and pains will be taken by the use of good stock, and by fidelity of work," Howe confessed, the quality of materials and labor would have "to compensate for the apparent disadvantage of inferiority in elegance and neatness of execution." Though "a blind man cannot finish a broom, or a brush, for instance, with that neatness and polish which a seeing workman can," Howe explained, "he can make as strong and serviceable an article, and he is willing to work for a smaller profit" (PR 1841, 16). He again urged the public to come examine the goods for themselves, assuring them that they would pay "not a cent more than the articles are really worth" (PR 1841, 17).

In order to make the goods made by his blind workers competitive in an increasingly difficult economy, one torn by panics and dominated by ever-increasing numbers of machine-made goods, Howe's only recourse was continually to cut the margin of profit the workers could expect to reap from the sale of their products. In so doing, he continually had to lower his, and the workers', expectations of earnings and the type of life those earnings could support. In his 1842 Annual Report he urged blind people of all ages to continue to seek for any respectable employment that would keep them from "eat[ing] the bitter bread of charity all their days. . . . Seek for employment, and work diligently at it; consider any occupation that is useful, to be honorable; and be satisfied with an independence, however humble the abode, or frugal the fare" (PR 1842, 16).

But to exist frugally on even the most humble fare, the workers first
had to earn a profit. By 1848 Howe admitted that the adult workshop had
yet to make any money to distribute among the workers, as the sales of the
blind-made goods did not begin to meet the cost of the workers' board, nor
the cost of materials, much of which were ruined in the process of training
the workers. Somewhat desperately, Howe again decided that the problem
lay in the public's attitude toward the blind-made goods, and their eagerness to perceive the goods as inferior and the purchase of them as a form of
charity. The cultural associations between blindness, dependence, and charity were too strong, Howe found, for the public readily to discern that the
blind workers operated on the same economic terms as sighted workers.
Because "many really good people are indisposed to mix up charity with
business," he reasoned, those who assumed that buying blind-made goods
would be a form of charity would refuse to purchase them. They might give
donations if asked outright, "but when they buy, they want to buy as cheap
as they can" (PR 1848, 15).

The difficulty lay in the fact that Howe was trying to insert the blind
workers into a new framework, a new set of meanings for blindness that
would move blind people from the rhetoric of charity and benevolence to
that of market economics. His main vehicle for this redefinition lay in his
assertions, both in his written accounts and through the school's curriculum, that the blind body could become a site of productive labor rather than
of helpless dependence. If he could prove to the public that blind workers
could become economically competitive, then he would break the equation
between blindness and dependency. When the capacities of blind bodies for
participation in civilized society were governed by the same market laws
that governed sighted bodies, Howe hoped, the blind body would cease to
signify suffering, and would thus be removed from the rhetoric of charity.

The sighted public, however, proved incapable of understanding the
meaning of blindness as anything other than misery. They continued to
respond to blindness with tender-hearted benevolence, despite Howe's ex-
hortations, and thus they continued to separate the feelings of benevolence,
which prompted them to be charitable to the blind, from their desire to
make good bargains, which prevented them from buying the blind-made
goods.

Equal in importance to the public's recalcitrance in accepting the blind
as economically competitive workers, however, were the difficulties Howe
faced in trying to make the bodies of blind students and adults into laboring
bodies that could function in a rapidly-mechanizing system of industrial

production. Howe had originally envisioned his blind workers fitting into a preindustrial model of production, one in which independent artisans, working by themselves in workshops connected closely to their homes, performed all the tasks necessary to produce a single item. By the mid-1830s, he recognized that this model was being superseded by new methods of production. The division of labor, and the increased capital resources of large-scale factory production, made his dreams of employing his blind workers as artisans obsolete.

In his 1843 Report, Howe was forced to acknowledge a range of difficulties his blind workers faced in competing with industrial modes of production. His discussion shows his inability to imagine the blind worker as anything other than an independent artisan who might own his own shop, and who had to compete with factory production. Blind artisans, Howe argued, were at a disadvantage to sighted workers because they could not operate on a large enough scale to guarantee a profit. When a sighted man started a manufacturing establishment for making brushes, for example, he could buy his raw materials wholesale, employ a number of workers to perform subdivided tasks, and make more brushes than he could sell immediately. The blind, however, could not command sufficient capital to pay for materials and the workers' labor without needing the immediate income from the sale of the finished goods. The sighted manufacturer could stockpile finished goods in hopes of commanding higher prices, while the blind had to sell goods at an immediate market price. In addition, the blind maker of brushes, with no capital funds, could not buy materials wholesale, and would have to pay more dearly for them. Most important, the blind worker could not use machines to speed up his production, but was limited to hand tools that could be used safely without sight. Working more slowly, and with little assistance, the blind worker would make fewer brushes, and could not stockpile reserves, but must sell his products as he made them, for whatever price he could. While some would prefer to buy brushes from the blind worker in order to encourage him, they would necessarily pay more for their brushes than if they purchased them from the sighted maker — and "this amounts to charity," Howe confessed, "and charity and trade go not long hand in hand together" (PR 1843, 13).

Another difficulty Howe's blind workers faced lay in competition with other laboring groups, especially those in other institutions. As Howe lamented in his 1858 Annual Report, blind workers could sometimes earn good wages recaning chair seats for individual families, but such work was irregular, and unreliable as a steady source of income. If the same blind workers tried to manufacture new cane chair seats, they competed with wholesale dealers who had labor contracts with state prisons and other public establishments that could command labor without having to pay the inmates a living wage. Similarly, wholesale manufacturers increasingly relied on piecework done in families, "at odd hours, in bad weather, perhaps by women and children," and paid a price for such piecework that was not meant to support a family (PR 1848, 63).

By far the most important feature of the new industrial modes of production that prevented blind workers from successfully competing for a share of the market was the use of mechanized production. While in previous eras, even as recently as twenty-five years earlier, Howe stated, blind workers might have been given their own corner of a shop, or run their own workshop, by the 1840s all the simple manual trades that required only strength and perseverance had been take over by steam engines and machines (PR 1848, 59). Any task not requiring vision, which was "simple enough for the blind to do," was soon taken over by another sightless being, a "man of wood and iron, who wants neither food nor wages, [who] has been made expressly to perform it" (PR 1846, 12). Picking oakum, for example, had been the exclusive prerogative of the pauper, the labor to which the old, blind, feeble, or otherwise infirm had been put in almshouses and asylums since their founding.

But, yesterday there came along a new and strange creature of wood and iron, that had teeth, but no stomach to feed, — that had body and strength, but no back to clothe, — that had limbs and fingers, but no nerves to tire; and he seizes a ton of junk, and with teeth and claws, tears it into more oakum in an hour than a whole almshouse full of paupers could pick in a week, and does his work, too, with a nicety and uniformity that they could never hope to equal. (PR 1848, 60)

Howe frames the advent of machine-based production as the arrival of a new kind of "man," or, more specifically, a new kind of *body*, which can work but needs no wages, no food, no clothes, and no rest; like the blind, the laboring machine-body Howe describes has no vision, but unlike them, it also has no stomach, no back, and no nerves.

Characterizing the blind human worker and the machine-worker explicitly in terms of bodily differences, Howe finally conceded that his efforts to claim equality for his blind workers had failed. His initial hopes had rested on the assumption that blindness was "a mere bodily infirmity or imperfection" that did not affect any important aspect of life. In confronting the inability of the blind to compete with the laboring machine-body,

Howe had to admit that blindness, because it was a bodily infirmity, did affect the whole person and social functioning. In the industrial mode of production, labor required not just a mind and hands, but a specific kind of body, as his description of the machine implies, a body the blind could never have. In admitting that blindness did signify, that it did make the blind body an unsuitable site for competitive labor in the context of industrial production, Howe acquiesced to defining the blind body as abnormal, as inherently different from the sighted body. Rejecting the blind body as a site of competitive labor power, he also decided that blindness was not a normalizable physical category; the blind body could not be dismissed as insignificant.

His failure to redefine the social meanings of blindness, however, came not from the recalcitrant bodies of the blind so much as from the immutable laws of economics that governed industrial production. Those factors which forced blind laborers out of economic competition were part of "the received rules of trade, according to which all such competition is fair and honorable, and by which the weakest must go to the wall," Howe agreed (PR 1848, 64). He acknowledged that the bodies of sighted workers gave them an advantage over blind workers, and did not "complain that the laboring man . . . should profit by the advantage which his eyes give him over the blind man, and take up his trade; . . . for such are the spirit of the age and the laws of trade, that all this is to be expected" (PR 1848, 64).

Forced by market relations to accept that charity and trade could not mix and that blindness and charity were more linked than he had anticipated, Howe attempted one last time to assert that the blind and the sighted were equal in economic terms. The problem with employing his blind workers lay not in the defects of the bodies of blind people, but rather in the way industrial capitalism redefined the meaning and function of *all* working bodies. Like his fellow reformers, Howe placed the body at the center of definitions of self and social relations; with the rise of industrialization, the conception of how bodies functioned as workers, as sites of labor and production, shifted radically.[16] Howe's use of bodily metaphors in his attacks on industrial capitalism reflect this focus on the physical, as well as his own concerns with the particular bodies of the blind.

Like his fellow reformers, Howe saw the predominance of machine-based production as a destructive force, one that would dehumanize all economic relations and hence threaten the foundations of all social organization. The machine-bodies which, with their iron fingers and teeth, could perform more labor than any worker, blind or sighted, were "like long levers in the hands of capital," Howe wrote, "which serve to raise the aggregate of production; but the fulcrum is apt to be the body of the poor, which is thereby ground to powder" (PR 1848, 60). The laboring classes, in Howe's metaphor, become the body of the whole society, which the machine-body crushes; in order to compete with the nerveless and stomachless machine-body, laborers must become themselves "unthinking, irresponsible machines" who perform the same task again and again in mechanical repetition. Turning thinking, feeling humans into nerveless machine-bodies encouraged workers to become irresponsible, Howe argued, because they no longer had to plan tasks with care and forethought, as independent artisans did. Rather than being worthy citizens through earning their own economic independence, such laborers became a threat to the republic; in becoming like machines, they lost the power to make decisions and judgments for themselves, and had no concern for the manufacturing process of which they were a coglike part.

When the body of the laborer is replaced by the iron body of the machine, and the human worker, to compete, must become himself mechanical, Howe proclaimed, the entire society — conceived of as the "social body" — suffers:

The laboring classes are as the feet of society; they support and carry the whole social body; but the system of irresponsible labor prevents their natural growth in a natural direction, as much as the iron shoe prevents the growth of a Chinese woman's foot. (PR 1848, 70)

Because a body will grow, Howe argued, if the social body's feet, in the person of the worker, cannot grow in understanding and responsibility, the higher human faculties, then they will grow in passions and appetites; "and when the feet of society are stunted in one direction, and overgrown in another, the whole body totters." Thus, Howe concluded, "Those who complain of the intemperance, the improvidence, the dishonesty, and the *strikes* of workmen, should recollect that the very object of the system is to prevent them from thinking, and that without thought and care there can be no virtue" (PR 1848, 70; emphasis original).

Figuring the operation of all economic aspects of society, including all forms of labor and production, as the functions of bodies that followed certain physical laws, Howe abandoned his hopes of normalizing his blind students by redefining the significance of their physical difference from the sighted. Rather, he accepted that blindness was a physical condition with far-reaching rather than minimal effects on all aspects of human development and endeavor. Blindness, rather than disappearing through proper training, became entirely determinant. The blind body became entirely abnormal. As such, it was necessarily a site of dependence rather than one of independent labor; the equation between blindness and dependence, which produced blindness as a sign eliciting a charitable response, was ultimately as determinant as the blind body itself.

Having come to the conclusion that blindness was ineradicable and incompatible with existing conditions of industrial production, Howe, like many who shared his idealistic reforming views, pinned his hopes for a solution to the problems of mechanized industrial production for both blind and sighted laborers on a dream of the millennial reorganization of society. Though he assumed that increased production, made possible by industrialization, would make life easier for all, as goods became cheaper and wealth was more equally distributed, Howe knew that that alone would not be enough to make his blind students equal to sighted workers in productive labor. As long as economic production was governed only by immutable laws based on individual self-interest and immediate profit and loss, the rule that "the weakest will go to the wall" would hold sway. A more enlightened organization of production, one that took into consideration something other than just the self-interest and profit of individuals, might recognize that "society belongs to us as well as we to it, and that by promoting the interests of all of its members we promote our own" (PR 1848, 64). In such a society, which focused less on the autonomy and independence of every individual and more on the networks of interdependence and fellow-feeling that held society together, there would be no necessary contradiction between the requirements of economics and the requirements of charity. Able-bodied productive members of such a society would not "think to do [their] duty to the blind, the deaf, and the infirm, by throwing on them gifts and alms, that crush the spirit while they seem to aid the body," Howe wrote. Rather, any tasks the blind or infirm could perform would be set apart and reserved for them alone, leaving the market open for free competition among forms of labor that required specific bodily configurations, such as sight, hearing, or strength, and preserving some useful and profitable employment for those with different bodies (PR 1848, 65). Blindness, like any other form of defect or infirmity, would thus come to signify a particular kind of economic pursuit, rather than a necessary exclusion from all forms of labor.

Howe went so far as to dream of a reorganization of production whereby the blind "may claim such labors *as a right*; for surely no right is more sacred than that of exercising one's talents in a useful and profitable manner" (PR 1848, 65; emphasis original). He based his argument on the claim that "every child born into the community has a right to food for his body and knowledge for his mind," and that useful employment should be similarly guaranteed, protected, and supported by the state, "for without it food and knowledge become but curses — they had better have been withheld" (PR 1848, 65).

How this reformation might come about, Howe did not pause to speculate; he envisioned this new society, however, as the perfection and fulfillment of both the democratic ideal of the rights of all citizens to "life, liberty, and the pursuit of happiness," regardless of bodily configuration, and the Christian ideal of universal human brotherhood. A truly Christian community, Howe argued, would recognize the right of all citizens to share in both labor and profits, with a spirit of brotherhood, cooperation, and mutual aid replacing competition, antagonism, and selfish interest. Under the present dispensation, Howe lamented, the doctrines of Christian brotherhood, and the emotions of benevolence and compassion, did not penetrate to the relentless laws of trade, and the blind, like the poor, were ground "between the upper and nether millstones of competition" (PR 1850, 38). Howe reiterated his acceptance that, in the current "spirit of the age," the rules of production that were so dehumanizing were "the legitimate effect of competition" and were not "cruel and unfeeling," but he longed for the day when "this transition state of society" would be over, and "the soul of commerce" would become more important than laboring bodies (PR 1850, 38). In such a community the physical differences between the able-bodied and the blind and infirm would cease to signify relations of benevolence and dependence, as all would be equal on economic and spiritual terms.

*   *   *

Having failed to erase the bodies of blind people as sites of difference, Howe began to anatomize them more fully, constructing the bodies of blind people as wholly determinant rather than inessential. Blindness, as a physical condition, had wide-ranging constitutional effects, he asserted. Using phrenological principles to declare that the mind functions like the body, he concluded that the lack of intellectual vigor among the majority of the blind students was produced by the lack of physical vigor in their bodies. That physical weakness came from their lack of mobility, as their blindness prevented their free locomotion and kept them from taking healthy exercise in the open air, and also from the fact that blindness was often only a symptom of a generally weakened, feeble, or otherwise defective constitution, which left many blind people prey to disease and early death (PR 1837, 3; 1841, 4).

"Thus, it is seen, that blindness is more than the mere privation of one sense," Howe declared; "it affects the whole physical and moral man" (PR 1841, 7). There could be no perfect development of any faculty or system that depended on physical organs — and, in Howe's view, all mental, moral, and emotional processes ultimately had their roots in some physical organ in the brain — when the absence of one organ perverted the workings of the entire body.[17] Figuring the individual body, like the "social body," as a unified entity whose individual parts affected all other parts, Howe decided that the blind were physically distinct from the sighted, and from the deaf, and that the meanings of the blind body placed the blind in a class of humanity, a species or race, all their own.

Howe found himself unable to write the bodies of the blind into normality. Rather, he reversed his earlier assertions that the blind were equal to the sighted, and instead insisted that blindness inevitably meant inferiority. As he became more convinced that physicality was indeed determinant, he increasingly focused his Annual Reports on anatomizing the differences between blind and sighted people, formulating "the blind" as an anomaly, an abnormal subgroup defined by the effect of their physical configurations on all aspects of their intellectual, moral, and material functioning. It being part of the duty of public institutions created for the welfare of dependent populations to "obtain and distribute all information they can respecting the interesting class of person" with whom they deal, Howe drew on fifteen years of close observation of blind people and on the statistical information gathered by other schools for the blind across the United States to conclude that the blind could never fulfill "the high expectations for independence originally held for them." Now that "the real capacities and conditions of the blind were known," Howe wrote, it became clear that "the infirmity of blindness is really greater than it has been supposed to be" (PR 1848, 34). In this spirit, Howe announced that

THE BLIND, AS A CLASS, ARE INFERIOR TO OTHER PERSONS IN MENTAL POWER AND ABILITY. (PR 1848, 34; capitalization original)

In his explanation of this pronouncement, Howe recounted his Lockean assumption that the mind did indeed develop from the senses, and that the absence of one sense must mean imperfect mental development; "To suppose there can be a full and harmonious development of character without sight is to suppose that God gave us that noble sense quite superfluously" (PR 1848, 37).

Those born blind, or who became blind in infancy, usually suffered from a constitutional infirmity, which Howe described as a "scrofulous character," indicating a "defective physical organization" that affected their entire being. "The inference, then, is plain, that the *naturally* blind must be, *as a class*, far inferior physically and intellectually to the seeing" (PR 1848, 41; emphasis original). For those who became blind by accident, rather than by constitutional defect, in early childhood or youth, before their mental and physical organs had developed fully, blindness similarly limited their potential, as the restrictions on movement entailed by blindness would prevent them from taking exercise and developing the healthy bodies without which there could be no healthy minds.

Anatomizing the bodies of blind people as determinant, as relegating "the blind" to a special class of humanity, Howe noted that those bodies were distinguished by more than just the lack of vision. Restricted from physical activity by their lack of freedom of movement, blind bodies had peculiar motions and habits; the blind tended to rock, twitch, and jerk, appearing awkward and uncouth. Their "pale faces, stooping forms, puny limbs, feeble motions, and hesitating tread" all marked them as a "separate race of beings" (PR 1847, 5–6). By comparison, the bodies of deaf people were less differentiated from those of full-facultied people; with full use of vision to aid them in locomotion and exercise, deaf bodies were "graceful and appealing" in appearance, carriage, and motion (PR 1847, 6).

Howe's work with other disabled groups, especially the deaf, led him to associate certain forms of physically determinant disability with particular formulations of social class. Where his early curriculum had promoted class stratification among the blind in order to emulate the educational distinctions made among sighted people, as another aspect of normalization, Howe's later written Reports attempted to define the specific meaning of blind bodies in class terms that maintained the idea that the blind formed a distinct species of humans, but one aligned specifically with middle-class values. Because "The eye ministers most to the body, its wants and pleasures," while the ear ministers "to the mind, its capacities and its affections," the loss of sight meant the loss of orientation to the body and to the material world, while the loss of hearing implied the loss of language, of social intercourse, and of intellectual stimulation (PR 1850, 37). To those who depended for their livelihood on manual labor, on the orientation to and manipulation of the material external world, blindness was a greater tragedy than deafness; for those who derived their living, or their pleasure in life, from the exercise of intellectual, moral, and social capacities more than from the exercise of animal and physical resources, deafness would be a greater tragedy than blindness. "He who prefers the body and its pleasures, the outer world, and beauty, would choose to be deaf rather than blind, but he who prefers the mind and the affections would choose to be blind rather than deaf" (PR 1850, 37). A wealthy man would choose to be blind, Howe concluded, because he did not need the economic independence gained by manual labor, which required sight, and he could still enjoy all forms of social intercourse requiring language. A poor man, by contrast, would choose deafness, and the sacrifice of those comforts and pleasures Howe considered luxuries, in order to be able to earn his living. Anatomizing the blind body as a middle-class body, as opposed to the working-class bodies of the deaf, he effectively removed them from the realm of physical labor. In so doing, of course, he removed the possibility that they might become self-supporting citizens through manual labor.

Accepting that the determinant qualities of blind bodies would always prevent the blind from becoming normalized, Howe turned his attention toward the possibility of eliminating blindness entirely from the human population. In the early days of his administration, while he had still hoped to train blind people to become economically self-reliant, Howe had insisted that within the "body social" there would always be both sighted and blind bodies; divine Providence and "immutable laws of nature" had decreed blindness an inherent part of the human condition (PR 1842, 15). The presence of blindness as a sign, like other forms of disability, was the Creator's way of insuring that the healthy would always be reminded of their charitable responsibilities toward the less fortunate (PR 1836, 13–14). By 1848, however, when Howe was anatomizing the physical limitations of blind bodies, he saw that he had committed a scientific as well as a theological error in declaring blindness inevitable. The theological error lay in his violation of his own Unitarian-millennial belief in the ultimate perfectibility of humankind. To insist that blindness would always be part of the human condition was to deny the human capacity to discover, through science, the divinely-ordained laws governing nature, and the human moral power to follow those laws, eventually achieving the physical perfection on which moral and intellectual perfection could be based. The scientific error, which paralleled and complemented the theological one as Baconian science complemented Unitarianism, was in ignoring the extent to which blindness was hereditary, the result of parental "error," and hence eradicable, if the carriers of the defective condition could be persuaded not to reproduce it in their offspring.

"BLINDNESS, OR A STRONG CONSTITUTIONAL TENDENCY TO IT, IS VERY OFTEN HEREDITARY," Howe proclaimed (PR 1848, 46; capitalization original). Violators of natural laws were visited with "inward infirmities," which, in "gross offenders, insures ailments visited on succeeding generations" (PR 1848, 47). "Diseased tendencies," such as a constitutional predisposition toward scrofula and blindness, resulted from an individual's own "intemperance and abuse," Howe declared; "not a single debauch, not a single excess, not a single abuse of any animal propensity, ever was or ever can be committed without more or less evil consequences" (PR 1848, 50). The abuse of the "animal propensities," which often came from the improper development of the higher moral and intellectual faculties, according to phrenological reasoning, could include all sorts of physical excesses, including drinking alcohol, smoking, sleeping too much or too little, eating too much or the wrong kinds of foods, and, of course, all manner of sexual excesses or vices, including masturbation and too-frequent intercourse.

Howe admonished, "if this world is a vale of tears, if it is full of deformity, and suffering, and sickness and crime," it is the result of imperfect social formations and individual efforts, rather than the will of Providence: "it is man, not God, that maketh it so" (PR 1848, 51–52). As a Unitarian, a doctor, and a social reformer who believed incontrovertibly in the perfectibility of humanity, Howe insisted that all social evils were the result of error, sin, and ignorance. "Our instincts revolt at the thought" of the inevitability of blindness

as irreligious, and reason, coming to the aid of our piety, points out to us that blindness is merely one of those manifold infirmities which are the consequences and the signs of the low and imperfect physical condition even of the healthiest community in the world. (PR 1849, 22)

Howe's rhetoric here emphasizes the semiotic function of blindness, and of disability in general. Naming blindness a "sign," he insists that blindness serves as a warning to correct physical and moral imperfections. Whatever his hopes for convincing the public that the blind were merely people without sight, he embraced the conception of blindness as having social meaning beyond the existence of the individual blind person. As a "consequence," blindness was the result of errors committed by a child's parents, or grandparents, who passed along a predisposition toward infirmity; as a "sign," blindness marked the individual as a person whose progenitors had committed some sort of sins against the natural laws of God and science.

As a sign of error or sin, blindness had multiple meanings in Howe's view. It signified past mistakes and also served as a warning to present generations of the consequences of their own actions. "When a child is born blind," Howe concluded, "it is, in some way or other, the fault of his parents or progenitors; and though they may have erred in ignorance, the will of God is made manifest by the result, — the child is blind that the sin may be avoided, and no other blind children be begotten" (PR 1849, 23–24). Though the blind person might be innocent of any personal wrongdoing, his or her body, with all its specific traits and characteristics, served as a "poster" describing for the sighted the wages of their own ignorance and sin.

Defining the blind body as a sign of sin in previous generations, Howe anatomized that body as having powerful meaning for the present generation. For the blind as well as the sighted, the physical defects that set the blind in a class apart could signify the possibility of repentance, or the possibility of further debauch and degeneration. Those people who heeded the message about the sins of progenitors made apparent in the bodies of the present generation of the blind would abstain from all indulgences that might cause or perpetuate the defect; those who ignored that message, blind or sighted, would threaten the health of future generations by continuing to engage in unwholesome practices.

Howe's rhetoric, in its allusions to "debauches" and "indulgences" of the body, codified certain forms of sexuality as dangerous; the dangers lay both in the capacity for certain forms of sexual practices to cause degeneration in the physical and mental health of individuals and in the possibility of perpetuating defects in future generations through procreative sexual practices. Like many Victorian social commentators, Howe insisted that the only safe and sanctioned place for proper sexual activity was within the confines of marriage, for the purposes of reproduction. Sexual acts performed for other purposes, including one's own pleasure, were defined as purely selfish, hence immoral, whereas sex undertaken to create a new (and helpless) life that would require one's self-sacrificing devotion and care was defined as acceptable and desirable. Sexual intercourse within marriage was thus safe because it could be oriented toward selfless reproduction rather than toward selfish pleasure.

What was made safe for able-bodied people when embedded in the context of domestic self-sacrifice, however, could never be made safe for disabled bodies. Even when the selfish pleasures of sexuality could be redefined as a form of selflessness when oriented toward reproduction, the interpretation of blindness and other forms of physical disability as incontrovertibly signifying suffering barred disabled people from reproductive sexuality. Only the most hardhearted could insist on engaging in even the most sanctioned forms of sexuality when those acts might result in the creation of a disabled — that is, a suffering and miserable — child.

In a plea that might have come from any mid-nineteenth-century sentimental novel or temperance tract, Howe insisted that the philoprogenitive instinct, which prompted protective feelings toward one's children, coupled with the innate sense of benevolence, would aid the moral resolve of blind or sighted adults determined to help perfect humanity. While admitting that there "may be those who will harden their hearts and stiffen their necks, and be willing to bide the consequences to themselves for the sake of sensual pleasures," Howe insisted that

there will appear in the far-off and shadowy future the beseeching forms of little children, — some halt, or lame, or blind, or deformed, or decrepit, — crying, in speechless accents, "Forbear, for our sakes; for the arrows that turn aside from you are rankling in our flesh."

Then many a woman will rouse herself to the stern duty of observance of every law of health, of abstinence from all luxury and slothfulness, for the sake of those dear ones that may be born to her; and many a man will abandon sensual indulgences which he would have clung to through life but for fear of cursing his offspring with hellish passions. (PR 1848, 50–51)

To prevent their own offspring from becoming signs of their wickedness, adults of both sexes should soar to "an exalted pitch of virtue" by "resolutely keep[ing] aloof from any relations of life that might cause them to hand down bodily or mental infirmities on the innocent ones of the coming generations" (PR 1848, 51).

Urging blind adults to abstain from the "relations of life" that produced physical pleasure or offspring worked to prevent the perpetuation of defect in Howe's dreams of achieving a perfected millennial society. But it came into contradiction with another of Howe's concerns about the problems of the determinant blind body. To keep blind men and women from wanting to marry and reproduce, Howe and other directors of institutions and asylums kept the sexes strictly segregated. Such segregation required constant vigilant supervision, which tended to undermine the students' sense of self-governance; worse, it encouraged the "evils which necessarily attend and follow so unnatural a condition of things." These evils, so "inevitable and irremediable" that "they need not be pointed out," existed "in soldiers and sailors, in monks and in nuns, in every community of adult persons of one sex" (PR 1849, 20–21).

Howe had come to an impasse in his anatomization of the bodies of the blind. If members of each sex worked and learned and lived together, they would want to marry; since marriage led to sexual reproduction, marriage between two blind people would be even more likely to perpetuate their defects. What was risky enough between two sighted people was prohibitively dangerous for a blind and a sighted person and virtually unthinkable for two blind people. But if members of each sex lived and worked separately, in "the unnatural families of the monastery and the nunnery," they would develop "such moral evils and such loathsome vices" as would surely exacerbate their defects and lead, like any physical debauch, to disease and early death (PR 1850, 26).

If "unnatural" families such as those found in sex-segregated institutions created "moral evils," Howe concluded, then "natural" families might provide the needed corrective for the problems of the determinant blind body. In this spirit, he declared that the blind needed, more than anything, "a comfortable home! Would that there were such for every blind man!" (PR 1850, 24). His first goal, then, was to remake his institution so that it reproduced the best aspects of home life, and in the 1850s he began to lobby the legislature for funds to establish a "cottage system" of residences for the students.[18] Each cottage was designed to look and feel as much like "a comfortable home!" as was economically feasible. Occupied by a small number of students and a matron, each cottage would reproduce what Howe considered to be the essential element of a family: consistent affectionate maternal care for each individual. "Our pupils are mostly of that tender age at which the domestic affections are putting forth their tendrils, and requiring something around which to cling," Howe wrote; the cottage system, centered around the matron, would ensure that the institution would "be made a substitute for home, as nearly as can be" (PR 1858, 8).

Though the cottages were still sex-segregated, with boys and girls living separately, Howe was convinced that the question of "unnatural" sexuality would never arise, in part because he believed children were inherently asexual and only learned "loathsome" practices from contact with vicious adults, and in part because he believed the maternal influence guaranteed by the presence of the matron of each cottage would continually sanitize and make familial the same-sex organization. This belief in the power of family life to transform potentially unhealthy forms of sexuality also underlay Howe's insistence that blind adults, too, needed "a comfortable home!" Though they could not form families of their own and risk passing their defective constitutions on to their offspring, blind adults would benefit greatly from becoming boarders in sighted families, and thus sharing (however vicariously) in the positive effects of family life. To this end, Howe urged the establishment of a special fund to supplement the meager wages of the workshop laborers so that they could afford to board with families outside the institution. Though some objected to the idea of the blind boarding with poor families, who needed the extra money the boarders would provide, Howe insisted that the benefits from being associated with any family, however impoverished, far outweighed the risk that blind boarders would be exposed to "ignorance and vulgarity" in such homes. Howe wrote that

the family relation is gradually refining men in this country, and wherever there is progress. By it the sexual relations have a chance to be spiritualized. Some of the best feelings and affections of our nature have free scope for development and for growth where the family exists, and where it does not, they have not. Better ignorance and vulgarity with these feelings and affections, than the learning of monks and the refinement of nuns without them. (PR 1850, 26)

Within "a comfortable home!" and in constant contact with a "natural" family, blind adults would benefit, not only from the sanitizing effects of family life on sexuality, but also from the constant circulation of "the best feelings and affections of our nature." These feelings, centered around the compassionate concern automatically provided for family members whose weakness made them dependent on the care of others, were precisely what was missing from the hardhearted rules of trade that made no allowances for the physical limitations of the blind. A "comfortable home!" would guarantee that each blind adult always had some sort of family who would provide the care the dependence created by the defects of blindness made necessary.

Though typographically Howe presented his solution of "a comfortable home!" as an exclamation, it represented for him more a surrender to necessity than a triumphant answer to the problems he had encountered during the first years of his administration. He had failed in his initial attempts to redefine the social meanings of blindness, to normalize blind people by training them for economic self-sufficiency and for integration into the sighted population. Rather, insisting that the blind body was wholly determinant, creating "the blind" as a distinct class apart, Howe concluded that the blind could have little or no productive role in an industrializing economy. Unable to propose any way to bring about reformations in the present conditions of capitalism, Howe resigned himself to a dream of a millennial reorganization as the only possible means by which the blind might become productive citizens. Meanwhile, the blind would continue to rely on the charity and compassion of others, as they had since the beginnings of Western civilization. Until the millennium arrived, the social meanings of blindness would remain substantially unaltered; underlying Howe's assertion lay the belief that, until that time, the blind would best be served by associating themselves with familially-based emotions, and by waiting patiently in "a comfortable home!"

3

Sentimental Posters

Samuel Gridley Howe could only dream of a transformation of society that would make the blind, and disabled people in general, into useful members of industrial society. Victorian fictional representations of disability actively worked to envision how such a reform might occur. Using the tropes of sentimental representation, which emphasize the centrality of fellow-feeling and empathy, these fictions agree with Howe's insistence that those emotions arise from, and are most prevalent in, familial life, and agree also in showing how necessary such values are to the care and well-being of the disabled. Unlike Howe, however, Victorian sentimental fictions do not confine their disabled characters solely to the home, patiently waiting for the extra-domestic world to change to accommodate their special conditions; rather, these fictions frequently show disabled characters as the bearers of domestic values beyond the boundaries of the home. Disabled characters in these works appear in the marketplace, not to be barred from production but to reform the essential selfishness of economic relations. What Howe had accepted as the immutable laws of trade are reworked in these stories, which show that the power of disability as a signifier of suffering and compassion is strong enough to erase and rewrite the heartless rules of economic competition.

Charles Dickens, among the best-selling authors in Victorian America, frequently presents disabled characters to debate the relation between economic and domestic values. In *Barnaby Rudge* (1841), for example, he employs a blind character to insist that the world of economics and the world of feeling and compassion must and always will remain separate. Stagg, a blind villain, pretends to be helpless in order to inspire the compassion (and the donations) of the sighted, who expect to respond to a blind person with care and tenderness. Dickens soon reveals that Stagg's dependence is an act, a show put on solely for economic reasons.

When the blind man comes to Mrs. Rudge's poor cottage, he asks humbly for water, but refuses food, as he had "through the kindness of the charitable" already eaten that day.[1] As soon as he has lulled Mrs. Rudge's idiot son Barnaby into a sense of security through his meek behavior, he reveals the true motive for his visit; after drinking some liquor, he attempts to extort money from the poor woman by blackmailing her. Pointing out how "pinched and destitute" she is, Mrs. Rudge follows Diderot's reasoning in attributing Stagg's hardheartedness to his blindness: "'If you had eyes, and could look around you on this poor place, you would have pity on me,'" Mrs. Rudge declares. Invoking sentimental logic and the law of sympathetic imitation, she exhorts him to "'let your heart be softened by your own affliction, friend, and have some sympathy with mine'" (*BR*, 424).

Both Mrs. Rudge and the narrator express surprise that Stagg's blindness has not increased his empathic capacities and made him more able to feel for the sufferings of others. The law of sympathetic imitation, as articulated by Hume, coupled with the ingrained association of blindness with suffering, seems to require that blind people would automatically feel compassion for others and expect such compassion in return. The blind person who does not show such feelings is abnormal and is represented as villainous; "the craft and wickedness of [Stagg's] deportment were so much aggravated by his condition," the narrator observes, because "we are accustomed to see in those who have lost a human sense, something in its place almost divine" (*BR*, 423). Mrs. Rudge, similarly, expects to see a blind person who is gentle, caring, and compassionate as a result of his own dependence. But Dickens takes pains to show how independent Stagg is: he travels alone, without a guide, and thus has no use for sympathy, for his own sake or for others. Rather, his interests are all economic and selfish; rather than empathizing with Mrs. Rudge's poverty because of his own understanding of dependence, Stagg asserts that such emotions are "'Beside the question, ma'am, beside the question. I have the softest heart in the world, but I can't live upon it. . . . This is a matter of business, with which sympathies and sentiments have nothing to do'" (*BR*, 424).

Stagg upholds the absolute separation of economic motives and sympathetic emotions in rejecting Mrs. Rudge's sentimental reasoning and declaring that his affliction, and her poverty, have no effect on his economic interest in extortion. In so doing, he explodes the sentimental association of blindness with a self-sacrificing goodness and increased empathic ability:

"Have I no feeling for you, because I am blind? No, I have not. Why do you expect me, being in darkness, to be better than men who have their sight — why should you? Is the hand of heaven more manifest in my having no eyes, than in your having two? It's the cant of you folks to be horrified if a blind man robs, or lies, or steals; oh yes, it's far worse in him, who can barely live on the few halfpence that are thrown to him in the streets, than in you, who can see, and work, and are not dependent on the mercies of the world. A curse on you! You who have five senses may be wicked at your pleasure; we who have four, and want the most important, are to live and be moral on our affliction." (*BR*, 429)

Stagg's villainy is overdetermined by his independence, his economic self-ishness, and his lack of any domestic or familial connections. Unique in Dickens's portrayal of blindness here is his refusal to allow blindness to mitigate or soften that masculine economic selfishness; rather than making Stagg a better man, more compassionate, or gentler, or kinder, his blindness makes his villainy seem even worse, though it also makes his insight about the social constructions of blindness more acute.

In this formulation, Dickens seems to agree with Howe's assertion that blindness and market relations are irreconcilable, that "charity and trade go not long hand in hand together." Blindness, creating dependence and evok-ing sympathy, requires a domestically-trained sensibility, attuned to re-sponding to the needs of others; this sensibility stands in stark contrast to the qualities of shrewdness and self-interest that characterize successful marketplace dealings. Stagg's villainy stems from his lack of any domestic ties or training, and is made more shocking because his blindness does not mitigate that lack of familially based empathy.

Dickens's portrayal of the interactions of the heartless blind villain with the impoverished and pitiable widow (and her idiot son) work both to ex-plode and to uphold the conventions of sentimentality on which most pop-ular cultural Victorian representations of disability relied. Stagg's speech points out that the conventional signification of blindness as a form of suffering automatically inserts the blind person into a sentimental frame-work of interpretation, where suffering leads to goodness, self-sacrifice, and an ability to feel for the sufferings of others. As a blind villain, Stagg under-mines that construction, yet the novel's depiction of his exploitation of Mrs. Rudge serves to reinscribe sentimentality, as the text urges readers to iden-tify with the widow's sufferings and want to alleviate them. In this regard the novel works to generate the feelings of compassion and empathy in the reader that were precisely the qualities so surprisingly absent in Stagg. Indeed, Stagg's villainy might be as much a result of his inability to read sentimental fiction, due to his blindness, as of his lack of domestic ties and his rejection of any but selfish economic values.

Sentimental forms of representation, particularly fiction, served as a way to expand the influence of the values fostered in the domestic sphere, as articulated by moral philosophy. David Hume and Thomas Reid argued that within the family the weakness or dependence of one member is guaranteed to elicit the love and care of a stronger member, as modeled by the relationship between mothers and infants. The basis for this relationship of compassion comes from the ideal of self-sacrifice and from the individual's ability to identify with, or empathize with, the condition of another; mothers thus identify with the helplessness of their infants by recognizing that they themselves were once so helpless and needed the self-sacrificing care for which their own infants are asking. This capacity for empathic identification, when given frequent exercise in the home, comes to govern all familial and extra-familial relationships, and can serve as the basis of all social organizations, from family to national government. The central assumption of this model of social formation is that humans have an innate capacity for empathic identification, which only needs to be properly developed, ideally in the family sphere. Once developed, this capacity enables everyone to read the natural signs of emotions instantaneously, and to respond to them with sympathy and concern.

Though sentimental logic posited the capacity for empathy as innate, needing only the appropriate familial models of mutual care and affection to be properly developed, such feelings, like muscles, also needed constant exercise to remain strong and powerful. Any encounter with a being whose state signified suffering or dependence was sufficient to strengthen existing capacities for empathic identification in well-brought-up individuals. Even more important, such encounters could work to develop an empathic capacity in people whose education in feeling had been stunted or neglected. For those like Reid's "unlucky boy" who had faulty upbringings, or even for villains like Stagg who had let self-interest suppress their feelings of benevolence and sympathy, contact with a being whose condition was unmistakably associated with misery or weakness could, in a sentimental framework, begin a process of reeducation, teaching the lessons that should have been absorbed in the family circle.

In stressing the social utility of beings whose existence signified suffering, and who thus served as pedagogical tools to educate and refine others' empathic capacities, sentimental logic does not differentiate between actual material beings and representations of them. Indeed, sentimental representations rely on the premise that there could be no important difference between the sight of an actual disabled person and the depiction of such a person in representational form, whether in a picture or in a verbal description; they would produce the same effect of sympathy and concern in the viewer or reader. Following Hume's logic again, sentimental representations insist that the natural signs of emotions, such as tears, would produce similar effects in an observer, regardless of whether that observer was imitating the production of physical or linguistic "tears."

So central is this idea of the power of linguistic descriptions to produce emotional effects in readers that sentimental representations cannot afford to assume that readers will know automatically how to respond to the linguistic descriptions of characters' natural signs. Rather, sentimental fictions constantly train readers how to respond by providing a variety of models that readers are urged to imitate. Assuming that all readers need a thorough education, or at least a refresher course, in sympathetic imitation, sentimental fictions rely on such devices as narrative interruptions, wherein direct address from narrator to reader can offer overt guidance in how to relate to a character's plight. When Harriet Beecher Stowe's narrator asks readers of *Uncle Tom's Cabin*, for example, if they have never felt the loss of a child, readers are told directly how to understand the feelings of Mrs. Bird, and how thus to identify with her as if she were a friend or neighbor. When the text has modeled for readers the proper responses to the linguistic representation of the natural signs of emotions, readers complete the process of identification by producing those same emotions, and their signs, in their own bodies. When a crying character makes a reader cry, the distinction between the linguistic signification of feeling and the physical signification of feeling collapses, as does any distance between reader and character.

In the case of disabled characters, particularly blind characters, this process of empathic identification is given further support by the semiotic significance of forms of disability. The depiction of a blind character is generally sufficient to provoke a compassionate response in readers, since readers already associate blindness with misery and suffering; before the reading process even begins, readers have already been trained in the proper ways to respond to blindness. Stagg's rejection of the meaning of blindness is thus even more surprising as the refusal of a seemingly universal signification. Readers are easily able to refrain from any empathic identification with his condition, and hence are able to see Stagg as a villain, because of his rejection of the meaning of blindness with which they are already familiar.

The sentimental element of Dickens's portrayals encourages readers to form empathic identifications with Mrs. Rudge, the poor widow, but not with Stagg, who rejects the entire premise of sentimentality in rejecting the conventional meanings of blindness. Mrs. Rudge thus becomes part of the

readers' textual "family," from which Stagg is excluded. By providing readers with substitute "families" in the form of characters with whom they
form empathic identifications, sentimental representations insist that the
ties of feelings are not limited to domestic-familial networks but can occur
anywhere, in any sphere. This explains in part why sentimental works
abound with orphans, widows, and other characters who are not part of
conventional family networks: by showing readers that characters who are
not blood relations will feel compassion for these family-less people, these
stories model how readers can extend their empathic feelings beyond their
own family members as well. Producing identifications between readers and
suffering characters, and between readers and the compassionate strangers
who care for the suffering characters, sentimental representations work to
ensure that empathic feelings will become universal, not limited to domestic
confines or familial relationships.

Sentimental representations, especially fictions, frequently demonstrate the power of empathic feelings by showing the movement of familial
values of compassion and benevolence from the domestic to the public
sphere. These fictions often use as the specific sign of these values a disabled
character or other figure—widow, orphan, pauper—who symbolizes suffering and the need for care. When such figures appear in the context of
economic relations in sentimental fiction, they highlight the inadequacy
and unfeelingness of marketplace self-interest so thoroughly as to discredit
those values completely. In the universe of sentimental fiction, empathic
emotions are superior to all other feelings (and to reason as well); when
brought directly into contact, and contrast, with public values, domestic
sentiments will inevitably conquer and reign supreme. To triumph, however, this movement of values must be unidirectional: the domestic, in these
fictions, must move out into the marketplace to enact its reforms. The
opposite movement, the penetration of economic values into familial relations, frequently appears in sentimental fictions as a direct threat to the
primacy of empathic feelings.

Dickens's depiction of Stagg's villainy relies on this formulation, as he
shows the devastating effects to the Rudge family when Stagg brings his
"matter of business" into a household where "sympathies and sentiments"
should hold sway. In so doing, Dickens presents both the sentimental and
anti-sentimental perspectives: Stagg's absolute separation of the realm of
economics from the realm of feeling, and his insistence on disrupting the
latter with the former, stand in sharp contrast to the values embedded in the
depiction of the impoverished widow whose home is ruled by love and

tender care for others. In showing the interaction between these two characters and the moral stance each represents, Dickens offers his readers a choice between an identification with Mrs. Rudge and a rejection of Stagg's formulations, or an identification with Stagg's hardhearted position and thus a rejection of the feelings prompted by the widow's predicament. The tension between these two stances or positions offered to the reader prevents *Barnaby Rudge* from falling completely in the conventions of sentimental fiction.

In other depictions of the relation between sentimentality and economics, Dickens displays a more traditionally sentimental understanding of the relationship between feelings and business; rather than insisting that the two are always necessarily separate and incompatible, Dickens, like other mid-century sentimental novelists, explores the possibility that feelings might have the power to reform or rewrite the dynamics of the marketplace.

In what may be the best-known fictional discussion of disability and economics, "A Christmas Carol" (1843) depicts the transformation of Ebenezer Scrooge from the selfish and hard-hearted businessman who cares nothing for other people's woes into a fully empathic subject, whose interest in money is superseded by his desire to alleviate suffering and create affectionate relations.[2] The story begins the transformation by showing Scrooge his boyhood self, and reminding him of his own dependence and suffering; Scrooge's biography becomes, in effect, the "text" through which he learns his first lesson in feeling for others. Witnessing his younger self alone, abandoned, and miserable, Scrooge sheds his first tears, the first natural signs of his emotional development.

Scrooge's next lesson in empathy comes from his supernatural observation of the Cratchit family, particularly of Tiny Tim, who "bore a little crutch, and had his limbs supported by an iron frame!" (CC, 94). Tiny Tim already knows his status as a cultural text: Bob Cratchit proclaims that Tiny Tim "'told me, coming home, that he hoped the people saw him in church, because he was a cripple, and it might be pleasant for them to remember upon Christmas Day, who made lame beggars walk and blind men see'" (CC, 94). Dickens has the crippled boy's father announce this to remind Scrooge and other readers how they too should respond to Tiny Tim's text. Scrooge provides a model for readers by reacting to Tim, and to the scene of happy family life in general, with "an interest he had never felt before" (CC, 97). He asks the Ghost of Christmas Present if Tiny Tim will live, feeling for the first time in his adult life some concern for the welfare of someone other than himself. When the Spirit announces that Tim will die if the future remains unchanged, Scrooge makes his first resolution to change the Cratchit family's condition.

Scrooge's feeling for Tiny Tim sparks his first stirrings of an empathic sensibility; his status as outside observer of the contented domestic scene also makes him long to be included in such loving and interdependent relationships, as he had been in the past. Scrooge's reformation occurs as the result of his being a witness to spectacles, to tableaux or dramas enacted before him, in which he participates only vicariously, through identifying with the emotions being portrayed. Thus Scrooge's transformation again provides readers with a model of how sentimental scenarios should affect them: they identify not only with the Cratchits and other characters, but with Scrooge's position as passive audience. Scrooge's transformation comes from the exercise of his ability to feel for those who are related to him only through economic ties; it is not his own son but the son of his employee who might die if he doesn't reform. The story shows Scrooge—and, by extension, the readers who also stand in Scrooge's position of observer— learning to supplement economic ties with emotional ones, rather than forcing the former necessarily to exclude the latter.

The final lesson in Scrooge's reformation is strictly sentimental: he witnesses his own deathbed, seeing that his greed has led him to die alone and unloved, and contrasts that barren death with the genuine love and grief the Cratchits feel for the loss of Tiny Tim. The Cratchits' response to Tim's death again provides a model for both Scrooge and readers, as they vow never to forget the crippled boy and to continue to use his memory as a kind of text, a reminder to be patient and mild and "not quarrel easily amongst ourselves, and forget poor Tiny Tim in doing it" (CC, 123). Scrooge's feelings both for himself and for the Cratchits marks the completion of his transformation into an empathic being. When he awakens and finds the world unchanged, Scrooge uses his new capacity for feeling to the fullest, and Dickens's narrator promises this new capacity will indeed transform the world, in ever-widening circles: "He did it all, and infinitely more. . . . He became as good a friend, as good a master, and as good a man, as the good old city knew, or any other good old city, town, or borough in the good old world" (CC, 133–34).

In this story, unlike *Barnaby Rudge*, Dickens unequivocally supports the power of sentimentality to transform audiences by providing them with an education in empathic feeling; he insists that this empathic education will necessarily make an individual change the way he acts in the world.[3]

Scrooge does not just learn to feel for the Cratchits, he acts on those feelings, radically altering the employer-employee relationship to accommodate his new identifications with the loving Cratchit family. Other sentimental fictions from this same era also asserted the power of empathy (and
the power of sentimental fiction to produce that empathy) to transform
economic relations. Perhaps the most detailed model showing readers how
to develop and use the powers of empathic identification in this way appears in Dinah Mulock Craik's *John Halifax, Gentleman*, which was a best-
seller in the United States from its first publication in 1856.[4]

Craik's story, as the title implies, delineates the characteristics relevant
to the title "gentleman." Rather than locating this status in possession of
property or bloodline, however, Craik's novel associates gentility with sentimental values and with the power to develop and use one's empathic sensibilities. Gentility, in her definition, is related to gentleness and is marked
by the deployment of a proper Christian moral sensibility and concern for
the welfare of others in all areas of endeavor, including the economic realm.
What makes John Halifax, the book's hero, into a "gentleman" is not the
wealth he gains through his honest work, but the love he generates and
earns through his treatment of his family and, by extension, his workers and
dependents.

The importance of empathic feelings, particularly in relation to economic relations, is evident from the opening scene of the novel. Phineas
Fletcher, a sixteen-year-old crippled boy, is on an outing with his Quaker
father, Abel Fletcher, when urgent business calls the father to his tanyard.
Unable to take his son, in his wheelchair, to his place of business, Fletcher
seeks help, offering to pay someone to escort his boy back home. John
Halifax volunteers, but refuses payment, scorning to take money for being
kind to a fellow human being. The father, impressed by Halifax's moral
rectitude, offers him a job in the tanyards; the son, gratified by the tenderness of Halifax's caring, wishes to adopt him as his brother.

Craik opens the novel by insisting, as did Howe and Dickens, that
disability and economic production cannot mix; Abel Fletcher cannot take
his crippled son into his place of business because the tanyard will not
supply the sympathy and care that Phineas's condition requires. Ensuring
Phineas's safe return to the domestic sphere requires the care of someone
whose feelings cannot be purchased by money, someone who is above mere
market relations. Eventually, Craik will show that John Halifax's gentleman
status comes as much from his economic probity, his loyalty, and his will-
ingness to give his employer an honest day's work as from his capacity for

empathic feeling; in opening the novel by showing how Halifax upholds sentimental over marketplace values, Craik insists that these domestically-based values are the more important of the two.

For Phineas, a motherless only child, Halifax's concern becomes the familial affection otherwise absent in his life. His father, too busy with his business interests to provide the affection and care Phineas lost when his mother died, has supplied him with paid attendants, who have tended to his physical needs but who could not be counted on to supply the genuine emotional care he has craved. Phineas reflects that his meeting with Halifax marked "the first time in my life I ever knew the meaning of that rare thing, tenderness," a quality that could never be purchased (*JH*, 21). In this initial formulation, what belongs to the domestic sphere — care and tenderness — cannot come from the economic sphere nor can a figure belonging to one cross over into the other. The paid attendant (an economically defined being) cannot provide genuine care, nor can Phineas, whose disability confines him to the domestic sphere (where such care is supposed to re-side) cross over into the marketplace. Craik shows Phineas actively at-tempting to leave the domestic realm in order to cement his friendship with Halifax, who dwells in the economic realm; at first he merely sits on the stoop of his house, waiting for Halifax's cart to pass by on market day, but eventually he asks his father to let him go himself to the tanyard. Despite his sense that his place of business is no place for his crippled son, Abel Fletcher relents, hoping that this indicates Phineas's desire to take an interest in his business and eventually to succeed him in it. Phineas, however, only wants to go to the tanyard to see Halifax; the business — both the tanning pro-cedures and the idea of business itself — make him feel ill, physically and mentally (*JH*, 23–24).

Phineas cannot cross easily between the two worlds, just as his father cannot leave behind the hardhearted values of the marketplace to offer his son the compassion he craves. Halifax, however, proves equal to both tasks, satisfying the father's need for a son who will be a shrewd business partner and the son's need for a brother/companion who will care for and protect him. In doing so, Craik begins to collapse the distinctions between the two spheres, defining Halifax's "gentleman" status as precisely that ability to function admirably in both worlds. Lest Halifax's tenderness toward Phi-neas tempt readers to associate him too closely with feminine ideals, how-ever, Craik takes pains to cast Halifax's emotions specifically in masculine terms: his tenderness, Phineas insists, is "a quality which can exist only in strong, deep, and undemonstrative natures, and therefore in its perfection is oftenest found in men." John Halifax, according to Phineas, had this brotherly sensibility "more than any one, woman or man, that I ever knew" (*JH*, 21).

Naming Halifax's tenderness as explicitly masculine, however, relegates Phineas to a feminine position in relation to him; his disabled body, which confines him to the domestic sphere and requires compassionate care, marks him as unable to participate in the masculine combination of business and empathy that characterizes Halifax. When the two sneak off to a playhouse to see Mrs. Siddons performing Shakespeare and the crowd threatens to crush the helpless boy, Halifax shelters him; "If I had been a woman," Phineas observes, "and the woman that he loved, he could not have been more tender over my weakness." Phineas's feminized condition, which was to him a source of humiliation and which aroused in other men a feeling of contempt, was to Halifax yet another condition "dealt by the hand of Heaven, and, as such, regarded by John only with compassion" (*JH*, 56). Phineas, feminized by his disability, evokes only the masculine tenderness of his "brother," showing that such a brotherly empathic sensibility will be available, even beyond direct family ties, for the protection of women, children, and other weak and dependent people.

Phineas's feminized position as dependent fluctuates to some extent throughout the novel. Craik's narrative, establishing Phineas as narrator and observer, depends on Phineas's continued presence in Halifax's life and endeavors; his crippled body signifies to readers the need for Halifax, as gentleman, to continue to provide him with care, and ensures that Phineas will never take up an independent existence of his own. Rather, Phineas exists, first as Halifax's dependent "brother" and object of his compassion, then as the bachelor uncle and observer in the Halifax household, serving as tutor to John's children as well as the narrator of the story. Craik makes much of Phineas's crippled condition at the beginning of the book in order to demonstrate how the bond of "brotherhood" forms between the two unrelated characters, and in order to show how Phineas's disabled body, while dwelling solely in the domestic sphere, moves into the marketplace to show Halifax's ability to use familial values even in the economic realm. As the novel progresses, however, Craik minimizes references to the disability that had dominated the first sections of the story. Phineas inexplicably ceases to need help in getting around, and while he remains too weak (and too disgusted by business) to earn his own living and establish his own household, he is never so ill as to be unable to participate fully in any of the Halifax family triumphs and trials.

Having inherited his father's property—though the elder Fletcher's business went to Halifax—Phineas is financially independent, but his money does not come from any direct participation in market relations. This allows him to function as an emotional touchstone or center by providing opportunities, both before and after Halifax's marriage, for Halifax and his wife to demonstrate the depth of their empathic sensibilities. Though he does not need their financial support, his disability still demands their compassionate care, and he remains the figure who proves the centrality of Halifax's empathic capabilities. Craik thus retains Halifax as the only figure who can successfully combine domestic and economic virtues.

Phineas's role as the object that can demonstrate and strengthen Halifax's compassionate capacities is necessary for the first third of the novel, in order to establish that Halifax's claim to gentility is based first and foremost on his inextinguishable reservoir of tenderness and fellow-feeling. Phineas's main function is to be a "poster child," a sign understood as meaning suffering, and as evoking sympathy and care, in all observers, whether in domestic or economic settings. Craik's novel is less about Phineas per se than about the effect Phineas's disability has on an independent adult white male. The story thus serves to model, for readers assumed to be physically independent (and white, if not exclusively male), their proper duties and responsibilities toward the disabled. Once this modeling is established, however, Phineas's role diminishes, which may explain why Craik ceases to mention his crippled condition further; certainly he is less believable as the object of Halifax's compassion as he becomes an economically independent adult.

More important, though, Phineas's function in sparking Halifax's compassion is superseded when John and Ursula's first child, Muriel, is born. At the christening it is discovered that Muriel is blind; throughout the rest of the novel, it is Muriel's blindness that serves to test the empathic sensibilities of all other characters, and thus to evaluate the extent of their gentility, regardless of wealth or title or appearance. Craik retains Phineas in the story by necessity, as he is the first-person narrator, but his role is reduced to that of observer and his function is to record how the family responds to Muriel's blindness.

The replacement of Phineas by Muriel marks a transformation in the definitions of Halifax's status as "gentleman" as well. Initially, as a penniless orphan, Halifax proved his capacity for gentility through combining his brotherly sentiments toward Phineas with his loyalty and devotion to his employer, Phineas's father. Craik presents the two qualities as inseparable, as two sides of the same coin. Rather than being seen as currying favor with his boss by caring for his crippled son, Halifax's honesty and industriousness in the workplace are echoed and reinforced by his masculine tenderness in the Fletcher home. As Halifax grows from boyhood to manhood, however, the requirements for adult selfhood shift as well. Rather than being the loyal employee, Halifax becomes the manager (and eventual owner) of the elder Fletcher's tanning enterprise. Craik shows his adult entrepreneurial sensibility as influenced by his affectionate and protective roles as husband and father, just as his apprenticeship had been influenced by his brotherly compassion for Phineas. Thus, as Muriel replaces Phineas as the primary object through which Halifax can demonstrate his adult empathic subjectivity, so his concerns as employer replace his concerns as employee as the means through which Craik can delineate the "gentlemanly" qualities of his adult economic self. Through structuring these parallels in the novel, Craik insists that the two aspects of selfhood are directly interrelated and inseparable: how one treats a disabled member of one's "family" indicates how one treats one's economic dependents, and vice versa. The movement from brother to husband and father thus parallels Halifax's progression from employee to employer, as both provide an indication of the validity of his claim to "gentleman."

Blind Muriel, the family's only daughter for thirteen years, becomes her father's favorite, whom he calls his "blessing." Craik describes Muriel as a conventionally angelic girl-child, who is never angry, restless, or sad; she is a "living peace," whose "soft dark calm . . . seemed never broken by the troubles of this our troublous world" (*JH*, 206). Muriel's blind purity also protected her from childhood illnesses and tantrums, as "her parents never had to endure a single pain" from her or for her; "even the sicknesses of infancy and childhood, of which the three [boys] had their natural share, always passed her by, as if in pity. Nothing ever ailed Muriel" (*JH*, 206).

Muriel's presence functions initially in the novel as a traditionally feminine domestic resource, ready to soothe away the cares and trials of the business world when Halifax returns to his home and family. "If at night her father came home jaded and worn, sickened to the soul by the hard battle he had to fight daily, hourly, with the outside world, Muriel would comfort him and creep into his bosom, and he was comforted" (*JH*, 206). Taking over what would usually be the wife's role, the angelic blind girl not only revitalizes the worn energies of the competitive businessman, but also sets a moral standard for behavior in the household—not through reproaches, but through her own always-exemplary behavior and through the disability that unfailingly summons a compassionate attitude. "No one could speak any but soft and sweet words when the blind child was by" (*JH*, 206). Because of Muriel's angelic presence, her brothers did not learn, as did other boys, "that a young man's chief manliness ought to consist in despising the tender charities of home" (*JH*, 297). Providing yet another model for the ablebodied male reader, they, like their father, promised to become men who had the "tenderness" Phineas found so masculine.

The power of Muriel's purity to restore faith and happiness in her worn-out father, and to inspire gentle compassionate behavior in her otherwise boisterous brothers, eventually extends beyond the limits of her own home and family. As Halifax prospers and becomes a mill owner, he begins to take his favorite child with him: "he got in a habit of fetching her down to the mill every day at noon, and carrying her about in his arms, wherever he went, during the rest of his work" (*JH*, 273). When Lord Luxmore, an unscrupulous nearby landowner, blocks the flow of the stream that drives Halifax's mill, he uses his entrepreneurial ingenuity to design and install a steam-driven engine to turn the mill wheel. Unlike other mill owners who attempted to introduce industrial machinery at the beginning of the nineteenth century in Britain, however, Halifax is saved from a Luddite rebellion, and the hostile uprising of his workers, because he has shown them his empathic side through Muriel. "Rough, coarse, blue-handed, blue-pinafored women of the mill" would stop and "look wistfully after 'master and little blind miss'" when they appeared. Phineas notes that he often thought

the quiet way in which the Enderley mill people took the introduction of machinery, and the peaceableness with which they watched for weeks the setting up of the steam-engine, was partly owing to their strong impression of Mr. Halifax's goodness as a father, and the vague, almost superstitious interest which attached to the pale, sweet face of Muriel. (*JH*, 273)

Craik here shows herself capable of imagining the kind of industrial reform Samuel Gridley Howe could only dream of. While Howe longed for a miraculous millennial reorganization, with no vision of how such a restructuring of industrial capitalist society might be achieved, Craik, as a writer of sentimental fiction, was eager to show exactly how domestic values, brought out of the home and into contact with the laws of market relations, would effect a radical transformation. While Howe felt it necessary to confine the blind to "a comfortable home!" Craik literally brings the blind girl, in her father's tender arms, out of the home and into the workplace to remind workers that the spirit of empathy and care can operate just as effectively in the industrialized factory as in the home. The paternal spirit that prompts Halifax to carry his daughter around the millworks reassures the laborers that he will show them the same empathic care, that they will not have to become unfeeling machine-like bodies in order to function in this new mode of production.

Even more than her depiction of Phineas, Craik's portrayal of Muriel emphasizes the social function of a disabled person as a "poster child," as a cultural sign that generates and guarantees a compassionate response. While Phineas served to show the effect of disability in summoning sympathy in an ablebodied and economically productive individual man, Muriel affects the entire workforce of Halifax's mill; Muriel has the greater effect because her signification is overdetermined by her blindness, her femininity, and her age. Phineas's crippled body moved between the domestic and economic spheres to show how John Halifax represented the best of the values of both worlds, while Muriel's body, literally carried from the home into the factory, works to redefine relations of production in the industrial arena. While Phineas's disability evoked sympathy in one man, Muriel's disability rewrites market relations on a larger scale, casting employer-employee relations as those of a father with his children. In so doing, Craik supports the Victorian convention that workers are dependent on the paternalistic care of the father/employer, but strengthens and expands that convention by insisting that the extension of familial sentiments and concerns to one's workers will transform market relations completely.

Renamed as caring father rather than merely employer, Halifax protects his employees as he would his children by standing up for the workers against their unscrupulous landlord, the same nobleman who diverted his millstream, even though he risks losing profitable business connections to him. If the laborers needed additional proof of Halifax's gentlemanly extension of familial affection to the workplace, it is provided in a scene where the disabled and dependent of all sorts enter into the Halifax family home for the yearly feast the Halifaxes provide for "the poor, the lame, the halt, and the blind," and anyone else who needed but could not return the kindness (*JH*, 248). In so doing they dissolve the distinctions between home and marketplace, between those who are family members related by blood and those who are not. The true mark of Halifax's status as gentleman,

Craik concludes, lies in his refusal to consider any differences among people except those which distinguish those who need care from those who are able to provide it.

*   *   *

Sentimental fictions portraying disabled characters rewrote the division between marketplace and domestic values by showing how disabled bodies, as signs generating empathic responses, evoked sympathy and kindness even in the midst of economic production. Authors like Dickens and Craik, by their insistence on the universal effectiveness of sentimentality, thus contradicted Howe's assertion that charity and trade were inimicable. They also invented a form of social utility for the disabled, where Howe had found only incapacity and the necessity for confinement to the domestic sphere. A disabled body could serve a useful social role in eliciting an empathic response from an observer and reminding an audience of their Christian duty to respond to suffering with compassion and care. But such a body had its limitations. Fictional and nonfictional representations of blind and disabled bodies agreed that disabled people could hardly fulfill any functions beyond their roles as "posters." As Craik illustrates through Phineas Fletcher, a disabled man cannot establish his own family network, but must always be on the margins of an ablebodied person's family. Enjoying Howe's dream of "a comfortable home!" without becoming a husband and father in his own right, Phineas's position reinforces both the idea that affectional ties are not necessarily linked to blood kinship and that a disabled body is necessarily an asexual, and specifically nonreproductive, body.

What Craik sketches in Phineas as the desirable familial relation for disabled males becomes a full-blown portrait when applied to females, as illustrated in her discussion of Muriel's future. The contradiction between the reproductive sexuality at the center of family life and the requirement that disabled bodies remain asexual is, in most sentimental fictional portrayals of disability, even greater for a disabled woman than for a disabled man because female social roles in sentimental fiction are focused almost exclusively around questions of wife- and motherhood. This contradiction prevents Craik from attempting to portray Muriel as anything other than a dependent child. In a conversation about the future, Muriel innocently asks about what she will be like as a woman, and stops the conversation in mid-sentence. "Somehow, she seemed so unlike an ordinary child," Phineas muses, that "none of us ever seemed to think of Muriel as a woman" (*JH*, 248).

To be a "woman," in nineteenth-century sentimental logic, meant being a wife and mother, which necessarily meant being reproductively sexual. The limited meanings available to define the social roles of a disabled body, conflicting with the limited meanings available to define the social roles of a female body, result in Muriel's slow but inevitable death. As her family role as comforter and role model is gradually usurped by her younger sister, Maud, Muriel's strength begins to fade; as she weakens, she tries to imagine herself

a woman grown. Fancy me twenty years old, as tall as mother, wearing a gown like her, talking and ordering, and busy about the house. How funny! . . . Oh! no, father, I couldn't do it. I had better remain always your little Muriel, weak and small. (*JH*, 284)

Muriel cannot envision herself taking her mother's role, like her clothes, which become a metonymic displacement for other functions she could never fulfill. Unable, however, always to remain "little Muriel, weak and small," she dies, escaping the contradiction between the ban on sexuality required by her disability and the cultural imperative for reproduction that would turn her into a mother, the only sanctioned role of female agency available in sentimental fiction.

The focus in Victorian sentimental fiction on female sexuality as the unnamed center of the domestic sphere and the source of the maternal-infant bond that is the model for all social relations stands in marked contrast to the representations of female sexuality in eighteenth-century sentimental fiction. As typified by Samuel Richardson's *Clarissa*, eighteenth-century sentimental novels showed seduction, as well as abduction, as the cause of female suffering requiring familial protection (or sparking paternal indifference). In so doing, they placed female sexuality at the center of the plot and of the emotions, though they also worked to make that sexuality innocent by portraying the heroine as a passive and ignorant victim of rapacious male lust.[5] The eighteenth-century version served as a kind of "training manual," advising young women about the dangers of male sexuality and telling them how to avoid the rake and choose the virtuous husband. As Cathy Davidson reads Mrs. Rowson's *Charlotte Temple*, one of the first American versions of the sentimental novel, women readers could use the plot to experience vicariously the thrills, and the costs, of seduction, weeping over the heroine's unwise decisions and learning, through their empathic identification with her, not to make the same mistakes.[6] In the nineteenth-century sentimental novel, however, particularly as produced by mid-century Anglo-American women writers, the portrait of female sexuality and desire that had formed the center of the plot has been superseded by a portrait of reproduction and motherhood. Replacing sexual feelings with maternal feelings, the mid-century sentimental novel advises readers, not about the proper way to bestow their virginity, but about how to acquire the empathic sensibility that will make them attractive to men as wives and mothers.

Female sexuality in the nineteenth-century sentimental novel becomes unrepresentable as something distinct and separate from motherhood. In *John Halifax, Gentleman*, Lord Luxmore's daughter, Lady Caroline Brithwood, has left her husband Richard, who has been labeled as a man of base character through his lack of concern for his employees, tenants, servants, and dependents. She intends to run off with a paramour, until Ursula Halifax reminds her of her "child which only breathed and died," and who "died spotless" as a result. "When you die," Ursula asks her, "how dare you meet that little baby" with such a stain on your soul? (*JH*, 230). Though Lady Caroline weeps heartfelt tears at Ursula's evocation of her motherhood and lost child, she finally does go off with her lover. In this character, Craik presents readers with a woman who clearly has her own sexual desires, but figures that woman in terms of frustrated or unfulfilled maternalism. Had Lady Caroline's baby lived, she would have devoted herself to its welfare and not focused on the gratification of her own selfish pleasures.

In sentimental works, sexual reproduction occurs almost entirely offstage; what is represented is always couched entirely in terms of emotion, rather than physical activity or sensual pleasure. The difficulty is to find a way to frame sexuality so that it is related to empathy and emotionality, the grounds on which all bodies are both equal and representable, and not in relation to pleasure, which is necessarily self-oriented and selfish. The solution most novels find is to displace adult sexuality onto parental emotions; sexual activity is acceptable (though still not directly representable) only because it leads to children and to the disinterested self-sacrificing love that is the foundation of all subsequent empathic social relations.

In sentimental fiction female sexuality thus functions as a powerful determinant of social role: characters are classified by whether they are allowed any form of sexuality, and then by how that sexuality is used. Adult female status is marked by the ability to become a sexual being, and moral standing is marked in turn by what kind of sexuality she exhibits. While adult female characters must thus choose between positive and negative forms of sexuality, most disabled female characters, whose function relies on their "poster" status, die before the choice needs to be made, and thus avoid the dual pitfalls of marital reproduction and extramarital immorality.

Those characters who remain forever children, by dying young or otherwise refusing to negotiate the hazards of adult sexuality, continue to function solely as signs reminding others of their emotional responsibilities toward the less fortunate. In Phineas Fletcher, however, Craik introduces a new conceptualization of disabled selfhood by showing him, not just as the object of Halifax's compassion, but as an adult, defined as an emotional agent who is able to provide care for dependents, particularly Muriel. Phineas's capacity for empathic agency, for active compassion on behalf of a less-fortunate or weaker person, represents a model of disabled adulthood that does not rely on either economic production or sexual reproduction; this model marks the beginnings of the possibility that disabled characters (and perhaps disabled people) might find some social function in this emotional agency, and thus escape having to remain forever objects of others' care.

In Craik's conception, however, gender proves powerful in limiting this new possibility for disabled adulthood through emotional agency. Muriel is not given this option by Craik because sexuality is too powerful a determinant of female adulthood. Were Muriel to grow up and marry, she would risk not only the reproduction of her defect but the loss of her status as "poster." As she became a mother, she would necessarily symbolize the ability to become completely self-sacrificing, erasing her own needs in favor of meeting the needs of dependent others; as such she would cease to symbolize the need for care itself. Girls like Muriel, Little Eva, and Little Nell, defined as "weak and small," retain their status as "posters" by dying before having to choose between becoming an empathic agent, a mother, or a selfish sexual being. More important, these characters die because the sentimental fictions in which they appear cannot imagine a model for female adulthood that encompasses the concept of "woman" as empathic agent defined as separate from sexual reproduction and motherhood.

Sentimental logic, because it relies on the infant-mother relation as the model for all empathic social relations, excludes any nonmaternal, nonreproductive model of female empathic adulthood. The limits of sentimentality thus occur at the threshold of representing adult sexuality in itself, even though that sexuality is the unnamed and unnamable core of the family structure which, as Howe asserted, is the best purifying and refining institution ordained by God. Muriel, Nell, Eva, and other purely sentimental heroines die on the brink of adolescence, at precisely the point where female embodiment, in order to lead to the adult relations of maternal-infant empathy, must lead to reproductive sexuality. While most adult women make the choice between self-sacrificing reproductive sexuality, as epitomized in Ursula Halifax, and selfish pleasure-oriented sexuality, as epitomized in Lady Caroline Brithwood, girl-children in sentimental fiction retain their status as the inspiration for exercising others' empathy and leading others away from selfishness by avoiding sexuality altogether. Their deaths allow them to continue to exist as educational "texts," as exempla that provide illustrations of natural purity and goodness, and which prompt others to feel and act similarly.[7]

Unable both to remain dependent empathic objects and to become maternal centers of a family through the unnamed activities of adult reproductive heterosexuality, such characters die from the contradictions inherent in sentimental logic. The two forms of embodiment — the embodiment of disability, which exists solely to produce empathic reactions in others, and the embodiment of sexuality, which exists in good people for reproduction and children, and in bad people for selfish pleasure — are mutually exclusive and contradictory. This explains, in part, why depictions of sexually active disabled adults still remain taboo in late twentieth-century culture; the expectation that disabled embodiment confines one to a necessarily asexual childlike status is coupled with the injunction against disabled bodies as sites of reproduction to ensure that disabled bodies, when representable at all, are inscribed solely in sentimental frameworks.

Working with these same assumptions about the relations among disability, empathy, and female sexuality, Charles Dickens agrees with Dinah Craik in depicting blindness as incompatible with any form of adult female sexuality, including motherhood. In this particular portrayal of the relationship between disability and sexuality, however, Dickens also emphasizes the unidirectional movement of values from domestic to economic spheres by showing the disastrous results of the intrusion of economic values into family life. In "The Cricket on the Hearth" (1846), Dickens presents a blind girl, Bertha Plummer, who lives entirely in the domestic sphere, where Bertha's father Caleb shelters her from all knowledge of evil or cruelty.[8] Bertha's existence in the home is thus portrayed as a fantasy of goodness and wholesomeness that simultaneously protects her from knowing the realities of the extradomestic world and entraps her in dangerous illusions. The dangers of Caleb's protective fantasy world are shown when the question of sexuality, which forms the center of family and domestic life, becomes the unnamed center of Bertha's romantic imaginings.

Dickens's story focuses on describing what constitutes a true "home," "family," and "marriage" by contrasting three different households and sets of relationships. John and Dot Peerybingle and their infant child (and their servant) stand as the existing ideal, complete with a cricket chirping happily on the domestic hearth. They are contrasted to Caleb Plummer, a widower, who contrives to make his daughter's life happy by lying to her about their poverty, and to Mr. Tackleton, Plummer's employer, a hardhearted toy manufacturer whose stinginess is the cause of the Plummers' woes. Tackleton wishes to marry May Fielding, and is shown early on to be an unsuitable mate because he fails to show any compassionate feelings for Bertha's blindness.

The Peerybingle household contains a constantly crying baby, whom the servant girl is continually trying to hush. Dickens repeatedly refers to the baby's crying as a comic trope, but his emphasis on the child also serves as an implicit reminder of the reproductive sexuality at the heart of the Peerybingle family. The stability of the Peerybingle family is threatened by the appearance of a man, disguised as a deaf old gentleman, whom John, a carter, brings home one night as a "package" that has been left to wait "until called for." Tackleton, out of sheer malice, tries to get John to believe that Dot is about to commit adultery with this disguised gentleman.

All the difficulties presented in the plot of the story arise from the interpenetration of the domestic and economic spheres. When Peerybingle brings his work home, in the form of the "package," his domestic relationships threaten to go awry. Plummer's problems stem from his attempt to shield his daughter from the knowledge that their home is not a paradise but rather serves as Plummer's workshop. Tackleton's unsuitability as a husband is made apparent through his inability to separate economic and domestic values, as he assesses all human relationships in monetary terms.

Caleb Plummer's particular conflation of the domestic and economic spheres results in catastrophe for his daughter: believing in his fantastic portraits of their comfortable home and his benevolent employer, Bertha falls in love with Tackleton. While overtly pointing out the dangers of an innocent and dependent blind girl falling for an unscrupulous and uncaring businessman, Dickens's story also reveals the dangerousness of Bertha's love in her hope of becoming a sexual adult, a wife and mother like Dot Peerybingle. The emphasis on adultery in the Peerybingle household, while not named explicitly, foregrounds the idea of sexuality as the basis of marriage and family; this is reinforced also by the fact that the Plummer household is not only poor but asexual, as there is no husband-wife partnership at its center.

As with Howe's and Craik's depictions, Dickens's story shows that sexuality becomes the limit of the blind person's ability to participate fully in domestic life. As such, sexuality also becomes the limiting point for the empathic capacities celebrated in the family and signified by the presence of disabled people inside and outside the domestic realm. While reproductive sexuality can be figured as the product of the desire, not for selfish pleasure but for dependent objects on whom to practice maternal self-sacrifice, such sexuality is inaccessible to disabled people, who are culturally enjoined from reproducing their defect. Sexuality defined solely as pleasure, by contrast, can only be represented as selfishness and vice, which become the antithesis of empathic feeling. Thus, while nondisabled bodies can be sites of reproduction without compromising the ties of empathy that form the basis of all social bonds, disabled bodies cannot. Dependent on empathy for their survival as well as for their social utility as "signs," blind people like Bertha are forced to remain on the margins of family life, barred from becoming the centers of their own families because of the contradictions between blindness and sexuality.

Tackleton, too, is left in a similar position at the story's end. The disguised old gentleman is revealed to be Edward Plummer, Bertha's brother, Caleb's son, who has returned from South America with a fortune. This explains why Dot was seen embracing him; it also allows Edward to rescue May Fielding from marriage to Tackleton by marrying her himself. The story concludes with Tackleton asking to be included in the restored family circles, now augmented to include Dot's parents, May's mother, and the family dog. Tackleton, like Scrooge, repents the errors of his hardhearted and selfish ways as he experiences the joys of the family hearth, but, like Bertha, remains on the edges of the circle, a bachelor who cannot form the center of a family of his own. Thus Dickens equates the businessman and the blind girl, as both are prevented from becoming the sexual center of domesticity: the one because of his lack of empathic capacities, as determined by his business dealings, and the other by the meaning of blindness as necessitating compassion, and the equation between reproductive female sexuality and empathic agency.

These forms of sentimental representation could not present blind or disabled characters as full adults, in the family or the marketplace, because they cannot represent blind or disabled characters as the necessarily sexual centers of family life, as mothers and fathers. Sentimental representations cannot inscribe disabled bodies simultaneously as sites of empathic feeling and of sexuality, whether reproductive or pleasurable. While working to establish that the empathic model of adulthood is operative and powerful in both the domestic and economic spheres, the insistence on family relations as the basis for all forms of empathic subjectivity, in the marketplace as well as the home, bars disabled people from full participation. Though "brothers" might run businesses, blind women can't be mothers, and thus they cannot hope to attain adult status on the same terms as the sighted, in either the home or the marketplace.

These fictions are unable to imagine a disabled female character who could be both the object of others' sympathy and concern and an emotional agent in her own right. Such a character could, like Muriel or Tiny Tim, remain a "poster" fulfilling an important social function by reminding the ablebodied of their Christian moral duty to care for the less fortunate, while also serving, like a mother, as a model for how to provide that care. Other representations of disability, both fictional and nonfictional, borrowed the idea of the centrality of empathy and compassion from sentimental logic, and took on the task of imagining what a non-sexually-based emotional agency might look like. In doing so, fictional and nonfictional representations raised questions about the parameters of this notion of adulthood and about its potential social utility. These forms of discourse, while insisting that the role of "poster" inspiring benevolence in others was still central to any question of the social roles for disabled people, began to rewrite the cultural meanings of disabled bodies as signs to include a wider notion of agency, one not dependent on either economic production or sexual reproduction.

4

The Angel in the Text

Maria Susanna Cummins's novel *The Lamplighter* (1854) imagines the possibility of a disabled adult woman becoming a model of empathic agency.[1] Emily Graham, blind since childhood, appears in this novel as the model of True Womanhood, whose example the uneducated orphan Gertrude Flint must follow in order herself to become an empathic adult, capable of unselfish compassion for others. Emily Graham thus marks a new development in the representation of disabled people: not herself a mother or wife, she nonetheless stands as exemplar of sentimental values that have their roots in maternal-infant relations, and as such demonstrates that disabled people, while remaining signs generating compassionate responses in others, can themselves accede to the empathic agency that is the hallmark of adult status within sentimental logic.

Cummins's portrayal of Graham emphasizes the idea that Emily's blindness, while remaining a sign of affliction and suffering, has also increased her capacity to feel for the plight of others and to work actively to aid them. In this, Cummins's novel agrees with the stance articulated by Mlle. de Salignac, who argued with Diderot's insistence that a blind person must always remain unfeeling. Diderot had based his conclusion on the assumption that the sight of the natural signs of distress, such as tears, was the only effective means to prompt the empathic responses that spurred individuals to act to relieve suffering; vision alone could provide the stimulus needed to make observers identify with a sufferer, reproduce the natural signs of suffering in themselves, feel powerfully the emotions that produced those natural signs, and then attempt to alleviate their cause. Mlle. de Salignac, offended at the suggestion that her blindness necessarily made her hardhearted, had responded by insisting that her own experience of misery, resulting from her blindness, was sufficient to enable her to notice and identify with another's woes.

Neither Maria Cummins's fictional portrayal of a blind woman nor

Mlle. de Salignac's autobiographical account provides a blueprint for how a blind person might become an empathic agent, other than to evoke blindness and gender as the natural determinants of the capacity for fellow-feeling. Both, however, insist that the lack of sight does not stunt their ability to feel. The difference between Diderot's view of vision and empathy and those of Mlle. de Salignac and Maria Cummins lies primarily in the way they understand the operation of signs. Diderot insists that the ability to understand another's feelings comes from a direct sensory apprehension of the natural signs another person produces: one must directly see tears, or smiles, or frowns, to reproduce those emotions in one's own person, and hence to experience them for oneself. Mlle. de Salignac, however, insists that the natural signs of another's feelings can be apprehended through means other than sight; her statements to Diderot imply that her blindness, as a form of suffering, combined with the sensitivity she posits as inherent in her gender training, provides another means of "reading" the signs produced by another — a means not dependent on direct sensory perception of material signs.

Mlle. de Salignac thus effectively separated the capacity to read signs from the capacity for sensory apprehension of those signs. In so doing, she articulated a shift in the conception of the relation between sensory perception and reading that provided a new way to understand how a blind person might become an empathic agent rather than merely a signifier of suffering. Disconnecting sensory perception from an understanding of signs had important repercussions for the education of the blind, deaf, and deaf-blind and provided an important foundation for the development of sentimental representation. A disabled person, particularly a blind person, who was able to find ways to "read" signs of emotions even in the absence of direct perception of the natural signs of those emotions could learn to identify with and feel for others, and thus learn to be an empathic adult, just as a nondisabled person could. The same process facilitated the linguistic education of those lacking a sense, such as sight or hearing: when alternative methods of signification could provide the same information usually given by a missing sense, there was no distinction between the ability to interpret signs of those who had sight or hearing and of those lacking one or more of those senses. Taken on a more general level, when direct apprehension of natural signs was impossible, through distance or the lack of a sense, or because the generator of those signs was a fictional rather than a real person, linguistic signs of emotions could produce the same effects as natural signs. The key, in each situation, was learning to read modes of signification that would provide the same information as natural signs.

Samuel Gridley Howe frequently argued that natural signs, such as those signifying emotions, were akin to the pantomimic gestural languages used by deaf people and by "primitive" civilizations; the hallmark of an advanced civilization lay in making the transition from using natural gestural language to using arbitrary language based on alphabetic characters.[2] Howe's pioneering work in educating blind and deaf-blind people relied on the idea that the blind could be taught to read arbitrary language by means other than sight; he developed his own raised alphabet with which to teach blind children and later developed a manual alphabet designed to convey the elements of arbitrary language to deaf-blind people.[3]

Howe insisted that the information conveyed by natural signs could just as easily and precisely be conveyed by arbitrary language; once one had access to arbitrary language, through speech or through reading, one did not need to experience natural signs directly in order to understand and respond to the emotions they signified. This is also the fundamental premise of sentimental representation: linguistic representations of natural signs serve as an entirely adequate substitute for the sensory apprehension of natural signs themselves. Diderot had gotten stuck on the idea that the direct perception of material signs of feelings was the necessary precondition for empathic identification; Mlle. de Salignac, like Howe and like sentimental writers such as Maria Cummins, believed that the lack of sight did not mean the lack of the ability to read in less directly material forms.

That arbitrary language could so effectively represent emotions in the absence of direct perception of natural signs meant that the empathic response triggered by natural signs could be produced through words, whether spoken or written. But while philosophers posited that the response to the direct perception of natural signs of emotions was immediate and inevitable, once a person had had proper familial training, sentimental writers feared that linguistic representations might not trigger responses so automatically and powerfully. Thus sentimental representations focus on training readers how to respond appropriately to linguistic signs of emotion, as well as on presenting those linguistic signs. Sentimental representations almost always provide some form of reading lessons for readers, modeling for them how to read linguistic signs of emotions, how to identify with the characters producing those emotions, how to reproduce those emotions in their own bodies, and then how to act on the feelings their bodies have affirmed.

Sentimental representations rely on a denominational model of language, insisting that words expressive of emotion are assumed to refer to some real feeling existing in actual persons. On this assumption, linguistic signs of emotions can serve as adequate substitutes for material signs. The relation between arbitrary linguistic signs and the material natural signs that give them meaning is cemented through the body of the reader of a sentimental text. The text stands in place of a material other person, producing words instead of the natural signs another's feeling body would produce. Readers respond to those words in the same way they would to the natural signs; they reproduce the signs of emotions for themselves. Rather than having one crying body prompt another perceiving body to cry, however, a sentimental text presents linguistic signs that prompt a reading body to cry; the material locus of the feelings shifts from the body of the sufferer to the body of the observer, who affirms the reality of the linguistically signified emotion by producing his or her own natural signs of that emotion. The ultimate meaning of the linguistic signification of feelings, then, lies in the reader's physical response to the words. In the traditional denominational view of language, words take their meaning from their connection to the perceivable objects they signify; in the sentimental reworking of that view, words take their meaning from the reader's response to those words and not from an original object the words supposedly represent. The truth or reality of a sentimental representation thus lies solely in the reader's embodied response to it, rather than in its faithfulness to some person or event outside the reading process.[4]

This distinction provides the means by which disabled people, particularly those lacking a sense, can become empathic agents in their own right and not remain merely "posters" or signs that help develop and strengthen the empathic capacities of others. Once a disabled person becomes a reader of arbitrary language, he or she is no different, in the ability to read, from an ablebodied person. The equality is marked by the capacity to feel; when a body can produce the natural signs of emotions when prompted by the linguistic representation of those emotions, there is no distinction needed, or made, whether that feeling, reading body is ablebodied or disabled. The ability to respond to linguistic signs replaces the ability to respond to natural signs, and in so doing erases any distinction between a body that can directly observe those natural signs and one that cannot; empathic agency is marked only by the capacity to reproduce emotions physically, and to act on those feelings, rather than on an original bodily capacity for perception. While the disabled body will still serve its cultural function as sign or poster, producing feelings in ablebodied others, within the logic of arbitrary language that body can also become a reading body, one that can respond, on equal terms with the ablebodied, to significations of emotions. Thus disabled people become identical with ablebodied people in their capacity to read and embody and act on signs of feeling, while still retaining their status as different by virtue of being the locus of those signs.

Maria Cummins's *The Lamplighter* illustrates these aspects of sentimental representation in allowing a blind woman to be the model of empathic agency for both characters and readers, while still retaining her status as "poster" generating empathic responses. Indeed, Cummins's novel could serve as an archetype of sentimental representation in a number of respects: it focuses on an orphaned girl, showing her lessons in becoming a "True Woman"; it provides numerous scenes of reading, modeling for its readers how they should respond to the linguistic representations before them; and it provides an adult woman as role model for the kind of womanhood the orphaned girl (and the novel's readers) should aspire to.[5]

Like other sentimental fictions, *The Lamplighter* emphasizes the importance of teaching readers how to read linguistic representations of emotions in order to extract the appropriate lessons from them. In order to be sure that readers know exactly how to read Emily Graham's examples, and her lessons with Gerty Flint, the orphan, the novel presents scenes of reading, showing again and again how to interpret stories which illustrate scenes of suffering or need. In so doing, the novel works to guarantee the success of its own representations by providing two layers of reading instruction: it shows characters reading stories, and learning to interpret them to extract a moral that will strengthen their empathic capacities, and it presents its readers with similar stories, acted out by the characters, providing readers with opportunities to imitate the interpretive strategies modeled by the reading characters.

The novel begins by showing that Gerty has the innate capacities for benevolence and fellow-feeling, but that these have been stunted and curtailed by the negative influences of her environment, as she is grudgingly being fed and housed by Nan Grant, a distant relative. Though she knows only kicks and blows, and as a result has a "little, fierce, untamed, impetuous nature" full of "angry passion, sullen obstinacy, and even hatred," Gerty also has a tendency toward love and gentleness (*TL*, 7).

[T]here were in her soul fountains of warm affection yet unstirred, a depth of tenderness never yet called out, and a warmth and devotion of nature that wanted only an object to expend themselves on. (*TL*, 7–8)

The "object" needed to call forth these undeveloped capacities appears first in the form of a kitten, whom Gerty loves. This love is marked as the seeds of Gerty's empathic sensibility, as Cummins notes that Gerty does not love the kitten selfishly, because the kitten loves her, but rather "she loved the kitten all the more for the care she was obliged to take of it, and the trouble and anxiety it gave her" (*TL*, 8). In sentimental logic, real love springs from one's perceptions of the weakness and need of another, and not from any calculation of what that other might offer to oneself.

Though her care for the kitten shows that Gerty has the potential for becoming an empathic True Woman, she has very few objects on which to exercise and develop her faculties of benevolence. Neglected in Nan Grant's household, Gerty is worse off than the "little drudges" she sees in her urban working-class neighborhood, not because she is beaten but because she has "nothing to do at all, and had never known the satisfaction of *helping* anybody" (*TL*, 8; emphasis original). Nan Grant abuses Gerty by actively beating her and by failing to provide her with any models of compassionate feeling in and of herself, or with any opportunities to do things for others. The most graphic example of this abuse occurs when Nan discovers Gerty caring for her kitten, and reacts by throwing the pet alive into a pot of boiling water. "The little animal struggled and writhed for an instant, then died in torture" (*TL*, 11).

Readers who have begun to identify with Gerty's loneliness, her youth, and the comfort she takes in caring for the kitten get their first lesson in the cruelties of the world in experiencing Nan Grant's complete lack of any empathic feelings for Gerty or her pet. Representing the worst-case scenario of an orphan with no family dependent on the care of strangers, whose benevolent capacities are too underdeveloped or stunted to offer any fellow-feeling or compassion for the orphan's helplessness, Gerty and the reader both encounter the hard, heartless world at its worst in Nan Grant. Gerty's reaction to Nan's gruesome murder of the kitten, however, shows the reader the consequences of living in a world without empathy:

All the fury of Gerty's nature was roused. Without hesitation, she lifted a stick of wood which lay near her, and flung it at Nan with all her strength. It was well aimed, and struck the woman on the head. The blood started from the wound the blow had given. (*TL*, 11)

Gerty's rage at seeing the kitten killed triggers her violence toward Nan. In sentimental logic, anger stands as the opposite of empathy, leading only to violence and destruction and the complete dissolution of all relational ties. Anger is equated with a lack of self-control, with an inability to step beyond one's own feelings of grievance or wrong and understand another's position. As such, anger is equated with selfishness and purely personal "passions" and "desires," which the True Woman must learn to subdue and replace with empathic consideration for others.

What historians of emotionology Carol and Peter Stearns have called the American "campaign to control anger" arose in the eighteenth century with the increasing separation of the sphere of economic production from that of the home and domestic life; in the nineteenth century, as that separation became more absolute, inscribed in ideologies of gender, family, and domesticity as well as in ideas about economic practices, the effort to banish anger from the domestic sphere increased. As the family and home became a sanctuary from the "heartless world" of selfishness and self-interest, so anger was depicted as the antithesis of family feeling and empathy.[6] Most of the advice literature that outlined rules for a happy marriage and a stable family life pointed specifically to anger as the most destructive element in domestic relations and urged family members of both sexes and all ages to expunge anger and quarreling by developing habits of self-control and submission. But while men were advised to suppress any angry feelings in the family circle (and to reserve them for public interactions with non-familially-linked men), women — at least True Women — were described as not having any such angry feelings at all. Advice literature, like sentimental literature, constructed anger and femininity as antithetical; as women were the heart of the home, the home too became a place where anger was banished, in order to foster and protect the empathic sympathies created in that environment. The "home," which the mid-century sentimental novel locates as a condition of heart and feeling, rather than blood relationship, class status, or money, was also marked as a place where only the "tender" emotions — love, sympathy, charity, benevolence — were permitted.

The "home" Nan Grant provides for Gerty is thus no home at all, as it is centered around selfishness, anger, and violence. When Nan throws Gerty out onto the snowy winter street, Trueman Flint, the neighborhood lamplighter, tries to stimulate Nan's (and the reader's) empathic sympathy by asking her " 'How'd you feel, marm, if she were found to-morrow all *friz* up just on your doorstep?' " (*TL*, 12; emphasis original). Nan, as one might expect, remains unmoved by Flint's reminder, and the elderly lamplighter takes Gerty home and becomes her protector and preceptor.

Gerty, and the reader, experience for the first time the love and caring of a real "home" and "family," provided by someone who has no blood relationship or other form of "interest" in the orphan girl. In becoming the object of Flint's benevolence, Gerty learns her first lesson in empathic domesticity. Because he takes care of her, she responds by wanting to do things for him; this follows Reid's principle of sympathetic imitation, as Gerty imitates the caretaking behavior she has seen Trueman Flint display, and which was missing from Nan Grant's household. When Gerty cleans up their rooms while True is working, the day becomes "marked in her memory as long as she lived," because it is "the first in which she had known *that* happiness — perhaps the highest earth affords — of feeling that she had been instrumental in giving joy to another" (*TL*, 27–28; emphasis original).

In addition to providing both Gerty and the reader with a model of disinterested care and concern, Flint also shows both the character and the reader how to develop empathic capacities through reading fiction. Gerty reads aloud to True "story after story, of little girls who never told lies, boys who always obeyed their parents, or, more frequently still, of the child who knew how to keep her temper" (*TL*, 66). While these stories provide yet another source for Gerty's empathic education, and give her models of characters her own age to emulate, they also provide Flint with opportunities to keep his sympathies well-tuned. Despite their difference in age, Flint's interest in Gerty's books

was as keen and unflagging as if he had been a child himself; and he would sit with his elbows on his knees, hearing the simple stories, laughing when Gerty laughed, sympathizing as fully and heartily as she did in the sorrows of her little heroines, and rejoicing with her in the final triumph of truth, obedience, and patience. (*TL*, 66)

This scenario shows readers how to read empathically, by describing Flint's reactions; it also shows that even those with well-developed sympathies can enjoy strengthening and stretching these faculties farther through the process of empathic reading.

Through showing Trueman's responses to Gerty's stories, Cummins insists that the development and exercise of an empathic subjectivity is not limited to True Womanhood. Rather, anyone who has ever experienced being helpless or dependent and relying on the compassion of others has the necessary germs of empathy. As Trueman points out, his own capacities for feeling came, not from his gender, but from having been "a little shaver" who knew "what a lonesome thing it was to be fatherless and motherless" (*TL*, 21). To bolster True's example of True Manhood, Cummins introduces another male character, Willie Sullivan, the son and grandson of True's poor neighbors. Showing that Willie is pious, dutiful, and industrious in caring for his mother and grandfather, Cummins also insists that he always displays "a sincere sympathy in others' pleasures and pains" (*TL*,

37).[7] With such capacities already in place, Willie shows how a boy might continue his training in True Manhood in order to become like Trueman Flint in adulthood.

Like Gerty and Trueman, Willie also strengthens his empathic capacities through reading and telling stories, providing yet another model for readers of how the act of reading is to affect them. Gerty and Willie read stories together and also create their own, imagining what life will be like as adults. Their visions of their future center on exercising their empathic capacities, as they plan how they will become wealthy and help all the poor and needy people they know. These stories provide hours of amusement for the two children, and the narrator makes a point of telling the reader that, in addition to entertainment, the value of such stories "undoubtedly lay in the disinterestedness and generosity of the emotion which occupied them; for, in the plans they formed, neither seemed actuated by selfish motives" (*TL*, 48). For those readers who might worry that reading fiction itself was a form of idleness, isolation, and selfishness, rather than a means of education, Cummins insists that reading and imagining can exercise one's benevolent faculties just as well as concrete action.

If Cummins's assertion about the value of such stories in employing Gerty's and Willie's unselfish capacities is insufficient to persuade some readers, she offers another model of reading in Trueman Flint's response to these stories. Like the stories Gerty read aloud, and like *The Lamplighter* itself, these fictions work to engage the sympathies of their audience and provide them with opportunities for empathic exercise. Like the novel's readers, Trueman "listens" while Gerty and Willie spin their tales of benevolence; True, a "simple-hearted and sympathizing" soul, laughs when they laugh, and cries when they cry, modeling the proper responses for readers. When Gerty tells Willie the story of "her childish griefs" at the hands of Nan Grant, both Willie and True prompt the empathic reaction readers should have: both "had heard the story before, and cried then"; both "often heard it afterwards, but never *without crying*" (*TL*, 33; emphasis original).

The tears which True and Willie, and the ideal novel reader, always shed over the pathetic story of a child's discovery of the cruelty of the fallen extrafamilial world, the lack of compassion and care available for those who need protection and help, are the text's assertion, in linguistic terms, of the characters' and readers' sentiments. Whoever cries "feels right," and that right feeling in the characters prompts them to provide the compassion missing from nonfeeling people such as Nan Grant. Ideally, readers who have followed the model presented by Trueman and Willie in responding to these stories will continue to imitate them in providing (or wanting to provide) sympathy and benevolence, if not for Gerty, then for others who remind them of her dependence and weakness.

As Trueman stated, his own memories of childhood dependence, of being a "little shaver," informed his desire to act as an empathic adult and to care for Gerty. Through the models of reading and empathizing presented for the "sympathetic imitation" of *The Lamplighter*'s readers, readers are encouraged to follow a similar process. Identifying with Gerty, readers experience her sufferings and abuse as if they were their own; remembering that suffering (or recalling their own and adding that memory to their textual experiences of Gerty's woes), readers desire to help Gerty, and fulfill that desire vicariously through Trueman and the other empathic adults. Ideally, that desire will remain unfulfilled, as the reader cannot enter into the text to assist Gerty; rather, it will remain when the novel is finished to prompt the reader to continue to use Trueman and Gerty as models for actions in the "real world" beyond the text.[8]

Sentimental novels like *The Lamplighter* provide linguistic representations of "suffering" in order to help develop the empathic capacities of readers. Identifying with characters who suffer and cry, readers also cry; their tears, in marking their identification with the character's feelings, also become a sign of readers' own "dependence" and "weakness"—a necessary step, in sentimental logic, to feeling for, and acting to care for, others also perceived as dependent. Sentimental fiction thus works to pull readers out of the world where material forms of power, such as wealth, voting rights, or physical force, hold sway, and to insert them into a represented world of arbitrary linguistic signs, where immaterial emotional power reigns supreme. Having experienced that world intellectually and physically, through comprehending the meanings of the printed words and through feeling the emotions they represent being produced in their own bodies, readers will carry those experiences with them when the reading and weeping are finished. The ideal reader of sentimental fiction, having "lived" in the created world where feelings are primary and powerful, will close the book to discover that that world really exists, in the domestic familial circle, and will work to make that world exist and function in extradomestic contexts as well.

*   *   *

The Lamplighter's first description of Gerty Flint, the orphan heroine, is of a child totally desolate and abandoned by all: "No one loved her, and she loved no one; no one treated her kindly; no one tried to make her happy, or cared whether she were so. She was but eight years old, and all alone in the world." The first chapter ends by calling for some being, "man or angel," who will "kindle a light" in the "[p]oor little, untaught, benighted soul!" of Gerty (*TL*, 4). As Nina Baym notes, the events of the novel supply Gerty with both: the man is Trueman Flint, the lamplighter of the title, who rescues Gerty from the abusive treatment of her guardian and provides her with her first lessons in empathy by responding to her weakness and need with kindness and care. The "angel" is Emily Graham, the blind daughter of a wealthy Boston businessman, who works to transform Gerty from the object of others' care into a caring adult subject in her own right (*TL*, xxii).

Emily Graham stands as the model of True Womanhood for Gerty and for the novel's readers; because she is also a disabled woman, and detached from sexual reproduction and maternal experience, she also stands as a model of disabled adulthood as empathic agency. She teaches Gerty the necessary traits of submission and self-sacrifice, defined in the novel as placing others' needs always before one's own, learning to feel for, and act to assist, anyone in a position of misery or helplessness. Emily teaches these lessons mostly by her own example; she has submitted to God's will that she be blind, and her suffering in that blindness serves as a constant reminder to her that others too may suffer, and need the care she can provide. Rather than giving her a reason to wallow in a slough of self-pity for her own woeful affliction, remaining always a dependent object of others' care, Emily's blindness, continually reminding her of her need for others' compassion, prompts her always to be ready to feel empathically for others. This becomes the hallmark of adulthood for female and for disabled characters: the capacity to recognize one's own dependence and the ability to use that dependence as the spur to work to care for others who are also dependent or in need. Indeed, these characteristics become the hallmark for any form of adulthood, including that of ablebodied males, as sentimental logic insists that everyone recognize the possibility of dependence and the need for interdependent networks of care.

When Gerty first meets Emily and learns that the older woman is blind, she is initially glad, because Emily cannot see how ugly Gerty is and cannot then reject her for that ugliness. This response, while pathetic, is shown to be selfish, oriented toward Gerty's own sensibility and not toward feeling for what Emily feels. Emily tells Gerty that she feels sad, and asks her to " 'think . . . how you would feel if you could not see the light, could not see anything in the world?'" This admonishment, addressed both to Gerty and to readers, makes Gerty "burst into a paroxysm of tears," a "natural sign" of her developing capacities for empathy. "'O!' exclaimed she, as soon as she could find voice amid her sobs. 'it's too bad! it's too bad!'" (*TL*, 54). Whether what is "too bad" is Emily's blindness or Gerty's selfish response to it is left to the reader to determine.

As illustrated in this scene, the first lesson on the road to becoming an adult empathic agent lies in learning to think what others are feeling before thinking of one's own feelings. This capacity is one of the most important characteristics of the maternal sensibility as portrayed in sentimental representations, as it guarantees that a child's needs will always come before a mother's own needs. By placing that sensibility in unmarried Emily Graham, Cummins disconnects it from its maternal roots and thereby universalizes it, insisting that all feeling beings, whether they are mothers or not, are capable of placing others' needs before their own. While sidestepping the question whether blind Emily could marry and have children, Cummins's use of Emily as the exemplar of self-sacrifice provides a model for disabled adulthood that does not rely on sexual reproduction, and thus creates an equality between disabled and ablebodied people.[9]

In this scene, describing her blindness as something sad and deserving of grief, Emily Graham serves both as a poster signifying misery and as an agent, actively showing Gerty, and the reader, how to overcome selfishness and how to use the emotions generated by the sign of her blindness as a lesson. Gerty's tears, and any the reader may shed over this scene, mark her understanding of blindness as a cultural sign of suffering, and also mark her successful comprehension of this lesson in "self-sacrifice." Once Gerty has cried, Emily soothes her, in a "sweet voice and sympathetic tones," reassuring Gerty that she is used to being blind and does not find it an unbearable condition. The sincerity of Gerty's dismay on discovering her selfish error becomes evident in the "natural signs" of emotion she displays, which Emily can "read" even without sight: "The tones of her voice, the earnestness and pathos with which she spoke, the confiding and affectionate manner in which she had clung to her, the sudden clasping of her hand, and finally, her vehement outbreak of grief when she became conscious of Emily's great misfortune"—all these serve as signs to Emily that Gerty has the rudiments of an empathic subjectivity (*TL*, 57).

Emily's first task in developing Gerty's sympathetic capacities lies in working "to cure that child of her dark infirmity," the temper and selfish anger which threatened to "cast a blight upon [her] lifetime" (*TL*, 63). She finds the key to taming Gerty's anger in Gerty's love for those who care for her. Loving True, and Emily, Gerty was always ready to obey them, and to control her own temper. True had developed that affectionate tie; it was Emily's task to inspire Gerty with a higher motive for action, one which did not depend on earning the approbation of her friends. Emily thus serves as Gerty's teacher in Christian as well as domestic values, teaching her to banish her anger by learning to obey "the spirit of her Divine Master," rather than her own will or the will of other humans (*TL*, 73).

By helping Gerty internalize the values of submission and selflessness, Emily hoped to create a womanly sensibility which would be "powerful to do and to suffer, to bear and forbear," even when separated from friends and family and their approval of her actions. Significantly, Emily frames this sensibility as "powerful," as a form of "doing" as well as "suffering." In using those words, Cummins declares that the ability to bear one's own trials without complaint or rebellion enhances one's ability to feel for and with the sufferings of others. One's own woes thus become the basis for a kind of action and power, as empathic feelings prompt one to act to assist and relieve others' misfortunes. An adult empathic sensibility is marked by these two poles of suffering and doing: in suffering, one becomes an object of others' compassion, helping others to exercise their empathic capacities; in doing, one becomes an agent, acting effectively on behalf of other sufferers, with whom one identifies. While suffering educates an individual in how misery feels, encouraging the empathic understanding of others' misery, by itself it can only place an individual in the position of object of others' care. Doing, taking active steps to help others whom one perceives as suffering, turns the sufferer from an object to an agent, from a dependent child to a capable adult.

In their first interaction, Emily exists as the object of Gerty's compassion so that she can gauge the extent and strength of that faculty in the child. In subsequent interactions she takes the position of empathic agent rather than object. In demonstrating for Gerty how fully one can minimize one's own afflictions through self-forgetfulness and caring for others, Emily provides a model for Gerty's own development more powerful than Trueman, Willie, or books could offer. Emily serves the same function for the reader, who sees a concrete example of someone with a "woeful affliction" (not just age or poverty) who yet puts others' needs and cares before her own. As such, Emily exists as the "angel" in the text, teaching both the heroine and the readers how to become fully empathic adult subjects.

While Cummins has Gerty encounter an actual woman in the novel, readers encounter only Cummins's linguistic representations of this textual "angel." The need for angels in the text comes from the fear of the absence of such angels in real life. In the increasingly urbanized and anonymous world of mid-nineteenth-century American culture, the frameworks of family life and maternal care that were presumed to train children (of both sexes) to empathic adulthood might be flawed or absent. Mid-century sentimental texts characteristically portray urban settings, not as realms of evil and vice in contrast to the purity of the countryside, as eighteenth-century sentimental works did, but in order to show characters asserting the presence and power of domestic values in the midst of the hostile urban environment.[10] In the "wide wide world" of strangers, who have no kinship or affectional ties to others, texts, and the angels they contain, take the place of family members and caring individuals to develop the empathic capacities of readers. When the angel in the house is no longer available to assist the poor orphan girl, on her own in the big city, the angel in the text must take her place in order to ensure that the empathic capacities fostered in the family circle will continue to exist as active forces, even in the absence of direct familial ties.

As the angel in the text for both Gerty and the reader, Emily "never forgot the sufferings, the wants, the necessities of others." This unceasing empathy, according to Cummins, who is in agreement here with Mlle. de Salignac's explanation of her own ability to feel, comes directly from Emily's blindness. Because "she could not see the world without," because she knew personally what it was like to suffer loss and grief,

> there was a world of love and sympathy in her, which manifested itself in abundant benevolence and charity, both of heart and deed. She lived a life of love. She loved God with her whole heart, and her neighbor as herself. Her own great misfortunes and trials could not be helped, and were borne without repining; but the misfortunes and trials of others became her care, the alleviation of them her greatest delight. (*TL*, 57)

Because her blindness and her necessary dependence had strengthened her empathic capacities, rather than being a passive object of others' concern and care, "Emily was never weary of doing good" (*TL*, 57).

Emily's position as the representative of adult empathic agency is overdetermined by her blindness and her True Womanhood; her status as angel in the text stems from the compatibility of the two conditions. Both femininity and blindness, in the ideology of domestic True Womanhood, resulted in forms of physical weakness, dependence, and reliance on the values of compassion and concern fostered in the family. While blindness was generally figured in sentimental representations as an affliction that would help the individual learn to "bear and forbear," femininity was figured as an asset. Thus Emily's blindness is redefined, not as a form of suffering, but as part of her True Womanly capacity for empathy.

The conflation of blindness and True Womanhood in this text works to reaccentuate and rewrite the social sign of blindness as necessarily meaning suffering and affliction. Though "so great a misfortune might well, and always did, excite the warmest sympathy" for Emily, "it was hard to realize that Emily *was* blind" (*TL*, 64; emphasis original). Because "there was nothing painful in the appearance of her closed lids, shaded and fringed as they were by her heavy eyelashes," and because there was never "any repining or selfish indulgence on the part of the sufferer," it was "not unusual for those immediately about her" to forget that she was blind (*TL*, 64). Friends would often "converse upon things which could only be evident to the sense of sight, and even direct her attention to one object or another, quite forgetting, for the moment, her sad deprivation" (*TL*, 64). Emily, of course, reacted to this "selfish" forgetfulness with resignation and acceptance: "Emily never sighed, never seemed hurt at their want of consideration, or showed any lack of interest in objects thus shut out from her gaze" (*TL*, 64).

Emily's blindness is erased by her ability to forget her own affliction and to refrain from reminding people of it when they fail to remember it. It is further erased, as Cummins emphasizes, by the lack of any physical signs of her blindness: her closed eyes look no different from those of the sighted. Emily's being is thus defined not as the product of her blind eyes but as the product of her abundance of feeling. In showing how easily Emily's blindness is forgotten by herself and others, Cummins declares Emily's equality with the sighted on the basis of her capacity for True Womanly self-sacrifice and empathy. This is the equality which Valentin Haüy sought in his eighteenth-century experiments with educating the blind, and which Samuel Gridley Howe sought in his nineteenth-century attempts to insert the blind into existing models of economic production. Where Haüy and Howe were frustrated by the physical limitations of blind bodies, however, sentimental fiction succeeds in claiming the equality of blind and sighted through erasing the physical differences and rewriting the body as a site of feeling and emotion, rather than of sensory perception.

Refusing to acknowledge as important the strictly physical and sensory distinctions between blind and sighted bodies, Cummins rewrites the meaning of Emily's blind body by depicting that body as central to her empathic capacities. Emily appears, not only as the equal of the sighted in her ability to feel, but as their superior, making her the most suitable teacher for Gerty. Rather than merely the best of mortal women, Emily's blindness has made her an angel, someone who, as Gerty exclaims, has "'been with God,'" and belongs "to an order above humanity" (*TL*, 64). Like an angel, Emily has transcended the merely material world of flesh and blood; her confinement to physical darkness has shown her an inner world of light and love that remove her from the necessity to perceive the outside world. As a disembodied angel, Emily becomes more than just a teacher. Rather, in Cummins's figuration, Emily's blindness makes her a Christlike manifestation of holiness and pure spirituality:

> God had chosen an earthly messenger to lead his child into everlasting peace; a messenger from whose closed eyes the world's paths were all shut out, but who had been so long treading the heavenly road, that it was now familiar ground. Who so fit to guide the little one as she, who with patience had learned the way? Who so well able to cast light upon the darkness of another soul as she, to whose own darkened life God had lent a torch divine? (*TL*, 67)

While Trueman Flint, the literal lamplighter, lights the first sparks in Gerty's soul by making her the object of his care, Emily lights the lamp of True Womanhood that turns Gerty into an empathic adult.

Because it has led her to angelic realms beyond the material world, Emily insists that her blindness, rather than being "'one of the dreariest misfortunes that can afflict humanity,'" is actually one of God's blessings. "'With eyes to see the wonderful workings of nature and nature's God, I nevertheless closed them to the evidences of almighty love that were around me on every side,'" Emily declares. "'And therefore did He, who is ever over us for good, arrest with fatherly hand the child who was wandering from the only road that leads to peace'" (*TL*, 397). With this philosophy, Emily articulates a basic premise of sentimental domestic Christian logic: "'it's all for the best, or it wouldn't be'" (*TL*, 91). Since everything that happens, for good or ill, is God's will, the only proper responses to any event are resignation, submission, and acceptance. While these strike modern readers as unnecessarily passive, in sentimental logic they removed any possibility of "affliction" or "misfortune." Blindness, or any other earthly trial, was given for a purpose, for the lessons it taught the individual in how to "bear and forbear." Because any "affliction" strengthened the empathic capacities of an individual, there was no such thing as "affliction," but only the misperception or misinterpretation of what is "for the best." In other words, the Christian element of sentimental logic erases the equation between disability and misfortune, at least temporarily, by insisting that all events are part of God's necessarily benevolent design.

Cummins's text thus shows the redefinition of blindness as disability in two ways: by showing that Emily's blindness enhances her ability to feel, thus making her the equal of sighted adults in terms of empathy, and by showing that there is no such thing as "affliction" in a world where whatever happens is "for the best." The former involves reaccentuating the meaning of Emily's body, placing the defining characteristics of her being not in her physical inability to see, but in her extraordinary abilities to feel. The latter involves rewriting the meaning of disability as suffering, refiguring blindness (or other disabilities) as forms of "text," as lessons to teach the disabled person the correct idea of God's benevolence. Both kinds of rewriting remove the disabled person from the realm of the ordinary — the first by redefining the meaning of the disabled body as having superior capacities, rather than as lacking, and the second by elevating the disabled person from mortal to angel, to one who walks with God. Emily's status as the angel in the text thus depends on Cummins's representation of her as having transcended her body and ascended into heavenly realms inaccessible to the nondisabled. While she thus serves as a proper teacher to train Gerty in the lessons of empathic adulthood, she is effectively removed from participation in the world in which she is preparing Gerty to operate.

Emily's success in teaching Gerty how to become an empathic adult is figured in the text by a role reversal. As Gerty's lessons in how to bear sorrow strengthen her ability to do for others, Gerty begins to become Emily's companion instead of just her pupil. The first marker of the shift appears when Gerty serves as Emily's eyes, providing her with descriptions of visual phenomena. As Gerty described a sunset, Emily listened and "experienced a participation in Gertrude's enjoyment" (*TL*, 196). Here Gerty functions for Emily as books had for Gerty and for the reader: she describes a scene imperceptible to Emily's physical perceptions, and Emily shares in Gertrude's feelings through the verbal portrait. Between the blind and sighted woman, just as between a reader and a sentimental text, sympathetic identification and linguistic descriptions produce the same emotional effect. In this scene, unlike others that show how texts of all kinds produce empathic responses, Emily appears as the empathizer, while Gerty produces the text that sparks her feelings.

In serving as the "text" through which Emily can experience the visual world, Gerty becomes Emily's teacher as well as her student. As the empathic connection between the two grows, Gerty's "lively sympathy, her constant devotion, her natural appreciation of the entertaining and the ludicrous, as well as the beautiful and the true," become an important part of "her earnest and unsparing efforts to bring her much-loved friend into communion with everything she herself enjoyed." Through experiencing Gerty's pleasure, Emily begins "to call into play faculties which blindness had rendered almost dormant" (*TL*, 128).

With this assertion, their roles are fully reversed. In demonstrating her capacities for active care as an empathic adult, Gerty provides yet another model for readers. Having learned, through the various "texts" presented in the novel, how to bear suffering and turn it into an opportunity to feel for others, readers need one final lesson in how to use those feelings in proper effective actions to alleviate misery. Gerty shows this, first by caring for Trueman on his deathbed, and then by functioning as Emily's caretaker and companion. In this regard, Cummins reinscribes Emily's blindness as a kind of disability, producing dependence and the need for empathic care. " 'She's blind, you know,' " True tells Gerty as he is dying, " 'and you must be eyes for her; and she's not over strong, and you must lend a helpin' hand to her weakness, just as you do to mine' " (*TL*, 94–95).

Where previously Gerty had been the child needing Emily's protection and guidance, now Gerty, "so bright, erect, and strong with youth and health" becomes "a fit protector for the others, who, in her sweet and gentle helplessness, leaned upon her so trustingly" (*TL*, 261). Gerty becomes the reader's model for how to use one's empathic feelings to take an active role in helping others. Previously Emily had served as the model for how to bear suffering without selfishness; their role reversal here shows Cummins's inability fully to depict blind Emily as "doing," as being an active empathic adult. Her capacities to feel for others are fully developed, and are indeed superior to those of the sighted, as a result of her blindness, but Cummins cannot present her as doing more than just feeling (and teaching). Cummins insists that disability does ultimately have an ineradicable meaning: it elevates one to angelic status, or limits one to the status of empathic object, but does not allow for full empathic participation in the merely mortal world.

Cummins's depiction of blindness, while granting Emily a form of adult subjectivity, works to circumscribe the effectiveness of that subjectivity. By making Emily into an angel, Cummins reinforces Emily's power as a role model and preceptor, but also effectively removes her from participation in earthly concerns. As Gerty becomes the model of the active type of empathic adulthood, she functions in part to protect Emily's angelic status by sheltering her from knowledge of the cruelties of the real world. While Gerty, having learned the correct way to suffer, to "bear and forbear," could accept any insult or cruelty directed at herself without anger or malice, "her blood boiled in her veins when she began to perceive that her cherished Emily was becoming the victim of mean and petty neglect and ill-usage" (*TL*, 242). Rather than confronting those who are abusing Emily and trying to force them to change their ways—an option which, the novel asserts, can only lead to more anger, disruption, and violence—Gerty opts for the power of self-sacrifice, working twice as hard to be sure that Emily does not "'*suspect* even that anybody could willingly be unkind to her'" (*TL*, 245). Cummins here suggests, as Dickens did with Bertha Plummer, that disabled characters (particularly women) might require a sheltered environment; in order to retain her angelic status, Emily may require the maintenance of a fiction that the world is always a good and caring place.

While Emily's angelic empathy can only work when she is sheltered from the realities of cruelty and unkindness, Gerty provides a model for readers of an adult empathic capacity that can function fully in the real world. Emily's blindness ultimately prevents her from leaving the domestic sphere; the lessons she teaches Gerty all occur in the confines of the home, and in the circle of "family" relations established by Gerty and Emily. In this, Cummins agrees with Howe's assertion that the blind need "a comfortable home!" rather than seeking definitions of adulthood beyond the domestic realm. Gerty, however, shows readers how a nondisabled woman, who can move between the domestic and extradomestic realms, can use her empathic capacities beyond home and family.

Gerty's ability to use her empathic capacities beyond the home appears as a result of a quarrel with Emily's father. Because he supported Gerty financially after Trueman's death, Mr. Graham expects obedience from his dependent. Rather than allowing her autonomy and judgment to be compromised by a sense of debt, however, Gerty insists that she has been trained all along to earn her own living, and not to depend on anyone but herself for support. Though Emily points out that "'the object, in giving Gertrude a good education, was to make her independent of all the world, and not simply dependent upon us,'" Mr. Graham reacts angrily to Gerty's refusal to obey his wishes, and Gerty leaves the Graham household (*TL*, 140). Mr. Graham warns her that she "'must take care of yourself, or trust to strangers,'" in an attempt to frighten Gerty into remaining with him.

Gerty proudly retorts, however, that she will "'neither look to him or any-one else for support; I intend to earn a maintenance for myself'" (*TL*, 146).

Supporting herself (and later becoming Emily's economic support as well) by teaching school, Gerty shows readers how to achieve economic independence without losing the empathic capacities she had developed in the Graham household. Finding herself blessed to be living in a world "which contained hearts so quick to feel, and hands so ready to labor" as hers, Gerty herself becomes the "text" embodying the two values necessary to success in both the domestic and extradomestic spheres (*TL*, 177). Both the ability to labor and the ability to feel define Gerty's version of adult womanhood. Of the two, the ability to feel comes first, as the more impor-tant trait, but the ability to labor, lacking in Emily because of her blindness, ensures that the emotional connections fostered by the empathic capacities developed in the domestic sphere will not compromise the independence gained by self-reliance.

Gerty thus combines the best of two models of adulthood in being able to function effectively in the economic sphere as well as having a well-developed capacity for empathic feeling and relatedness. Her ability to com-bine these two forms compatibly stands in contrast to other formulations of adulthood in the novel. Emily, for example, exemplifies the highest capaci-ties for empathic feeling but is unable, because of her blindness, even to hope to attain economic independence; her father provides an example of financial independence but stunted emotional capacities; the Grahams' housekeeper, Mrs. Ellis, demonstrates the problems of financial depen-dence paired with emotional disconnection. Gerty, in successfully uniting empathic relatedness and economic independence, provides the final model for readers to follow, in showing how her training in True Womanhood enables her to function in the extradomestic world, bringing the values and lessons she learned from Emily in the domestic sphere to bear beyond the confines of the home.

By bringing her empathic sensibilities into the world outside the do-mestic sphere, Gerty shows readers how they too can turn their feelings into concrete actions to reform the cold, cruel world. In so doing, Gerty — and Cummins — insist that there is no necessary separation between the domes-tic and public realms. Traditionally, the domestic sphere is figured as the only place producing empathic feelings, learned through the affectionate ties produced by kinship and caring, while the economic sphere is governed solely by relationships forged by money and self-interest, rather than by mutual concern and compassion. The domestic sphere is populated by lov-ing friends and family, while the economic sphere contains only unfeeling strangers; in the latter world, there can be no assurance that the dependent, whether children, dying people, blind people, orphans, or women, will find any protection or sympathy. When the empathic capacities developed in the home are deployed in this uncaring world, however, Cummins, like Dickens and Craik, hopes that the economic sphere will be transformed.

She shows this transformation beginning through erasing the category of "strangers," defined as people who feel no bond toward other humans, and who thus will not act to aid or comfort others unless prompted to by money or other forms of self-interest. Just as she erases blindness from the category of "affliction," portraying it instead as a form of angelic "blessing," so Cummins discards the concept of "uncaring strangers," insisting instead that all people, whether known or not, whether related or not, have the power to feel for, and care for, all others.

Gerty once again provides a model for readers of how to expunge the notion of "strangers" from the extradomestic world. As a friendless orphan cast out on the harsh world, Gerty discovers that "the bounty of strangers" is available and abundant.[11] Her adventures in the novel stand as illustrations, both to other characters and to readers, that the world which has been "'called cold, selfish, and unfeeling'" has to Gerty been kind and caring (*TL*, 185). In discussing the nature of the world with Gerty, a potential suitor urges her to discard her "romantic" notions about the kindness of strangers and to acknowledge that "'this is a world where people must look out for themselves.'" Gerty, rejecting both the suitor and his worldview, asserts that her "'sympathies have not been exhausted by contact with the world,'" but rather have been strengthened by seeing how much love and care the world contains (*TL*, 235–36).

At a resort in the Catskills, Gerty shows readers again the power of the "romantic" view of reality. On seeing an unknown man asleep, having a nightmare, Gerty does not pause to think of her own safety (or of propriety), but promptly tries to soothe the man, because she "forgot that he was a stranger," and "saw only a sufferer" (*TL*, 275). In the purview of her empathic subjectivity deployed outside the home, there can be no such thing as a "stranger" to whom one does not respond; there are only perceptions of others' suffering and pain, which automatically stimulate one's compassionate faculties and hence the desire to assist the sufferer. The identification and sympathetic imitation dictated, biologically as well as morally, by a well-developed empathic subjectivity create bonds between all who perceive and all who suffer, thus erasing the category of "strangers" as those with whom one feels no connection.

For readers, the final example of how to use their empathic capacities to care for others, and to erase the category of "stranger," occurs when the suffering sleeper awakens. Seeing Gerty's eyes "glistening with the dew of sympathy," he warns her not to "'weep for a stranger,'" but to save her tears for her own woes. She replies, in classic sentimental logic, "'If I had not had sorrows already, . . . I should not know how to feel for others; if I had not often wept for myself, I should not now weep for you'" (*TL*, 276). The stranger reveals that he hates the world as a cruel and unkind place, full of the "'shafts of malice, envy, and ill-will'" that mark "'selfish, base, and cruel humanity'" as a whole (*TL*, 304). Looking at the resort crowd to prove his point, the man sees in the random collection of "strangers" proof that human nature, as seen beyond the domestic sphere, is essentially selfish and uncaring, essentially unempathic. Gerty, of course, refutes his conclusion by referring to her own experiences, thus reminding readers as well of the lessons they have been subjected to in reading the text. When the man asks if "'heartless strangers [have] deserved the love you seem to feel for them,'" Gerty responds, with words and natural signs, for herself and for the readers: "'Heartless strangers!' exclaimed Gertrude, the tears rushing to her eyes. 'O, sir, I wish you could have known my Uncle True, and Emily, dear, blind Emily!'" (*TL*, 278).

5

Institutional Sentimentalism

The cultural associations between disability and sentimentality framed disability as a signifier of misery or suffering prompting the compassionate response of others. Elaborated on and celebrated in the pages of sentimental fiction, these associations provided the predominant social meanings of disability — meanings that educators like Samuel Gridley Howe were trying to dispel through their work with disabled populations. So long as the public thought of disabled people, along with other dependent populations, as "burdens thrown onto society by God's providence" in order that "the suffering of others" might "draw out virtue and charity," Howe noted, the blind would never be fully integrated into sighted culture, and would forever remain the objects of charity, rather than being recognized as competent self-sufficient adults (PR 1849, 26).

The prevailing view of disability focused on its inevitability — God had always afflicted, and would always afflict, certain people with forms of suffering — and on the social utility of that inevitability: a benevolent God had designed the world so that disabled people's sufferings had a positive result, in that they conjured up the highest feelings in others, and prompted them to imitate Christ in caring for these less-fortunate ones. Howe's efforts to rewrite this paradigm focused initially on erasing the notion of blindness as suffering by trying to insert his blind pupils into existing frameworks of economic self-sufficiency that would assert their equality with the sighted; when this failed, Howe worked to rewrite the other dimension of the prevailing attitude, insisting that blindness was not, in fact, inevitable, but could be eliminated from the general population through scrupulous attention to laws of health and the absolute prohibition of reproduction among the blind.

In objecting to the familiar association of blindness with suffering and with charity, Howe claimed that such an attitude was merely "a license of speech," a convenient way of talking about blindness, rather than a necessary fact about the blind (PR 1849, 26). With this label he implicitly notes that this view of the blind is a discursive construction, a product of a form of speech or set of cultural meanings assigned to blindness as a social signifier. Though Howe does not name a specific source for these meanings, they were created and reinforced throughout the nineteenth century in the forms of speech and imagery fostered in sentimental representations. Surprisingly, however, given Howe's objections to this portrayal, his own Annual Reports, during the first twenty years of his administration, use the same tropes and conventions as sentimental representations, and for the same purposes. Whether or not he was aware of it, Howe's own writings employ sentimental figures of speech and sentimental constructions of disability as a means to encourage his audience to identify with the people he is depicting and to see them as feeling beings like themselves.

The Annual Reports from the early 1830s through the mid-1850s are vexed documents, marked by paradox and contradiction, as Howe addressed his ideas to two distinct audiences, using two different rhetorical modes and incorporating contradictory sets of assumptions about the education of the blind and their positions in American society.[1] As a result, Howe's Reports outline contradictory modes of constructing the social meanings of blindness and the strengths and limitations of blind bodies.

On the one hand, his Reports were always addressed "To the Public," imagined as the enlightened citizenry of Massachusetts, intelligent laypeople of both sexes who wanted to see their tax monies spent wisely and who also believed in ideals of democratic equality and Christian benevolence. This audience already knew the traditional sentimental associations between disability and suffering and would be likely to respond to sentimental portrayals of disability with donations, if not with other forms of charitable care. These readers needed to be persuaded that Howe's institution was primarily benevolent, that it was as much like a home environment as could be managed on an institutional level. This audience was thus provided with details, employing sentimental conventions, of the daily workings of the school, and the studies, health, and recreation of the students. Through sentimental rhetorical devices, Howe effectively created sets of identifications between his blind students and his sighted readers; these identifications, in turn, enabled sighted readers to think of blind people as similar to themselves rather than a separate race of beings. Having emphasized the similarities between blind and sighted, Howe could then use sentimental scenarios to begin to rewrite the age-old associations between blindness and suffering, persuading his lay audience that blind students were no different from sighted students in their emotional capacities for happiness and for empathic agency.[2]

While recognizing that his lay audience would respond most readily to sentimental rhetoric, the prevailing popular mode of representation, Howe was simultaneously aware that his Reports were increasingly influential among the growing body of professionals who were exploring the best means to cope with the social problems posed by dependent and disabled populations. Addressing this latter audience, more concerned with the intellectual and physical characteristics of dependent and disabled populations than with their status as domestic and emotional beings, required a different rhetorical mode, one that focused on statistically provable trends observable in aggregate populations rather than on the achievements of individuals. By the late 1840s Howe was insisting that it was the duty of institutions for dependent and disabled populations "to obtain and distribute . . . correct information" about the "class of persons" institutionalized; though the findings might be unpleasant to readers who expect to hear marvelous stories about phenomenal successes, Howe warned, it was incumbent on all men of science to "keep back no truth that could lead to a more perfect understanding of the subject" (PR 1848, 29–30).

In doing this we shall not transcend our office, because public charitable institutions have other duties besides the care and culture of their immediate inmates, and among those duties is the gathering of knowledge on all subjects closely or remotely connected with the infirmity under which those inmates labor. (PR 1848, 43)

As a result, beginning in the mid-1840s Howe's Reports increasingly focused on providing statistical information about the blind population as a whole, and on anatomizing the blind "as a class," finding them inferior to the sighted in virtually every respect.

The sentimental and scientific modes of portraying the characteristics of the residents of his institution frequently appear side by side in Howe's Reports, providing a paradoxical portrait of the blind. The passages meant for professional readers, detailing statistical trends in the blind population as a whole, focused attention on "the blind" as a distinct group, emphasizing their abnormality, their absolute difference from the sighted population, and hence their disability, the ways in which they were inferior to the sighted and required lifelong institutional care. Meanwhile, the passages employing sentimental rhetoric, addressed to caring lay readers, took an opposite approach. These passages discussed blind students as individuals, often by name, placing them in groups and categories recognizable in the general sighted population; in such descriptions a blind student might be described as a son or daughter, brother or sister, or playmate and scholar, rather than as an anonymous member of the class called "the blind." This emphasis on individual identity highlighted the similarity between blind and sighted people, naming blind people as normal, as capable of the same kinds of familial and social relations as sighted people, rather than as a class apart, a separate race of beings.

These two kinds of meanings exist side by side not only in Howe's Reports, but in the nineteenth-century American cultural understanding of the social meanings of blindness and of disability in general. Howe's writing about the inability of the blind to fit into prevailing structures of economic production and sexual reproduction, which are echoed in fictional representations of disabled people, tended to produce images of the blind as "other," a group unable to participate in the activities of daily life that are the hallmarks of normal adulthood. His sentimental representations of blind individuals, however, portrayed them as similar to the sighted. Constructed as like the sighted, blind people could then be integrated into "normal" adult life — in the domestic sphere, if not in the economic realm. Howe's Annual Reports, in their sentimental aspects, end up in agreement with the fictional portrayals of disabled characters in arguing that in the domestic sphere the blind have the same abilities as the sighted; additionally, Howe and the sentimental fiction writers agree that it is in the domestic realm where questions of adulthood or agency will arise, even as that agency is denied to disabled characters in any other arena of adult activity.

Like the authors of sentimental fiction, Howe was aware that disability, when removed from the privacy of the domestic sphere and put on display in the public realm, could serve as a "poster" to stimulate compassion and benevolence in the general public. While Dickens and Craik had insisted that Tiny Tim and Muriel Halifax appear in public in person to remind people of Christ, and of their duties to the unfortunate, Howe went one step farther in portraying the building housing his blind students as itself an adequate "poster." Col. Thomas Handasyd Perkins had donated his mansion to Howe in 1834, with the stipulation that it become the new home for Howe's expanding school. Though grateful for the gift, Howe soon lamented that the site was too retired; in 1836 he negotiated to sell the Perkins mansion in order to purchase a former hotel, which, in addition to housing more students, would also be more easily viewed by the public.[3] In his pleas for funds to make this purchase, Howe argued that a more visible

Figure 2. The Perkins Institution and Massachusetts School for the Blind, circa 1900. From postcard, author's collection.

institution would be a more effective "monument to benevolence," reminding passersby "every day and every hour, of their duty to the unfortunate" (PR 1836, 10).

By 1839 Howe had relocated his school in this former hotel, and his metaphoric portrayal of the effect of the sight of the building became more infused with sentimental assumptions, as he claimed that the physical prominence of the institution would promote a "contagion" of virtue to counter the viciousness of urban life: "vice is contagious, but so is virtue, and a school for the blind, calling into exercise, as it so strongly does, all the kindly and benevolent feelings of its neighbors and visitors, thereby increases and strengthens them" (PR 1842, 15). The building alone would thus function the same way that sentimental fictions did, as a means to exercise and strengthen the capacity of the able-bodied to feel for the disabled. As he wrote privately to fellow reformer Horace Mann, the increase in the number of such facilities would furnish "more occasions for the *exercise* of the benevolent affections."[4] On this basis, Howe urged the establishment of more such institutions, "Not for the blind alone, . . . but for the sake of the community, and for the cause of humanity" (PR 1842, 15).

If the exterior of the institution building could produce a powerful sentimental effect on observers, what went on within those walls had even more potential to be framed in sentimental terms. Howe's Annual Reports throughout the 1840s and 1850s, in presenting statistical trends about blind populations, became increasingly pessimistic about the possibilities of situating the blind in any kind of productive economic situation or normalized physical classification; they also became more insistent in describing the blind as ideally suited for domestic life. Because of this, paradoxically, the Reports that are most reliant on anonymous scientific data to prove the unfitness of the blind for participation in most arenas of "normal" life are also the most reliant on sentimental rhetoric to demonstrate how perfectly blind people fit into domestic arrangements. In these Reports, Howe takes great pains to articulate in detail the importance of home life for both blind and sighted people and to describe his school as functioning more like a middle-class family than like an anonymous institution full of uncaring strangers.

Having failed to find economically productive roles for his blind students, Howe had instead offered a wish for "a comfortable home! Would that there were such for every blind man!" (PR 1850, 24). Having anatomized the blind as physically inferior to the sighted in virtually every regard, Howe proceeded to follow sentimental logic by arguing that the same physical defects that made them weak and helpless made them "nestle more closely to the bosom of humanity," and rely more than sighted people on "the closest relations of sympathy of heart and of mind" (PR 1849, 30; 1851, 14). A blind man, in Howe's depiction, had "more need than others of the comforts and joys of domestic relations" because "his infirmity increases, not lessens, his desire for them, and increases too his capacity for their enjoyment. . . . for while his infirmity does not lessen the strength of those affections, it increases his need and his desire for their exercise" (PR 1850, 25). In the confines of "a comfortable home!" blind persons would be sure to find the care and sympathy which their defective bodies required.

Howe's encomium to the "comfortable home!" like those found in the pages of sentimental fiction articulated many of the most firmly held and beloved ideals of middle-class Victorian American culture in insisting that home and family life represented the highest levels of moral development and provided the foundations for all forms of public and private virtue:

Now, there has never been contrived, and there never can be contrived, any institution or community to meet the wants of the social nature, and gratify the yearnings of the soul, as does the institution of the family, ordained of God. No other calls into healthy play so many faculties and sentiments of the human mind and heart; no other so elevates what is low, and purifies what is selfish. (PR 1850, 24)

Chief among the advantages and powers of family life, Howe noted, were the continual efforts of all family members to create, maintain, and strengthen the atmosphere of empathy and care which is the hallmark of sentimental representations, and which Howe had found so strikingly absent in economic relations. In "a comfortable home!"

woman spreads around her softening influence; love, sanctified by marriage, becomes spiritual . . . brothers and sisters are ever weaving in its walls the tender ties of affection which prepare their own hearts for wider sympathy with mankind, while, by continually drawing on the fountains of parental affection, they prevent them from being chilled into selfishness, even by the winter of age. (PR 1850, 25)

In the domestic realm, children learned, via their affectionate ties to parents and siblings, to treat all humans with the same familial compassion. In such an environment, Howe insisted, blind people would receive the same tenderness as sighted dependents. More important, those who learned to care for the needs of others in the family might well carry their concerns outside the domestic realm, and into "wider sympathy with mankind," thus working to transform the heartless public world into the caring interdependent society the authors of sentimental fiction so thoroughly envisioned.

The domestic sentiments, in Howe's metaphor, would keep the "fountains" of affection flowing by continually circulating care and concern from parent to child, and eventually, as parents grew old and weak and children grew strong, from child to parent. Such circulation would prevent the hearts of parents from freezing into a selfishness brought about by increased need, just as it prevented the hearts of children from freezing into a callousness brought about by adult strength and lack of need. This spring of human affection, flowing within the walls of "a comfortable home!" Howe concluded, "indeed furnishes the true elixir of life" (PR 1850, 36).

The blind even more than the sighted, Howe noted, needed to drink deeply of that "elixir of life." Blind adults (in Howe's terms, specifically "the blind man") needed "the love and loyalty of a wife, the affections of children, and the tender regard and tried fidelity of friends," because their defects required the tenderness guaranteed in the realm of domestic emotions. For the blind, Howe insisted, the exercise of the domestic affections was "the most harmless intemperance"; that "the blind man intoxicates himself by daily draughts" of that "elixir of life" was not only necessary, but highly desirable (PR 1850, 36).

In Howe's metaphor, the family serves as a perpetual fount of affection, whose flow accomplishes two things. It purifies and cleanses whatever is low or base, particularly forms of sexuality, by transforming them into the opportunity for self-sacrificing love. Howe wrote that "the family relation is gradually refining men in this country, and wherever there is progress. By it the sexual relations have a chance to be spiritualized" (PR 1850, 26). For the blind man, who cannot participate directly in even the most purified forms of domestic sexuality, the affections that circulate from the fountain provide a harmless intoxicant, of which he should partake daily. Here Howe replaces the forbidden physical pleasures of sexuality with the pleasure of intoxication; he further refigures the intoxication of the body, one of the anathematized forms of physical excess that could lead only to dissolute habits and viciousness, as the intoxication of emotions, a form of excess that can have only positive results. In doing so, Howe rewrites the sentimental scenario in which drunkenness leads inevitably to the destruction of affections and the disintegration of family life. Getting drunk on love in the family, for Howe's blind man, becomes a harmless indulgence, one that solidifies rather than dissolves the bonds that hold families, and societies, together.

The image of the blind man getting drunk on the waters of domestic affection provides a radical revisioning, made possible through sentimental rhetoric, of the cultural meanings of the blind body Howe was simultaneously constructing through his use of scientific rhetoric. The blind body that was not a fit site for excess or debauch of alcohol or sex becomes a fit site for the indulgence of excessive feeling. Rather than being defined by its defects and weaknesses, as it had been in relation to economic production and sexual reproduction, the blind body here is defined by its superior need and capacity for affectionate emotions. Relegated by lack or weakness in other realms to the domestic sphere, within the confines of Howe's lovingly-described "comfortable home!" the blind body demonstrates a superior ability to function in an emotional framework. The blind body in the home can do the "work" of feeling as well as any sighted body, whereas in the marketplace the blind body, like any feeling body, cannot compete with unfeeling machine-bodies. In fact, Howe insists both metaphorically and literally that the blind body can do the domestic work of feeling *better* than the sighted body; so powerful is the capacity of the blind body for feeling that there can be no concept of intemperance or excess, or any amount of feeling that can harm it. Even the deepest draughts from the fountains of affection, Howe asserts, will only strengthen the feeling bodies of the blind. Within the home, the defects of blind bodies turn into assets; what made them abnormal in the public realm makes them supernormal in the domestic realm, as they have more of what that sphere requires. Indeed, Howe concludes, the physical infirmities of blindness that had made the blind inferior in all respects to the sighted in public endeavors have given him "in all that regards his moral nature and his social affections . . . capacities far higher than . . . those of ordinary men" (PR 1850, 25).

Having thus found the appropriate locus in which his blind students could be defined as normal, if not superior to the sighted, Howe's use of sentimental rhetoric worked to prove that his institution itself was such a "comfortable home!" Addressing directly the fears of the lay public, and particularly of parents of prospective pupils, that any state-funded public institution must necessarily be run according to a strict economy, whereby financial concerns took precedence over emotional ones, Howe continually insisted that his school would surround its young students with the same quality affectionate care and sympathy as they would find in their own homes. In fact, Howe argued that, while his school replicated the most positive aspects of a family home, it was better than a home in that it provided blind children with a learning environment free from the often-restrictive qualities of parental affection. Parents, particularly mothers, were in Howe's view likely to oversentimentalize their afflicted children and to become overprotective of their supposed weaknesses; in their efforts to protect their blind children from any potential danger or injury, Howe frequently warned in his Annual Reports, mothers would prevent them from becoming as physically strong and independent as they might otherwise be. His school, by contrast, would not smother children with overprotective maternal concern, but would supply them with healthy amounts of sympathetic affection and kindness, just as would be found in any home full of able-bodied sighted children.[5]

In this spirit, Howe filled page after page of his Reports with descriptions of the familial bonds formed between teachers and students and among students. In many such descriptions Howe asserted that the blind students were eager to forge "the tender ties of affection" common among siblings, and he used distinctively sentimental rhetoric to illustrate this phenomenon. For example, in reporting on the sudden death of a female student, Howe chose to describe her as a sentimental heroine, whose life

and death illustrated a number of useful moral lessons, rather than supplying—as one might expect a doctor to do—the medical facts about her
demise. Martha Granger, in Howe's portrayal, had sustained a tragic loss in
her early youth, being "stricken blind when just commencing an education." Knowing that blindness was inextricably associated with grief and
suffering, Miss Granger initially "drooped in silent but uncomplaining sorrow" at her fate, until the news that a school for the blind had opened
"revived hope and promised happiness." The opening of Howe's institution, Howe's narrative insisted, promised that the rescue of the forlorn
heroine was at hand; with the support of her family, especially the encouragement of "a fond mother," Miss Granger "resolved to forgo for a while
the consolations of home and friends" and to make her way among strangers, in order to pursue "the opportunities for acquiring knowledge" (PR
1838, 3n).

Miss Granger, in Howe's prose, was bravely willing to leave the comfortable care of her parents and relatives, whose familial love for her
prompted a great sense of protection for her afflliction, and to risk living
among strangers, who might prove heartless and unfeeling, for the sake of
relieving the dark misery of her ignorance through education. At the Perkins Institution, however, Miss Granger found, according to Howe's description, a home as caring as the one she had left. She readily made friends
with the other students and with her teachers, and when she suddenly
became ill the members of the school cared for her. When she "sickened, a
brain fever followed, and she died," the inhabitants of the school gathered at
her bedside to comfort her last moments and to mourn her passing. From
this story, Howe draws a moral that springs directly from the assumptions
of sentimental fiction:

she died not in the midst of the stranger; and her relatives had the satisfaction of
knowing that, by her amiable and interesting manners, she had already secured
many warm friends, who watched over her anxiously and unceasingly to the last,
and followed her, weeping, to the grave. (PR 1838, 3n)

In Howe's portrayal, Miss Granger's demise, like the death of Muriel Halifax or Little Eva, served as an education in feeling, not only for the blind
students who displayed their capacities for tender emotions at her deathbed, but also for Howe's readers, who, like readers of sentimental fiction,
might shed a tear both for Miss Granger's death and for the fact that it
occurred among such loving friends.

Howe's use of sentimental conventions in his description of Miss
Granger's demise serves the same function as sentimental representations in

fiction. First, Howe works to create a means for readers to identify with the heroine whose suffering he portrays; by naming her directly, as "Martha Granger" rather than as "a blind student," Howe encourages his readers to understand her as an individual rather than as an anonymous member of a class. Then, he describes Miss Granger's emotional response to becoming blind, drawing on the assumptions sighted readers would have about such a tragedy, and prompting readers to recognize Miss Granger's feelings as identical to their own in such a situation. As Howe describes Miss Granger's family relations, focusing on her "fond mother" and her courage in determining to leave that family to pursue her education, readers recognize a scenario sentimental fictions have trained them to read, and hence recognize Miss Granger as a familiar figure whose emotions are no different from their own. Having thus created powerful sets of identifications between character and readers, Howe then shows Miss Granger's death, urging readers to respond to that scenario by emulating the emotions he describes in the blind students who weep over her deathbed. By stimulating the affectionate and sympathetic capacities of his readers, Howe, like the authors of sentimental fiction, provided readers with an opportunity to strengthen their empathic abilities, with the idea that those readers might close the book resolved to use their feelings to alleviate misery wherever they encountered it. More important for Howe's purposes, however, the creation of the empathic bond between readers and Miss Granger, and between readers and the blind students in general, required that readers recognize his "characters" as feeling beings, as emotional agents no different from themselves. Attributing to these "characters" the same emotions they would feel in similar situations prevented readers from understanding the blind as primarily disabled, marked by their differences from the sighted.

While Howe's use of sentimental tropes in his accounts of the workings of the school worked to create the identifications that would rewrite the cultural meanings of blindness being reinforced in the scientific rhetoric of his Reports, Howe did not need to rely solely on his written descriptions to create emotional bonds between his blind students and the sighted public. Unlike the authors of sentimental fiction, Howe could augment his descriptions of the blind pupils by letting the public see these "characters" for themselves, without the mediation of writing. Throughout the first twenty years of his administration, Howe staged exhibitions of his students, both in and outside the Perkins Institution, to demonstrate first-hand the success of his theories and methods of education.

From the school's beginnings, Howe stressed the importance of keeping the the doors open to "the public," so that the taxpayers whose money supported his work could see what he was accomplishing. In 1832, during the first year of his "experiment," when Howe taught his original six pupils in his father's house, visitors could drop in at their convenience. After the first six months of instruction, Howe arranged to display his students' accomplishments to the Massachusetts State Legislature; this exhibition so impressed the legislators that they voted an annual appropriation of six thousand dollars. When the school moved to the Perkins mansion, Howe set up regular visiting hours, and invited the public to view the blind students every Saturday from 3 to 5 p.m. Eager to show his students' progress, Howe was loath to enforce his stated visiting hours strictly; visitors were likely to drop in at any time, asking (and receiving) permission to observe the blind students at whatever activity was currently underway. In addition to these opportunities to observe the students at their work or play within the walls of the institution, Howe frequently staged exhibitions of his pupils before potential donors, parents, and legislators. In 1837 the performance of three Perkins students before the Ohio legislature prompted that body to authorize funds for a census of blind people in Ohio and for the establishment of a school for blind children. A similar exhibition before Congress was part of Howe's (unsuccessful) plan for a national library in raised print for the blind.[6]

These exhibitions consisted largely of displaying the intellectual and manual skills the students had learned. They focused on demonstrating to the public that the students had mastered a curriculum quite similar to that offered in the Boston public schools, which again reinforced the idea that this tax-supported institution was helping to create beings who were not different from other school-aged children. A typical exhibition might include blind students solving mathematical problems, reading aloud from raised-print books, using relief maps to show their knowledge of geography, displaying simple manufacturing skills, executing gymnastic drills, and, of course, performing vocal and instrumental music. Visitors to the institution were likely to see similar skills exhibited, though perhaps in a less-organized fashion; those who dropped in might witness classes in intellectual common-school subjects or manufacturing skills, or simply watch the students at play during their frequent recesses.

These opportunities for the sighted public to observe the blind students directly served a multitude of purposes for Howe. First of all, they offered incontrovertible proof to skeptics that the achievements Howe had proclaimed in his written Reports about his blind pupils were indeed true;

anyone who had any doubts about his claims, Howe wrote, was invited to "see for himself" what the blind students were capable of (PR 1842, 26). In this stance, Howe adhered to a materialist perspective, in which direct sensory perception offers a more reliable form of proof than a written account of an event; this perspective supports the denominative view of language, in which words derive any definitive meaning from the concrete referents to which they refer. In this logic, Howe's written accounts were only as true as the skills of his pupils could demonstrate and confirm. By staging exhibitions and holding open-house visiting hours, Howe insisted on the veracity of his Reports by showing that his words did indeed describe existing conditions accurately, and that they could be verified by direct observation.

In so doing, Howe addressed a concern, prominent in antebellum American culture, about the authority wielded by written texts and that wielded by direct observation and experience. In the transformation from an oral-based to a print-based culture, anxieties arose concerning the reliability of the disembodied voice contained in a written text. In an oral culture, or one in which written texts circulated only among a small population or geographical region, the veracity of a statement was backed up by the audience's knowledge of the moral stature of the author and his or her reputation for honesty and reliability. In a culture where printed texts circulated among a wider audience, however, readers might not know the author, or his or her reputation, personally; the question of the veracity of the written text was thus thrown into question. Without other structures, such as professional credentials or certification programs, to confirm the status of the author as reliable expert, the reading public during this transitional period might necessarily remain skeptical about Reports such as Howe's that claimed almost miraculous achievements. Lacking the credentials organizations like the American Social Science Association and the American Association of Instructors of the Blind would begin to provide after the Civil War, Howe had to rely on demonstrating the observable reality behind his written words to prove to the skeptics in his audience that his written accounts were indeed believable.[7]

The need for directly observable proof of Howe's written accounts came from the same sets of cultural assumptions as did Howe's own increasing reliance on statistical evidence and analyses of aggregate populations: both addressed concerns raised within the science of the time. While answering in objective scientific form the doubts of skeptics, however, the exhibitions of the blind students also served a decidedly sentimental purpose. The direct experience available through the exhibitions would appeal, not only to observers' rational judgments, but to their emotional sensibilities as well; following Diderot's logic, which Howe cited directly, the sight and sound of the blind students would provide a more immediate and more powerful stimulus to the audience's feelings than could a written account (PR 1843, 4). Through the exhibitions, the "spectacle of the poor sightless creatures and of what was being done for them"[8] had the power to move audiences to feel for, and act generously toward, that group of people "whom misfortune has thrown on the sympathy and charity of their more favored fellows" (PR 1839, 11).

The exhibitions and visiting opportunities, offering to audiences a direct experience of the blind students, served to reinforce the truth of the written accounts, but they were also constructed by those written acounts, especially in regard to their sentimental significance. Howe's written descriptions of the exhibitions, and of the sights audiences were likely to see when they dropped in during the institution's weekly visiting hours, serve to frame for audiences the meaning of what they witnessed. Like sentimental fictions, which teach readers how to respond to the images and scenes before them, Howe's written Reports worked to show readers how to interpret what they were seeing in the exhibitions, with the hope of rewriting the cultural expectations and sets of meanings associated with blindness that the audience brought with them to the "spectacle." Through his written accounts of the exhibitions, Howe prompted audiences to see his blind students, not as some alien race of beings or as sufferers needing sympathy and charity, but as happy children, just like sighted ones, who were capable of the full range of human emotions, including the capacity to feel and act on behalf of less-fortunate others.[9]

In the earliest descriptions of his work with blind students, observers placed Howe, rather than the students, in the forefront, framing him as the sentimental hero. Elizabeth Palmer Peabody, visiting the school in 1832, when Howe taught his six students in his father's home, recounted going "to see this hero . . . wholly absorbed, and applying all the energies of his genius to this apparently humble work, and doing it as Christ did, without money and without price."[10] Naming Howe as the heroic "man of feeling," a character made familiar through eighteenth-century sentimental representations, Peabody foregrounded Howe's "humble" and charitable attitude, rather than the accomplishments of the blind students. Rather, she took it for granted that readers, being presented with a depiction of blind children, would assume that those children were pitiable and in need of sympathetic care, even if the efforts expended on their behalf proved to no avail. The scene thus centers on Howe's Christlike offering of his time and energy without thought of reward, whether financial or in the form of successfully educating his students.

Howe's descriptions of his students' work minimize his own role, though later observers such as Charles Dickens would again see Howe, and not the students, as the hero of a sentimental drama. Instead, Howe focuses on describing what visitors would be likely to see when they attended an exhibition or an open-house; more important, he works to explain to his readers the differences between what they expect to see and what they will see, and to describe to them how they should react when they do observe the blind students directly. Writing about a typical exhibition, Howe noted that virtually all audience members expected to see blind students exhibiting the traditional cultural meanings they had come to associate with blindness, including misery, suffering, and an inability to perform basic tasks, or to perform them only with great effort and not well. "Whenever there is a public exhibition," such audience members "look on the preparations with a doubtful eye," expecting to respond to "the array of sightless beings with feelings of compassion amounting to pain." But, Howe insisted,

the moment [the blind students] take their books, and, running their fingers along the lines, begin to read aloud, there is a mingled feeling of relief and admiration, which shows itself in smiles and tears. There is hardly a person who can witness this, for the first time, without deep emotion. (PR 1846, 18)

The emotions observers feel on watching the blind students at work shift from painful expectations of suffering and sympathy to "relief and admiration," expressed in "smiles and tears," as observers — and readers of Howe's written accounts of those observers — learn new sets of cultural meanings to associate with blindness.

The blind students in this example still serve as "posters" to arouse feelings in sighted observers, and to strengthen their capacities for empathy. The meaning of those "posters," however, begins to shift in Howe's descriptions. While the old significance of blindness as necessarily associated with suffering and dependence does not disappear completely from the observers' frames of reference, Howe provides a new overlay, insisting that the prevailing new meaning of blindness will be one of competence and pride in skills learned. Audience members will thus have new emotions aroused by the sight of the blind "posters": rather than feeling only pity and compassion for the less-fortunate, they will begin to feel pride and admiration for the accomplishments of the students — emotions very similar to what they would feel for their own children's achievements.

By trying to rewrite the kinds of emotional responses visitors should expect to experience on seeing the blind children, Howe works to create identifications between his audience and his students, so that the sighted public will view the students as just like normal children, rather than as a class of suffering recipients of charity. His descriptions of how visitors should respond to seeing the students in the institution itself create these identifications even more powerfully than his descriptions of how audiences should respond to exhibitions held outside the school. Visitors to the school may expect to feel trepidation when approaching the walled grounds of a state-run institution, expecting to find "inmates," Howe warns; rather, they should be prepared to experience the institution as a home, just like their own, where children learn and play. "The visitor who approaches our house," Howe warned, "nine-tenths of whose numerous inmates are groping in darkness, feels a melancholy presentiment that sights of suffering, and sounds of sadness, must there await him." The visitor who already knows the established meaning of blindness, and expects to weep over the pathetic sight of blind children, enters a "house" full of children, and "soon finds that he alone is sad, and that children who sit darkling at their books, or run fearlessly about at their play, are as contented and happy as those whom he left in the enjoyment of sun-light without" (PR 1842, 3).

Describing the school specifically as a home, Howe urges his readers to think of his institution in association with all the images that "home" conjures up in the American cultural imagination. Associating the school thus with existing notions of family and childhood, rather than with existing notions of "institutional care," Howe attempts to overwrite the existing meanings linking blind people with misery and dependence and instead to paint a portrait of blind children as happy, contented, playful, and joyful. Students who are members of this "home" are part of a new kind of "family," who, as indicated in Howe's description of Martha Granger's death, share all the joys and sorrows, all the feelings of mutual care and concern that a regular family would feel.

The outside observer, Howe warns, is likely to bring only the old expectations of misery and dependence when he enters the institution, and thus is likely to miss the fact that the blind students are fully capable of joy and of empathic agency, just like sighted children. Indeed, the existing meanings of blindness the sighted observer brings to the institution are the likeliest means by which blind children learn that they ought to feel miserable, Howe warns. The assumption of pathos, Howe reminds his readers, comes from a sighted person's sense of how tragic the loss of sight would be; blind children do not repine over their loss. "To the blind child," Howe reminds his readers, "existence itself is a great boon." It is only when "others point out their privation" to the blind children, "or shock [them] by those well-meant, but injudicious expressions of pity, which visitors are too apt to make," that the blind students discover that they ought to be anything other than happy and playful (PR 1842, 3).

Insisting that the prevailing cultural associations between blindness and misery do not occur to the blind children themselves but are meanings told to them by injudicious visitors, Howe concludes that the social meanings of blindness are in fact constructions, and therefore variable. The existing meanings of blindness, and of disability in general, as signifying suffering, weakness, dependence, and difference are powerful, Howe admits, and are likely to color what observers expect to see when visiting the school. Howe's efforts to rewrite these existing meanings, or to provide a new layer of meanings to mitigate if not replace them, focus on portraying the blind students as just like sighted ones, as happy children who live securely in a homelike environment, and who learn skills in which their parents, teachers, and friends can take pride. Using sentimental conventions to create identifications between his descriptions of his pupils and his readers, Howe retains the idea that the blind, like the disabled in general, serve to generate strong emotions in readers; he works to shift the kind of emotions these "posters" create, however, from feelings of pity and charity to feelings of relief, joy, and wonder.

As his sentimental descriptions created a resemblance between the "family" of the blind and their teachers and the families of sighted children and adults, Howe attempted to "normalize" the blind students as domestic beings, even as his scientific descriptions created them as an abnormal class in relation to economic production. In this domestic context, Howe insisted, blind children and adults had capacities equal to, if not superior to, those of sighted people. Claiming their equality thus on the basis of their emotional capacities, rather than on their ability for economic production or sexual reproduction, Howe opened the possibility that the primary social function of the blind lay not just in being "posters" to arouse the empathic feelings of others, but in becoming feeling beings, empathic agents, in their own right, fully able to identify with the emotions of others and to act to alleviate others' suffering and misery.

Laura Bridgman

The most famous disabled person in the United States in the middle of the nineteenth century was also the most famous inhabitant of the Perkins Institution: Laura Bridgman, the first deaf and blind person to be successfully educated.[1] Thousands of people followed published accounts of her miraculous rescue from the prison of her deafness and blindness and her ascent into human realms. Bridgman became Samuel Gridley Howe's showpiece, proof that no living soul was so deeply interred as to be unreachable, and proof also that Howe's educational methods, and his reports of his work with his blind students, were sound and reliable. The voluminous accounts of his work with Bridgman Howe published in his Annual Reports were widely reprinted in newspapers and magazines throughout the United States and Europe.[2] Bridgman came to represent the entire catalog of cultural attitudes toward disability. In Howe's descriptions, as in those of numerous other observers and commentators, Bridgman served as a source of scientific information for a professional community; more important, she signified a range of sentimental attitudes toward disability, from her status as a "poster" who could summon the empathic feelings of the ablebodied to her status as a feeling being who could work to alleviate the sufferings of those less fortunate than herself.

Laura Dewey Bridgman was born on a small farm outside Hanover, New Hampshire in 1829. After a normal infancy, she contracted scarlet fever at the age of two, which destroyed her sight and hearing completely and left her virtually devoid of any sense of smell or taste as well. In 1837, a student at nearby Dartmouth College saw Bridgman and spoke about her to Dr. Mussey, the head of Dartmouth's medical department. After visiting the Bridgman farm, Mussey wrote to Howe, who was already well known as a pioneer in the education of the blind, asking if anything could be done for her. Howe leaped at the opportunity to try his hand at a task that had been mentioned by various philosophers and educators but never attempted. Accompanied by his old friend Henry Wadsworth Longfellow, Howe went to Hanover to see Bridgman; having determined that there was no deficiency in her intellectual capacity other than that occasioned by her sensory deprivations, Howe persuaded her parents to let him take her back to the Perkins Institution to undertake the task of her education.

From the beginning, Howe framed Bridgman's education as an "experiment" with a dual purpose. On the one hand, the dictates of humanitarianism, as well as the principles of Christianity, prompted Howe's efforts to rescue Bridgman's human soul from its state of ignorance and isolation. On the other hand, Bridgman provided an unprecedented opportunity to confirm or refute Locke's premises about the relations between sensory perception and intellectual functioning and to investigate more closely the question of the relation between sensory perception and language acquisition. Howe wrote

It struck me at once that here was an opportunity of assisting an unfortunate child, and, moreover, of deciding the question so often asked, whether a blind-mute could be taught to use an arbitrary language.[3]

The philanthropic importance of rescuing Bridgman, Howe noted, guaranteed that "No pains or expense will be spared in efforts to develop the moral and intellectual nature of this interesting child," while the scientific importance of her education mandated that, simultaneously, "no opportunity [will be] lost, of gathering for science whatever mental phenomena her singular case might furnish" (PR 1838, 8).

Howe's work with Bridgman focused specifically on the acquisition of language because that was the key factor in determining Bridgman's status as a human being. Though "It was considered doubtful when she came whether it would be possible to teach her any regular system of signs by which she could express her thoughts and understand those of others," Howe wrote, "it was deemed highly desirable . . . to make the experiment" (PR 1838, 7). Without such a signifying system, the "personage" in the physical frame "was unknown to [Howe], and to all, save in her outer aspect"; only the acquisition of language would prove if Bridgman were "fully and normally human."[4] Howe insisted that the only sign system appropriate to a "fully and normally human" being was alphabetic arbitrary language rather than the mimetic gestural language used in the education of the deaf. Following the denominational view of language, Howe thus commenced Bridgman's education in language by familiarizing her with sets of labels in raised type and encouraging her to associate those labels with the objects the words represented. Once she had mastered this task, Howe cut the labels into their individual letters, and helped Bridgman unscramble them, until she could reliably place the letters "e, k, y" in the proper order and associate them with the object "key," and so forth.

Over the first months of this work, Bridgman made good progress in learning the basic fact of denomination, that words represent tangible objects. Because of Howe's method, however, she failed to understand the idea that language is also a complete system of signification that does not rely on the material association of word and object. Howe himself was aware of this limitation, noting that, however well she learned to label objects, until she had mastered the principle of language as a system through which every idea could be expressed, his work with Bridgman was like "teaching a very intelligent dog a variety of tricks." Eventually, however, Bridgman did finally make the leap of understanding necessary to prove herself a "fully and normally human" language-user. By the end of three months of lessons, "the truth began to flash on her," and she was "no longer a dog or parrot, [but] an immortal spirit, eagerly seizing on a new link of union with other spirits!" (PR 1841, 26).

The key to becoming fully human, in Howe's conception, lay in this ability to forge "links of union" with other "spirits," so that each person's internal thoughts and feelings could be shared with others. Such links were made possible in the sighted and hearing population by two forms of language: the observation of the natural language of emotions and the powers of sympathetic imitation, which led to an empathic identification, and the use of arbitrary language to communicate in words those emotions which others would then identify with and respond to. Both forms of language helped to create a society of interdependent sympathizers; without the links forged by natural and arbitrary language, each individual would remain isolated in the privacy of his or her own thoughts and feelings. Bridgman's "imprisonment" in the confines of her deaf-blind body served as an illustration, for Howe, of an extreme version of such isolation. Her acquisition of arbitrary language liberated her, as it supplied the only other medium by which, in the absence of direct observation of others' natural signs, communication and relational bonds could be established to make her part of a caring human family.

The public who read Howe's accounts of Bridgman's liberation from her isolated state agreed that her success in acquiring arbitrary language was one of the miracles of the century, and she eventually became the central attraction at the Perkins Institution. At first, Howe guarded Bridgman carefully. Although she was "an object of great interest, and hundreds of people would come here to see her if they were allowed," Howe wrote to Bridgman's parents in 1838, after the publication of his first account of her education, "I do not wish her to be made an object of envious gaze, [or] allow her to be seen except by very few."[5] With the publication of each year's Annual Report, however, came more information about Bridgman's successful transformation into a human being, and with it more demand from the public to see her progress for themselves. In 1840, Howe began to include Bridgman regularly in the weekly exhibitions. The crowds eager to see the phenomenal child quickly grew so great, "and press[ed] so closely around Laura, that we are obliged to surround her desk by settees, thus making a little enclosure" to protect her from the visitors who wanted to touch and talk to her.[6]

Howe's Annual Report of 1841 included an extensive account of Bridgman's education. This account was widely reprinted, in the United States and in Europe, and attracted nation- and worldwide interest in Bridgman's accomplishments and in the man who had made them possible. Sophia Peabody Hawthorne asked permission to sculpt a bust of Bridgman; Lydia Sigourney wrote a poem in her honor. Charles Sumner and Henry Wadsworth Longfellow, accompanied by Julia Ward, were among the thousands of visitors who flocked to the Perkins Institution specifically to see Bridgman.[7] Howe declared:

She has come into human society with a sort of triumphal march; her course has been a perpetual ovation. Thousands have been watching her with eager eyes, and applauding each successful step. . . . Perhaps there are not three living women whose names are more widely known than hers; and there is not one who has excited so much sympathy and interest. (PR 1850, 48)

Among those who helped to spread Bridgman's fame, and to spark the "sympathy and interest" her case aroused, was Charles Dickens, who visited the Perkins Institution in 1842, and included in his *American Notes* a description of his encounter with Bridgman, as well as lengthy reprints of Howe's 1841 Annual Report about the girl.

Dickens's attraction to Bridgman came in large part from his ability to describe her as a sentimental heroine, the equivalent of his own Little Nell in his recently published novel *The Old Curiosity Shop* (1841). And Dickens's desire to create a sentimental portrayal of Bridgman came, in turn, from Howe's use of sentimental assumptions and conventions in his voluminous accounts of Bridgman's education. Howe's descriptions of Bridgman's education as a "triumph," as the miraculous rescue of a human soul, as the transformation of a merely animal physical being into an "immortal soul" who could communicate all her thoughts and feelings to others, relied on sentimental ideals, which made Bridgman a heroine—and Howe her hero. His accounts of her, while continuing to present to a scientific audience the factual details and principles of his methods, enthralled his lay audience precisely because they presented her in the same terms as a fictional sentimental heroine. Indeed, according to Julia Ward Howe, "the appearance of his annual reports was waited for almost as are the numbers of a serial in a magazine" (PR 1889, 150). Just as American audiences clamored for the installments of Dickens's latest serially-published novels, so too they were eager to hear the most recent developments in the case of this living sentimental heroine, as well as to see her for themselves at the Perkins exhibitions.

The accounts of Bridgman, primarily authored by Howe but echoed by virtually every other nineteenth-century writer who described Bridgman, use sentimental tropes to articulate the cultural meanings Bridgman's story illustrated and affirmed. Like sentimental fictional representations of disabled characters, these nonfictional accounts insist that Bridgman arouses the humanitarian feelings of the ablebodied. Many accounts, including Howe's, go beyond this view of the cultural significance of disabled people as objects to insist that Bridgman as sentimental heroine also had the capacity for empathic agency; as language put her into contact with other humans, so it enabled her to understand others' sufferings, to feel for others' woes, and even to act on their behalf to relieve them. The employment of sentimental tropes in these descriptions works to depict Bridgman, and by extension the disabled population she represents, as identical to nondisabled people in her emotional capacities, which are the most important attributes of a "fully and normally human" being.

Howe was acutely aware that his written accounts of Bridgman presented far more than just a description of his methods for her education. Though "the simple story of the past sufferings and . . . dreary isolation of Laura Bridgman" might not be poetic enough to "'adorn a tale,'" Howe noted in his first Report about her that it would "furnish much to 'point a moral,'" and "to interest and instruct readers" (PR 1838, 11). Like the story of the orphaned Gerty Flint in *The Lamplighter*, one of the morals illustrated by Bridgman's story was the importance in sentimental logic of human relationality. Like a sentimental novel, accounts of Bridgman begin by emphasizing her "dreary isolation" and lack of any connection to human caring. In Howe's words, she was "a human soul, shut up in a dark and silent cell," with "all the avenues to it . . . closed"; despite her imprisonment, however, she strove to make connections with others, as her soul was "active and struggling continually not only to put itself in communication with things without, but to manifest what is going on in itself" (PR 1838, 6). Without such an effort to forge relationships with others,

in this total darkness — this dreary stillness — this isolation from all communication with kindred spirits, the immaterial mind must have remained in infantile imbecility . . . or have attained a perception of its loneliness, only to pine and die at the discovery. (PR 1838, 11)

But with the aid of her heroic rescuer, who supplied her with the means to put herself in emotional and intellectual contact with the world around her, Bridgman neither repined nor died, but like a sentimental heroine, became "more active and more cheerful" (PR 1838, 11–12).

Dickens's description of Bridgman, too, framed her as a sentimental heroine, completely isolated from human connection and thus in grave need of rescue.

I sat down . . . before a girl, blind, deaf, and dumb; destitute of smell; and nearly so of taste: before a young creature with every human faculty, and hope, and power of goodness and affection, inclosed in her delicate frame, and but one outward sense — the sense of touch. There she was, before me; built up, as it were, in a marble cell, impervious to any ray of light, or particle of sound; with her poor white hand peeping through a chink in the wall, beckoning to some good man for help, that an Immortal soul might be awakened.[8]

Like Howe's description, Dickens's focuses on the idea of Bridgman as a prisoner in a cell, framing her soul as having all the necessary traits that would mark her as fully human — specifically, the "power of goodness and affection" — and her body as the limiting factor, the unfeeling "marble cell" that prevented her from connection with others. The pathos of the "poor white hand" emphasizes how helpless she was, imprisoned in this disabled body, able only to make a gestural signal to any potential rescuer.

Unlike Howe's account, Dickens's description of Bridgman foregrounds Howe's own role, framing him as the heroic "good man" whose sympathies were aroused by the sight of Bridgman's "poor white hand" and its feeble beckoning. Dickens follows this discussion of Bridgman's initial state of isolation by admitting his view as retrospective: "Long before I looked on her, the help had come," in the form of "her great benefactor and

Figure 3. Dr. Howe and Laura Bridgman. From Michael Anagnos, ed., *The Educa-tion of Laura D. Bridgman*.

friend . . . Dr. Howe."[9] Like Trueman Flint, or any other character in a sentimental novel who saves a heroine from a life of isolation and misery, "Dr. Howe" serves as a moral lesson for readers; Dickens wants to "hope and believe" that "'there are not many persons who, after reading these passages, can ever hear that name with indifference."[10]

Howe's stature as the noble rescuer, and Bridgman's as the grateful recipient of his care, are illustrated in the engraving that appeared in the summary account of Howe's work with Bridgman in the 1889 Annual Report (Figure 3). Here Bridgman sits like a doll on Howe's lap, clutching some thread that connects her small hand with his large one. They are taking a break from their lessons, as shown by the alphabet blocks strewn across the table, and Bridgman seems to be patiently awaiting the next exercise, since she is facing the table and showing only her profile to the viewer; the pose suggests that she is aware only of Howe's physical presence, and of the lessons they are undertaking, and is unconscious of anyone observing her. The full-face portrait of Howe, by contrast, emphasizes his powers of sight, in contrast to Bridgman's blindfolded blind eyes, as well as his large size in relation to her smallness. His erect head and steady gaze suggest a firmness of purpose, as does the direction of his look, slightly to the left of and beyond the viewer, which suggests a man preoccupied with the importance of his work and thoughts. Clearly this is a portrait of the man Dickens finds so heroic, and of the helpless child who is being rescued by his compassionate care.

For both Howe and Dickens, Bridgman's story illustrated not only the central importance of human relationships, but also the power of suffering to arouse empathic feelings in others. In this, Bridgman served as a quintessential "poster child," whose status as "suffering" was overdetermined by her deafness and blindness, her isolation, her age, and her gender. As Howe put it,

Human sympathies are always ready to be poured out in proportion to the amount of human suffering. The privation of any one sense is supposed to be a dreadful calamity, and calls at once for our sympathy with the sufferer; but when a human being is known to be deaf, dumb, blind, without smell, and with imperfect taste, that being excites the tender compassion of all who feel. . . . When the supposed sufferer is a child—a girl—and of pleasing appearance, the sympathy and interest are naturally increased. (PR 1841, 23)

Like disabled girls in sentimental fiction, such as Muriel Halifax, Bridgman served primarily to summon the compassionate feelings of the ablebodied.

Her life story was to be "as a lamp set on a hill" illuminating "the most gratifying" aspect of her accomplishments, which was "the amount of tender sympathy in her misfortunes, and of real interest in the attempt to lighten them, which has been shown by thousands of sensitive hearts" (*ELB*, 77, 163).

Howe continually emphasized that the "moral" Bridgman's story pointed lay in "the importance which, despite their useless waste of human life and human capacity, men really attach to a human soul" (PR 1850, 48). While Bridgman should be properly grateful for all that had been done on her behalf, Howe insisted that the nondisabled public

owes to her something for furnishing an opportunity of showing how much of goodness there is in them; for surely the way in which she has been regarded is creditable to humanity. . . . The treatment she has received shows something of Human Progress . . . as millions of people recognize a duty and a privilege to protect and cherish her. (PR 1850, 48)

This " 'child of misfortune,' " Howe concluded, had been sent by God to help elevate the best moral qualities of human kind: she was

destined to be the instrument of great good, not only by drawing forth the sympathies and putting into exercise the kindly emotions of others, but by teaching them how great may be improvement under the worst difficulties, how pure and elevated may be even uncultivated human character if only removed from bad influences, and how joyous may be existence under the darkest cloud. (*ELB*, 203)

Merely through "the silent show of her misfortunes, and her successful efforts to surmount them," Bridgman made the public better people, and the world a more humane place (PR 1850, 49).

While foregrounding the importance of Bridgman's status as a sentimental heroine capable of arousing empathic feelings in others, Howe also worked to show that Bridgman was not merely the object of compassion for the ablebodied. To emphasize her misfortunes and difficulties too fully, Howe knew, would be to focus attention too completely on her afflictions and on the misery generally associated with those afflictions. Rather, even as he listed all the factors which contributed to the conclusion that Bridgman must be helpless, isolated, and miserable, Howe insisted that this conclusion might be the false creation of ingrained social attitudes. While describing her as "deaf, dumb, blind, without smell, and with imperfect taste," and as "a child — a girl — and of pleasing appearance," Howe also named her as "the supposed sufferer," implying that perhaps her condition was only pathetic to observers who chose to see her that way (PR 1841,

23). The former view highlights Bridgman's disabilities, the factors that isolate her and mark her as different from others — and which are the basis of the world's interest in her (and in Howe); the latter view highlights Bridgman's normality, the result of her successful acquisition of language, and the ability of her soul, once disinterred, to triumph over the limiting conditions of her body.

Howe's efforts to supplement the image of Bridgman as dependent sufferer with one of her as a normal girl are echoed in Dickens's portrayal as well. Having described Bridgman as the isolated girl "built up . . . in a marble cell," beckoning to a good man to rescue her, Dickens concludes his observations by showing her as she existed after Howe had taught her arbitrary language. In Dickens's final portrait, she sits happily ensconced in her parlor, like the heroine of a sentimental novel who has been rescued from imprisonment and restored to the bosom of home and family:

Her face was radiant with intelligence and pleasure. Her hair, braided by her own hands, was bound about a head, whose intellectual capacity and development were beautifully impressed in its graceful outline, and its broad open brow; her dress, arranged by herself, was a pattern of neatness and simplicity; the work she had knitted lay beside her; her writing-book was on the desk she leaned on.[11]

Dickens here describes all the attributes associated with a normal girl, whose intelligence adds to her beauty and grace, who can braid her own hair and dress herself with neatness and simplicity, who is never idle, but always has knitting in hand, and who is able to record her thoughts in her writing-book. Like Howe, Dickens wanted his portrait of Bridgman to show that her dual disabilities, while contributing to her suffering, had ultimately worked to shape her spotless character. "From the mournful ruin of such bereavement," Dickens concluded, "there had slowly risen up this gentle, tender, guileless, grateful-hearted being."[12]

Dickens's sketch of Bridgman, while highlighting her domestic capacities, makes little note of what for Howe was the central purpose of teaching Bridgman arbitrary language: to enable her to establish normal relationships with others. Dickens paints Bridgman as still alone, though capable of writing in a book; Howe's portraits, by contrast, focus on how the acquisition of language put Bridgman in constant contact with the people around her. As he noted from his earliest work with Bridgman, Howe's goal was to provide her with the means to "shadow forth . . . the ideas that were passing in her own mind," and to understand the ideas of others in turn (PR 1841, 31). His descriptions of Bridgman's efforts to connect with others consist of relatively unemotional accounts of the lessons in language acquisition that he and Bridgman's other teachers pursued, combined with sentimental scenarios in which the emotional power and importance of this acquisition of language is displayed. After describing the painstaking procedures he used to familiarize Bridgman with concrete nouns and other parts of speech, Howe includes an account of Bridgman's mother's first visit to her daughter in the Institution.

> The mother stood some time, gazing with overflowing eyes on her unfortunate child, who, all unconscious of her presence, was playing about the room. Presently Laura ran against her, and at once began feeling of her hands, examining her dress, and trying to find out if she knew her; but, not succeeding in this, she turned away as from a stranger, and the poor woman could not conceal the pang she felt, at finding that her beloved child did not know her. (*ELB*, 21)

But before the reader could burst into sympathetic tears for the "painful distress" of the mother whose child fails to recognize her, Howe noted that the gift of some items from Bridgman's home, coupled with a teacher spelling the word "mother" into Bridgman's hand, turned the scene from one of tragedy to one of joy, as "at once the truth flashed on the child," and "with an expression of exceeding joy she eagerly nestled to the bosom of her parent, and yielded herself to her fond embraces" (*ELB*, 22).

Howe's use of sentimental tropes in this scenario highlight the two most important "morals," or cultural meanings, that Bridgman's story illustrated. On the one hand, the pathos of the child's inability to recognize her own mother emphasizes Bridgman's status as an "imprisoned" soul, an isolated being whose lack of connection to maternal affection must necessarily mean that she is suffering or miserable. On the other hand, the happy ending, wherein arbitrary language enables Bridgman to know her mother, and thus to gain access to an abundance of love and joy, emphasizes her transformation from pathetic object to normal child. Many of Howe's descriptions of Bridgman, especially in his earliest accounts of her, juxtapose these two morals and use them to reinforce each other. In his 1840 Report, for example, Howe insisted that

> it would be difficult to find a child in the possession of all her senses . . . who is more contented and cheerful, or to whom existence seems a greater blessing than it does to this bereaved creature, for whom the sun has no light, the air has no sound, and the flowers no color or smell. (*ELB*, 24–25)

In one sentence, Howe names Bridgman as both contented and bereft, both cheerful and cut off from the most common sources of joy and beauty in the world. He thus prompts his readers to understand Bridgman as both triumphant and pathetic, and in related degrees: the more isolated she is by her multiple disabilities, the more miraculous her transformation into a normal happy girl.

In other descriptions of Bridgman, Howe eschews the pathetic, with its emphasis on her disabilities, in favor of illustrating her normality, her similarity to sighted and hearing children. Howe's accounts of Bridgman throughout the 1840s claim normality for Bridgman by supplying numerous examples that demonstrate that Bridgman's "moral nature, her sentiments and affections" are "equally well developed as those of other children." Indeed, his descriptions of her might serve as a catalog of desirable Victorian virtues:

In her moral character, it is beautiful to behold her continual gladness, her keen enjoyment of existence, her expansive love, her unhesitating confidence, her sympathy with suffering, her conscientiousness, truthfulness, and hopefulness. (*ELB*, 21)

By showing repeatedly that there was no difference, in terms of capacity for affectionate human relationships, between Bridgman and sighted and hearing children, Howe prepared his readers to identify her with their own children, and thus to understand her, and the other residents of the Perkins Institution, as "fully and normally human" like themselves.

The majority of Howe's descriptions of Bridgman, after her triumphant acquisition of language, insist that Bridgman is just like other children; he echoes Unitarian assumptions about the innocence and joyousness of childhood and describes Bridgman in the same terms and settings found in sentimental fictional stories of normal happy children from the mid-nineteenth century. In his 1843 account, for example, Howe portrays Bridgman as having every virtue which could possibly be associated with a thirteen-year-old girl:

[S]he begins the day as merrily as the lark; she is laughing as she attires herself and braids her hair, and comes dancing out of her chamber as though every morn were that of a gala day; a smile and a sign of recognition greet every one she meets; kisses and caresses are bestowed on her friends and her teachers; she goes to her lesson, but knows not the word *task*; she gaily assists others in what they call housework, but which she deems play; she is delighted with society, and clings to others as though she would grow to them; yet she is happy when sitting alone, and smiles and laughs as the varying current of pleasant thought passes through her mind; and when she walks out into the field, she greets her mother nature, whose smile she cannot see, whose music she cannot hear, with a joyful heart and a glad countenance; in a word, her whole life is like a hymn of gratitude and thanksgiving. (PR 1843, 24)

In this description, which Howe acknowledges may be deemed the "extravagant" expression of a "partial" and "fond friend," but which he insists is scrupulously true, Bridgman is placed in a plethora of familiar sentimental tropes (PR 1843, 24). First, she is associated with nature, rising like a lark and later acknowledging nature as "her mother," whose bond with her supersedes the need for any direct sensory perception of the natural world. As a child of nature, Bridgman is unfailingly contented, as the words "laughing," "dancing," "gaily," "play," "happy," "smiles," "pleasant," "joyful," and "glad" emphasize. She is also an able and eager member of human society, as, after rising like a lark, she appears neatly attired in human dress, with hair she has braided herself, ready to strengthen her bonds with others through greetings, kisses, and caresses. Her participation in both educational and domestic forms of work shows her ability to become a productive citizen of the society to which she belongs, while Howe insists that her cheerfulness removes any onus the idea of "work" might have, as she labels housework "play" and doesn't know to call lessons "tasks." Her natural state of joy, combined with the firmly-forged ties that bind her to her community of loving and working friends, makes it possible for her to be happy even when alone, in contrast to the dreary isolation and loneliness which, in Howe's descriptions, characterized her pre-linguistic state.

Among the most normal of Bridgman's characteristics, according to Howe, was her capacity to form friendships with the other residents of the school. Always eager to meet and talk to anyone she encountered, Bridgman, like any sighted and hearing girl, was especially fond of chatting with her favorites, via the manual alphabet which Howe had taught her and which most of the residents of the female wing of the school had learned in order to communicate with her.[13] When she encountered one of her special friends, Howe noted, there was

instantly a bright smile of recognition, an intertwining of arms, a grasping of hands, and a swift telegraphing upon the tiny fingers, whose rapid evolutions convey the thoughts and feelings from the outposts of one mind to those of the other. There are questions and answers, exchanges of joy or sorrow; there are kissings and partings, just as between little children with all their senses. (*ELB*, 20)

In this passage, the only evidence of any difference between the interaction of these two girls and that of two sighted and hearing girls appears in the description of the manual alphabet being "telegraph[ed] upon the tiny fingers." That distinction is minimized, however, as the description then focuses on what the means of communication is able to accomplish—

"questions and answers, exchanges of joy or sorrow" — which again are no different from what would be accomplished through oral speech between two sighted and hearing girls. An insistence on the disabled status of the participants as blind and deaf-blind would prompt readers to imagine both as pathetic sufferers; Howe's avoidance of such a portrayal instead encourages readers to imagine the interaction of these two Perkins students as identical to that of their own girl children.

Even more crucial to Howe's claims of Bridgman's normality than her ability to form friendships was her ability to put aside her own feelings and troubles in order to identify with, and feel for, the problems of others. No capacity was more central in claiming fully human status than the ability to rise above one's own afflictions in favor of assisting less-fortunate others. Becoming an empathic agent was the culminating step in a disabled person's evolution from "poster" to person; as Emily Graham insists in *The Lamplighter*, only when one could put away one's own woes in order to work to alleviate the sufferings of others could one claim to be "fully and normally human." Howe, adopting this sentimental principle, is careful to provide examples of Bridgman's expanding empathic capacities as proof of her full moral development. Noting that Bridgman is not like other children, in that she "does not cry from vexation and disappointment" when she does not get her way, Howe explains that this difference is not due to any absence of feeling, but rather to her emotional maturity, and her ability to eschew merely self-centered concerns. Her tears, rather than marking only her own feelings, demonstrate her capacity for sympathetic identification with, and imitation of, others' emotions: "the fountain of tears . . . is seen when her companions are in pain, or her teacher is grieved" (*ELB*, 47).

Bridgman could sometimes perceive the emotions of others for herself, in feeling the flow of tears or noting a change in breathing patterns in her teacher's body; more often, however, she relied on linguistic descriptions of what others were feeling to understand their emotions. As in sentimental fiction, these linguistic representations were sufficient to produce the natural signs of emotions in Bridgman's own body, as evidenced by her readiness to cry when others were upset. She responded to stories with the same intensity with which she responded to the humans in her environment; Howe notes that, whenever she heard a (real or fictional) story about someone who had done something wrong, she was moved "to apologize for the person who appears to be in the wrong, and to say. . . . *He did not mean to do wrong*" (PR 1842, 30; emphasis original). Similarly, when Bridgman herself did something wrong — Howe is scrupulous about including accounts of such incidents, so as to highlight Bridgman's normality — and her teacher "lets her know that she is grieved," she shows her "tender nature" through "ready tears of contrition" and "earnest assurances of amendment" which are prompted, not by any fear of punishment, but rather by the desire "to comfort those whom she has pained" (*ELB*, 45).

Howe's accounts stress that Bridgman's sensitivity to the feelings of others prompted her to want to act on their behalf, which was the true sign of her accession to empathic agency. Like an ideal child in a sentimental story, Bridgman, when given any treat, was "particularly desirous that those who happen to be ill, or in any way afflicted, should share with her . . . even if it be one whom she dislikes." Whenever she learned of a Perkins resident who was ill, she was eager to be of assistance; "She loves to be employed in tending the sick," Howe testified, "and is most assiduous in her simple attentions, and tender and endearing in her demeanor" (*ELB*, 45). Her efforts to care for others were not limited to her immediate peers, however. Howe and her other teachers noted that her "sympathy is ever ready to flow for those who are afflicted," and for "those who are suffering everywhere," citing an example of Bridgman writing a condolence letter to a woman, whom Bridgman had once met, whose child had died (*ELB*, 174, 194). A more widely cited example, one that appeared frequently in the reprints of Howe's Annual Reports in newspapers and magazines, described how Bridgman, learning of the Irish famine in the late 1840s, endeavored to sell some of her embroidery work in order to buy a barrel of flour to send to Ireland. This work of selfless charity was cited by Thomas Carlyle, when he was asked what great or noble thing America had accomplished, as his sole example.[14]

Perhaps the most moving opportunity to demonstrate Bridgman's empathic capacities arose when a twelve-year-old deaf-blind boy, Oliver Caswell, entered the Perkins Institution in 1842. According to Howe's descriptions, Caswell did not have the natural quickness in learning Bridgman had shown, in part because he began his education later than Bridgman had, but he was nevertheless successful in learning the manual alphabet well enough to hold conversations with other people, to write letters, and to read the Bible. In some memoranda which Howe did not include in his regular Reports about Bridgman and Caswell, but which were published after his death in the 1889 Annual Report, Howe noted that, from the moment Caswell arrived at the school, Bridgman "took great interest and pleasure in assisting those who undertook the tedious task of instructing him," particularly because she could thus help put Caswell into communication with people who loved and cared about him. In Howe's scenario, Bridgman, like a loving little sister, would

take his brawny hand with her slender fingers, and show him how to shape the mysterious signs which were to become to him the keys of knowledge and methods of expressing his wants, his feelings, and his thoughts; so that he might have free and full communion with father, mother, brother, sister, and friends of all degrees. (*ELB*, 198)[15]

Howe confessed himself so moved by this image of the deaf-blind girl forgetting her own afflictions to help the deaf-blind boy become connected to the world of compassionate family and friends that "no scene in a long life has left more vivid and pleasant impressions on my mind than did that of these two young children of nature, helping each other to work their way through the thick wall which cut them off from intelligible and sympathetic relations with all of their fellow-creatures" (*ELB*, 199).

"Would that the picture could be drawn vividly enough to impress the minds of others as strongly and pleasantly as it did my own!" Howe proclaimed in his memorandum. Apparently someone attempted to do just that, as there exists an oil painting, by "D. Fisher," of Bridgman and Caswell at their lessons (Figure 4). Howe's memorandum offers a detailed description of the painting, which may well have been painted to fit his words, rather than his words describing the painting, since the memorandum laments the absence of such a picture (*ELB*, 199).[16]

I seem now to see the two, sitting side by side at a school desk, with a piece of pasteboard, embossed with tangible signs representing letters, before them and under their hands. I see Laura grasping one of Oliver's stout hands with her long, graceful fingers, and guiding his fore-finger along the outline, while, with her other hand, she feels the changes in the features of his face, to find whether, by any motion of the lips or expanding smile, he shows any signs of understanding the lesson; while her own handsome and expressive face is turned eagerly toward his, every feature of her countenance absolutely radiant with intense emotions, among which curiosity and hope shine most brightly. Oliver, with his head thrown a little back, shows curiosity amounting to wonder; and his parted lips and relaxing facial muscles express keen pleasure, until they beam with that fun and drollery which always characterize him. Laura shows seriousness amounting to anxiety; and expressions of hope, mingled with those of doubt and fear, depict, as in a clever pantomime, the ever-changing emotions of her awakened mind. (*ELB*, 199–200)

The picture as painted differs from Howe's description, in that Bridgman is not feeling Caswell's face for signs of his reactions to the lessons, but rather has one hand guiding his fingers and the other supporting the book he

Figure 4. Laura Bridgman teaching Oliver Caswell. From *Proceedings at the Celebration of the One Hundredth Anniversary of the Birth of Dr. Samuel Gridley Howe, Nov. 11, 1901*.

reads from. This difference highlights Bridgman's position as teacher and Caswell's as her pupil by minimizing references to her deaf-blindness; the only visual cue to her disability is the blindfold she wears over her eyes. Otherwise, her attentive attitude, face turned toward Caswell, implies that she might be looking at and listening to the boy, while his closed eyes and the face turned away from both Bridgman and book mark him as inattentive to all visual cues. As in the woodcut of Bridgman and Howe, the teacher is depicted as larger than the student, and the position of the hands lends an air of authority and competence to the one directing the lesson.

If this portrait of the deaf-blind girl helping teach the deaf-blind boy to read is such a moving illustration of Bridgman's capacity for empathy and active service, why does Howe's description of this scene appear only in his unpublished memoranda and not in any of his published Annual Reports? In those voluminous Reports, neither the sketches of Caswell's education nor the accounts of Bridgman's education and accomplishments contain any reference to Bridgman's becoming Caswell's teacher. The answer lies in Howe's misgivings about the full development of Bridgman's intellectual and moral character. Probably Bridgman, though she knew Caswell, never served as his teacher; Howe's description, like the picture, represents a sentimental fantasy rather than a reality. Howe had profound doubts about Bridgman's capacity to use arbitrary language fluently, given his reliance on a denominational view of language and his insistence that a clear understanding of words comes primarily from a thorough knowledge of the objects words represent, and it is unlikely that he would have encouraged her to attempt the job of teaching language to Caswell. Similarly, Howe had doubts about Bridgman's capacity for empathic agency; though he provided to the public numerous examples of her concern for others, he did not fully believe that the motives for her actions sprang from a true understanding of the beauty of selflessness rather than from a love of the approbation such actions garnered.

Most if not all of the published examples of Bridgman's benevolence were founded in fact, and testified to by Bridgman's female teachers and caregivers as well as by Howe, but he doubted the motivations that prompted those benevolent actions. Perhaps, in writing his vision of Bridgman teaching Caswell, Howe wished that his scenario might yet prove true, and that Bridgman might become the sentimental heroine he, Dickens, and a host of others had painted her as being; as a scientist, however, he could not bring himself to publish an account of Bridgman that was more imagined than actual. As Howe's doubts about the true nature of Bridgman's intellectual and moral capacities grew through the middle and late 1840s, his published accounts of her grew less laudatory and more cautious. While he still worked to prove that she was "fully and normally human," and just like sighted and hearing people in her moral character, particularly in her ability to form relationships with others, Howe increasingly included doubts and disclaimers in his descriptions of her development.

His doubts focused on the question of whether a person as afflicted as Bridgman could ever truly rise above the limiting conditions of her physical being in order to think more about the welfare of others than about her own. In his 1845 Report, he included an excerpt from the journal of Bridgman's teacher, Miss Wight, which raised the question whether Bridgman understood the meaning of benevolence:

Talking with Laura about being kind and benevolent. She began to give me a long account of little kind things she had done. After a time, I told her that sometimes people did kind things that their friends might praise them, and think they were very kind and benevolent. We talked of it some time, Laura's face growing more and red. (*ELB*, 147)

Howe worried that it was only Bridgman's love of approbation and praise that motivated her to act on behalf of others, rather than a developed capacity to put others' concerns ahead of her own. As a follower of phrenology, Howe believed that the capacity for benevolence and selflessness was innate in the human mind; like all other capacities, it needed to be exercised and strengthened in order to develop fully. For this reason, Howe wrote, "it has ever been a subject of anxiety with me to have her furnished with opportunities of exercising those virtuous dispositions in the various offices of charity and love, knowing well that they need exercise, just as much as do the mental faculties" (*ELB*, 173–74). Such opportunities seemed rare, however, as Howe noted that Bridgman "has necessarily been in the less blessed situation of receiver, and seldom in that of giver, of favors and kindnesses"; given the dependence on the care of others which her deafness and blindness necessitated, Howe concluded, "it is most remarkable that she has not become very selfish and inconsiderate of others" (*ELB*, 173).

In addition to forcing Bridgman into the position of receiver rather than giver of care, her disabilities provided another obstacle to the development of her innate capacities for benevolence and empathy, according to Howe. Her isolation worked "to narrow and limit her circle" of acquaintance and affection, he wrote; "her heart, cruelly hedged in, is forced at each remove to recur to self." More important, her lack of perception of sight and sound severely limited her ability to perceive the natural signs of others' emotions, which in turn prevented her from identifying with, imitating, and hence understanding those emotions.

She has fewer means of exercising her sympathies than we have, — we who in every waking moment have forced on our eyes constant marks of human feeling in the countenances of others, and on our ears constant sounds that should appeal to our hearts for sympathy. (*ELB*, 134)

Unable to perceive, and hence respond to, the signs that would normally arouse her sympathies, Bridgman could not develop the capacities which would enable her to forget her self in the active service of others. On this basis, Howe concluded that any disability, "any departure from the moral and healthy condition of the body; any ail, or pain, or deformity, or maim, is very apt to contract the circle of the sympathies, by forcing the thoughts to dwell on the centre of self" (*ELB*, 134).

The dangers inherent in Bridgman's sensory isolation and her inability to perceive the signs of others' sufferings lay beyond the mere arrest of the development of her power for empathic agency. Because "everybody can be useful or agreeable to her in some way or other," while "she can be of little use to them," Howe worried that she might begin to consider such "kindly offices" as "something due to one's merit, and to be claimed as a right," rather than received in humility and gratitude. The tendency to take these kindnesses for granted, as being only her due, might "have a hardening effect on her affections," making her more demanding and self-centered, and thus even less able to show any genuine concern for the welfare of others. Even worse for Bridgman's moral character, in Howe's view, was the possibility that "she may be made vain by being so much caressed," and begin to think only of herself as the rightful center of attention, to the exclusion of all others (*ELB*, 137).

The concern that Bridgman's dual afflictions might make her self-centered and vain bothered those, including Howe, who desired to portray her as an idealized sentimental heroine whose afflictions had only refined and purified her moral qualities. Thomas Carlyle, having read Howe's 1841 Annual Report on Bridgman, wrote to Howe that Bridgman was "one of the beautifullest phenomena at present visible under our Sun." She seemed to him the quintessential "good little Girl," and he noted that "no Goethe's Mignon, in most poetic fiction, comes closer to one than this poor Laura in prose reality and fact."[17] While enthusiastic about Bridgman's ability to serve as a sentimental signifier, arousing the compassion of others, Carlyle also expressed horror at the thought that Bridgman herself might become aware of being the center of so much attention and care. "One painful apprehension haunts me," Carlyle wrote to Howe,

that *she* learn at last how wonderful she is, — and have all the vanities and base confusions that yet lie safe as sediment and basis at the bottom of her character, stirred up and sent floating aloft, to the darkening, sickening and ruining of it![18]

In contrast to Howe's public portrait of Bridgman, which insisted on her innate qualities of goodness, Carlyle's vision here emphasizes the "sediment" of selfishness that lay at the bottom of her character, and threatened to cloud the purity of her being, were she to become aware of being the center of so much attention.

Both Howe and Carlyle wanted to guard against Bridgman becoming "a lion, than which hardly a greater misfortune can befall a woman" (PR 1843, 37). Both agree that a necessary quality of "womanhood," or of "good little Girl"-hood, is unselfconsciousness, a lack of awareness of one's own position in the world, or of how one is perceived by others. The opposite of this kind of unselfish and unaware womanliness is what Howe names as being "a lion," that is, proud and self-centered, aware of one's status as the center of attention. This metaphor appears in Howe's journal entries, as well as in Julia Ward Howe's *Reminiscences*, about their wedding tour to Europe in 1843–45:

The story of Laura Bridgman was already well known in Great Britain, and [Howe] was most heartily and cordially received. The philanthropists were eager to see and hear this man who had brought a soul out of prison. He was everywhere in request to dine with and address learned bodies, was indeed . . . "a first-class lion" . . .[19]

Howe's journal entries imply that, while "lionization" is not good for any human ego, it is more acceptable for a man than for a woman, whose modesty and unselfconsciousness must always keep her from becoming the center of attention. Both Carlyle and Howe want to preserve Bridgman from "lionization," from being aware of the worldwide fame and attention her education has attracted, so as to preserve her status as a figure who can model for others all the traits which are ideally associated with a disabled person who is also "a child — a girl — and of pleasing appearance." In this, they want Bridgman to be like a fictional character, who exists to demonstrate sentimental virtues but cannot be aware of her status as idealized image, or of the audience who read her as such.

Howe worried that it might not be possible, given the difficulties created by her disabilities, to keep Bridgman herself from becoming vain and self-centered, but he did his part to insist, in his written representations of her, that she remained unaware of the attention she attracted. Though she was the object of "great curiosity" to the public, and thus subjected to "the closest scrutiny" by observers, the fact that "thousands have been watching her with eager eyes" had not changed the fact that she was "all unconscious of their gaze" (PR 1850, 47). The girl who was so constantly watched, and yet who had no awareness of being watched, Howe named "a curious and an interesting spectacle" (PR 1850, 47). By naming Bridgman as spectacle, Howe reinserted her into a sentimental framework. One of the staples of sentimental representation was the tableau or set scenario, wherein a character functioned as an object to generate emotions in observers; such a scenario became a spectacle when the object that stimulated others' emotions remained unconscious or unaware of the effect it produced. In a sentimental representation, when a character expresses an emotion, and an observer mirrors that emotion, a relation of reciprocity is established; but when an observer's reaction is prompted by a situation of which the character is unaware, the observer becomes a spectator, and the character the spectacle.[20] The former situation recognizes a mutuality of subjectivity between character and observer, as both feel the same emotion; the latter, however, distinguishes between the feeling subject, the perceiver, the one who looks, and the object that produces the feeling, the one who is looked upon and remains unaware of being observed.

As spectator and spectacle, the interaction between reader and character, in the case of fiction, borders on voyeurism; similarly, the scenario described by Howe, where Bridgman endures "the closest scrutiny" of visitors yet remains "all unconscious of their gaze" is also voyeuristic, as sighted people look at objects whose status as object is marked by their inability to look back. Charles Dickens was particularly fascinated by this aspect of his visit to the Perkins Institution, noting that the blind boys he watched at play could not see him, though they continually called out to a teacher to "'look at me!'"[21] Dickens's descriptions of Bridgman, too, highlight her lack of consciousness of being observed, as Dickens places her in a set scene: first as a prisoner in a "marble cell," and then as a normal girl in a domestic parlor.

Dickens's attraction to Bridgman came in part from his interest in her as a voyeuristic object; he read her and wrote about her as a sentimental heroine through the lens of his own character Little Nell from his recently-published novel *The Old Curiosity Shop*. That Dickens associated Nell and

Bridgman is illustrated in the fact that, as a result of his visit to Perkins and to Bridgman, he paid for a raised-print edition of *The Old Curiosity Shop* to be printed and included in the Perkins library, where it was one of the few works of fiction available for Bridgman herself to read.[22] Twentieth-century literary critic Elizabeth Gitter, in investigating the similarities between Nell and Bridgman, suggests that Bridgman functioned for Dickens as "a curiosity, a symbol, an allegory," just as Nell did.[23] Both were dependent on others for information about the world; more important, both were under constant scrutiny and surveillance, of which they were unaware. The constant and lascivious stares of Quilp, who watches Nell and makes jokes about marrying her, highlight the sexual voyeurism inherent in such scrutiny. Like Quilp (though less evil-intentioned), Howe highlights Bridgman's help-lessness and attractiveness in noting that she is "a child—a girl—and of pleasing appearance." Gitter notes that, though Howe's account of Bridgman purported to be a "disinterested, scientific case study," he could not resist the sentimental portrayal of Bridgman's disabilities as forms of suffering that led to an angelic resolution. "As Howe 'beholds' her, the living Laura is transformed, estheticized, and fetishized"; described in sentimental terms as pure and innocent, "Howe's Laura is, as much as Nell, a source of spiritual inspiration and aesthetic pleasure," if not of sexual fantasy.[24]

Whatever his doubts about Bridgman's actual abilities to be selfless and unconscious of her status as poster, Howe's written accounts of her insist on her status as voyeuristic spectacle who, like Nell, offers observers a chance to watch without the objects of their scrutiny returning their gaze. In Laura Mulvey's analysis of the way voyeurism operates in film, the unseeing object of scrutiny becomes "a bearer of meaning, not a maker of meaning."[25] As unconscious objects of another's gaze, both Bridgman and Nell become opportunities for watchers to spin their own fantasies. In Nell's case Quilp's fantasy is directly sexual, while in Bridgman's case both Howe and Dickens fantasize sentimental meanings, representing the deaf-blind girl as the epitome of innocence, cheerfulness, and domestic saintliness. For both Bridgman and Nell, however, their status as spectacle, as object or fantasy, precludes their being recognized as subjects in their own right; they remain bearers of meaning, symbolic objects, rather than makers of meaning, people who can speak for themselves about their own experiences and thoughts.

Though Howe attempted to "rescue" Bridgman from being relegated to this status by insisting that she had the capacity to become an empathic agent, a feeling and acting being in her own right, ultimately his insistence on her agency collapsed under the weight of her significance as sentimental object, and his own doubts about the extent of Bridgman's agency. Like the Perkins building itself, Bridgman existed, in Howe's Reports as well as in Dickens's account, as a kind of "monument," functioning chiefly to elicit the feelings of others, rather than to express her own emotions and to act on behalf of others. In 1850, in what would be his last full Report on Bridgman, Howe reiterated that she was

utterly dependent on human sympathy and aid for the continuance of her happiness, and even of her life. She can appeal only as she has done, by the mute exhibition of her helplessness, for that sympathy and aid. (PR 1850, 89)

Howe's dismay at the failure of his "experiment" is evident in this passage. Despite his hard work in helping Bridgman acquire language, and despite his hopes that she might become "fully and normally human" through being able to form relationships with others, he is left describing the twenty-one-year-old woman in the same terms Dickens used to describe the eight-year-old girl who first attracted his attention: she remains unable to do more than have her "poor white hand peeping through a chink in the wall, beckoning to some good man for help."

A large part of Howe's disappointment in the results of his "experiment" with Bridgman came from the failure of his plans for her religious education. He had hoped to keep Bridgman from any external knowledge of religious ideas or doctrines in order to see what ideas about God emerged innately; he wished by this to prove the truth of Unitarian doctrines about the native purity and innocence of the human soul. But Howe could not, in all conscience, isolate Bridgman completely from intercourse with those around her; the whole point of providing her with arbitrary language was to give her the ability to communicate and form relationships with other people. Because of his own duties and the gender arrangements of the Institution Howe could not be with Bridgman twenty-four hours a day; once he had formulated the methods for her education, he left most of her daily lessons and all of her personal care to her female teachers. In the female wing of the institution, where Bridgman dwelt all her life, religion was a primary topic of conversation; despite Howe's injunctions to the female residents to avoid all talk of religious matters with Bridgman, such discussions were inevitable. Bridgman, throughout her adolescence, became increasingly interested in religion — the more so because discussion on this topic was forbidden by Howe — and increasingly agitated at Howe's failure to answer her theological questions.[26] Eventually someone acquainted Bridgman with the basic tenets of Calvinism, thus ruining Howe's hopes to prove the truth of Unitarian beliefs. Bridgman remained obsessed with religious concerns throughout her life, which added to Howe's disenchantment with the results of his "experiment."

A large part of Howe's reluctance, or inability, to discuss religious matters with Bridgman came from his doubts about her linguistic abilities, as he was reluctant to introduce to Bridgman words that could not be directly associated with concrete objects. Howe's denominational view of language insisted that words represented objects, and that a clear knowledge of the meaning of words depended on a clear understanding of the properties of the objects words represented. Though he was initially certain that such knowledge of objects could come through any combination of sensory perceptions, as he worked with the blind and deaf-blind he became convinced that the lack of sight created a crucially important lack in the connection between the properties of objects and the meanings of words.[27]

The blind, Howe concluded, could never understand certain words or phrases because they have "never experienced the sensations which they are intended to express." A vast number of the words in any language are made up of "words significative of sensations which arise in the mind in consequence of the action of the external senses," Howe explained; the blind learn words significative of sight as "figures of speech, and attach to them some kind of meaning, but not precisely such as other men do." Thus the blind never are able to associate "clear and definite ideas with every word," and thus cannot use words "with propriety and precision" in the way sighted speakers and writers do (PR 1847, 11–12). The lack of "precision" in language use, according to Howe, caused enormous problems in communications and social relations for the sighted as well as for the blind. The problem lay in the danger that a speaker or writer might

contract the habit of not examining closely the evidence given by the senses, and consequently that his ideas will be vague and indistinct. Inattention to those qualities of things which are the objects of sense leads to inattention to words which are the signs of these objects; and inattention to words makes the meaning of language obscure and equivocal, and obscurity of language causes evil without end both in school and in after life. (PR 1847, 36–37)

Laura Bridgman, unable to perceive the sight, sound, smell, or taste of objects, was thus in Howe's view quadruply barred from the hope of using language with any precision, and this exacerbated Howe's reluctance to

Figure 5. Laura Bridgman, circa 1878. From Mary Swift Lamson, *The Life and Education of Laura Dewey Bridgman: The Deaf, Dumb, and Blind Girl*.

introduce Bridgman to theological terms and concepts that had no concrete referents in the first place.

Howe's view of language convinced him that, no matter how well developed were Bridgman's moral and affectionate capacities, she could never be "fully and normally human" in regard to language use. His understanding of her linguistic limitations relegated her again to the status of a pathetic object who could only display her afflictions to arouse the emotions of others and a silent figure who could not use language precisely enough to represent herself to others. Though she was a "speaking subject," in that she could use the manual alphabet to communicate her thoughts to others, she could only "speak" to those who knew that alphabet, and only a few among the Perkins teachers and residents had mastered the skill of translating finger motions into arbitrary language.

Howe had taught her to write, in the "square hand" used by the blind, and writing constituted her main means of communicating with anyone who did not know the manual alphabet. Charles Dickens's description of Bridgman as the rescued sentimental heroine shows her posed with a writing-book open on her desk, but he does not show her in the act of writing, or speculate about what she might have written there. Howe's accounts of Bridgman did include excerpts from Bridgman's diaries that illustrated her comprehension of his lessons, but because such excerpts tended to show the flaws in her language usage as much as her developing abilities, Howe cited them infrequently.[28] As an adult, at the request of some friends, Bridgman wrote a brief autobiographical account of her earliest days at the Perkins Institution, but that autobiography was never published.[29] When the Swedish novelist Frederika Bremer visited her at Perkins, Bridgman enquired "whether she found that writing books 'paid well.'" Bremer responded that her novels paid "pretty well," and Bridgman asked Bremer " 'Do you think, if I should write a book, it would pay well?' " (*ELB*, 196). There is no record of Bremer's answer, nor of any attempt on Bridgman's part to write a book for public sale.

Bridgman became a writing subject only in limited forms, through letters, diaries, and her autobiography, all of which were unpublished and therefore inaccessible to all but a handful of readers. Rather, she remained the written-about, serving as a symbol to be described and interpreted by others, an image to be manipulated by authors like Howe or Dickens to serve their own ends. Howe's need to claim Bridgman's equality with the sighted and hearing on the basis of her emotional capacities required him to portray her in a sentimental framework where the feelings she aroused in others and the feelings which others' woes aroused in her would take center stage. His doubts about both her ability to understand the idea of benevolence and her linguistic ability prompted him to relegate her to "poster" status in that framework; in Howe's representations, Bridgman still functioned best as an object to arouse compassion in others. His portrayals of her as object thus focused on her disabilities, on the factors that made her forever dependent on the charity and kindness of others.

Can the Blind Girl Speak?

In Maria Cummins's novel *The Lamplighter*, the blind heroine Emily Graham insists that the hallmark of an empathic sensibility, and particularly a womanly sensibility, lies in the ability "to do and to suffer, to bear and to forbear." In this motto, Graham also sums up the available cultural meanings defining the social roles of disabled people in mid-nineteenth-century America. In the sentimental frameworks used in fictional and institutional representations, disabled people were depicted first as suffering beings, people who had to bear the afflictions God had given them. The image of disabled people as sufferers created their social function as "posters," as objects whose plight could arouse the compassionate feelings of others, who would then be prompted to care for them. Disabled people became the bearers of a certain set of cultural meanings, speaking of the need to extend the tender emotions of sympathy and care fostered in the domestic sphere to the "wide wide world," which was increasingly dominated by self-centered economic and political concerns.

Both fictional and institutional discourses, however, worked to supplement the role of disabled people as objects, as silent icons, by portraying them as being able to "do" as well as to "bear." The ability to feel for and act on behalf of less-fortunate others stood as one of the hallmarks of moral and social worth; the fictional and institutional portrayals of disabled people as empathic agents helped form identifications between disabled and able-bodied people, and served as the basis for claiming disabled people as equal, in emotional capacities, to the ablebodied. Though the institutional representations might raise some questions about whether people whose existence was marked by dependence, and hence the need to be the recipients of others' care, could ever truly act from selfless motives, the sentimental fictional portraits of disabled characters like Emily Graham firmly upheld the idea that disabled people were completely capable of both doing and bearing, of being empathic actors as well as "posters."

Emily Graham's assertion of the need to do and to bear, as a summary of social roles available to disabled people, however, leaves out another dimension, one that the successful education of disabled people throughout the middle of the nineteenth century made possible. Educated disabled people began to write about themselves for themselves. As authors, disabled people who expressed their own ideas and conceptions in writing added a third quality to Graham's list: in addition to being objects who could "bear" and agents who could "do," disabled authors became selves who could "speak," who could represent their own experiences, for themselves and others, without the intervention of ablebodied interpreters. As such, they participated in creating the social meanings associated with forms of disability, rather than being merely the bearers of such meanings, and in doing so helped to confirm the idea that disabled people were no different from ablebodied people.

This chapter examines what may well be an undiscovered genre of nineteenth-century American literature: the autobiographical writings of disabled people. I do not know how extensive such a genre may be; the few examples I have found have come to me by chance, as the result of my habitual haunting of second-hand bookstores and my work in the archives of the Perkins Institution. As my work has focused on examining the social construction of blindness as a paradigm for other forms of disability, I have concentrated on the autobiographical writings of blind people, two of which this chapter discusses in detail.[1] Whether the patterns I identify in these writings by blind women hold true for other disabled authors must await the discovery and examination of more examples of this as-yet-unexplored genre.

Both Mrs. S. Helen deKroyft's *A Place in Thy Memory* (1849) and Mary L. Day's *Incidents in the Life of a Blind Girl* (1859) use many of the conventions of sentimental representation, a fact that is not surprising given the dominance of sentimentalism in mid-nineteenth-century popular culture in general, and in depictions of disability in particular. More striking, perhaps, is that both autobiographies also use many of the conventions of slave narratives, and for the same purposes.[2] Like slave narratives, blind autobiographies tend to include an elaborate apparatus of authentication, including letters and testimonials from sighted people (often ministers or directors of institutions for the blind) confirming that the author of the volume really is blind, and really did write it him- or herself. Like slave narratives, blind autobiographies include direct appeals to readers to work to alleviate the conditions of misery and affliction described in the book; such appeals often focus on how readers can make financial contributions, both through purchasing the volume and through donating money to organizations that assist the sufferers. And, like slave narratives, blind auto-biographies insist that the author is trying valiantly to create or assume a form of independence through writing the volume. Rather than depending solely on the support of others (nonslaves, nondisabled) for their mainte-nance, the authors of both genres are to be praised for their efforts at becoming self-sufficient, as well as for their insistence on being taken as authors on the same terms as other adults. These last two characteristics are to some extent contradictory, as both genres attempt to portray the suf-ferers as striving for independence while still requiring assistance and char-ity; this contradiction is more prevalent in the blind autobiography, which is more directly a volume produced and marketed to generate financial support for the author, rather than moral support for a political cause.

Blind autobiographies also existed as a means by which blind people could attempt to attain financial support, if not independence, through a type of work that did not require a specific bodily configuration. The trans-lation of their stories into printed language obscured the defects of their blind bodies, since their writing was equal to that of the sighted, but also foregrounded the forms of affliction and suffering caused by those different bodies.[3] Autobiography thus functioned, like slave narratives and senti-mental fiction, as a genre which highlighted the cultural meanings associ-ated with different bodies, but which also transcended or corrected the oppressions and limitations of those cultural meanings by insisting that bodies that wrote were all the same. As authorial subjects, blind authors, like women writers and authors of slave narratives, could claim equality to "normal" (white, male, sighted) authors on the basis of linguistic skill, without regard to their bodily configurations; like slave narratives, blind autobiographies provided a forum for authors to assert, in their own terms and words, their existence as recognizable selves, rather than as silenced nonselves, as objects. In both genres, the objects of others' discourses begin to speak for themselves, and to assert the terms of their own sense of subjectivity through articulating their own experiences. In so doing, both types of authors reinscribe the meanings of their different bodies in ways that claim their equality with the "normal," but without necessarily erasing the specificity of their particular forms of "abnormal" embodiment.

*   *   *

Mary L. Day's *Incidents in the Life of a Blind Girl* uses conventions from sentimental representations and from slave narratives to portray herself as an object needing care, as an agent able to work to care for others, and as a self who can write about, and hence define for herself, her own experiences. Like Gerty Flint among the more triumphant heroines of sentimental novels, and like the majority of heroes and heroines of slave narratives, Day positions herself as both an object of others' care and sympathy, in response to her "affliction," and as an independent being, marked by her ability to support herself through her own economic efforts, to "own" herself and enjoy the fruits of her own labor.

Day's autobiography was published in 1859, in the same year as Harriet Wilson's *Our Nig*[4] but two years before Harriet Jacobs's *Incidents in the Life of a Slave Girl*.[5] Like Jacobs's text, Day's work comes with many of the features identified by James Olney as conventions of the slave narrative genre: a portrait of the author, a title page testifying to her identity and authorship, testimonials from reliable sources certifying the truth of the story, a poetic epigraph, a narrative which begins "I was born," and which continues to give an account of parentage, cruel treatment at the hands of others, and a successful rescue or escape from her plight.[6] Day's book includes an engraved portrait, in which her heavy-lidded eyes mark her status as "other," followed by a title page that attests to her status as "author," naming her specifically as "A Graduate of the Maryland Institution for the Blind" and noting that "Mary L. Day" holds the copyright to the volume (Figures 6 and 7). A Preface by "S.S.R." testifies to Day's blindness, her authorship, and the fact that her story is unembellished truth; a second testimonial exists in the book's dedication to the "Rev. Jno. McCron, D.D.," whom Day names as her "cherished friend, proven counselor, guide, consoler" (Day, iii–v).

The book begins with these sentences: "Gentle reader, although this will be a sad, painful story, yet it is truthful. I was born in Baltimore, Maryland, in the year 1836" (Day, 7). While the classic slave narrative form begins with establishing the existence of the author, in the statement "I was born," Day's story begins with establishing the presence of the reader, naming him or her specifically as "gentle"; this sentimental strategy of direct address frames readers from the outset as sympathetic beings who are prepared to feel compassion for the heroine of this "sad, painful story." Like the slave narrative, however, Day's story insists from its first sentence that it is truthful, rather than fictional. Day's strategy in doing so is similar to that of the authors of slave narratives; just as the purpose of a slave narrative is to provide a picture of " 'slavery *as it is*,' " free from any acts of *poiesis*, so the purpose of Day's narrative is to provide a picture of what blindness is

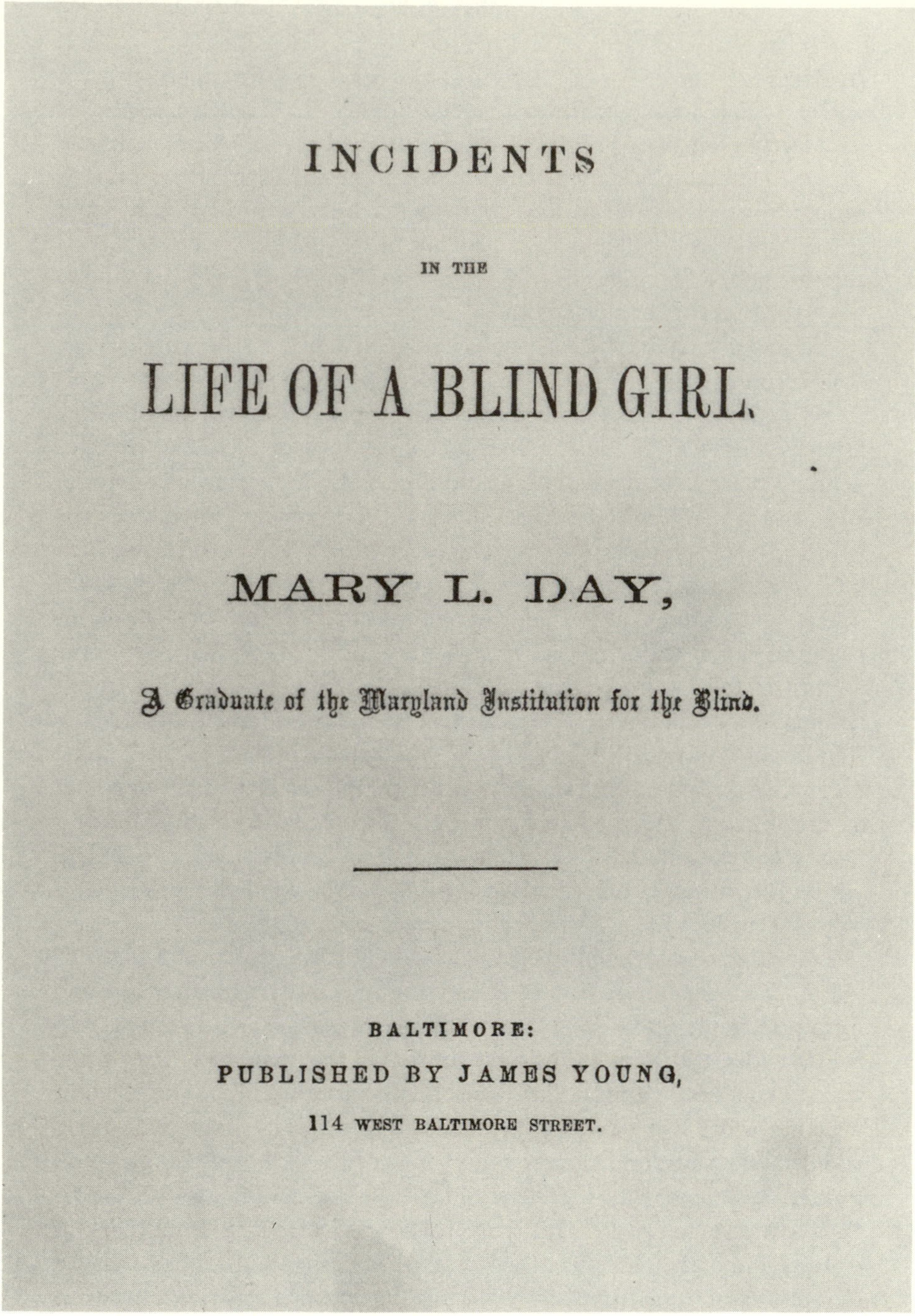

INCIDENTS

IN THE

LIFE OF A BLIND GIRL.

MARY L. DAY,

A Graduate of the Maryland Institution for the Blind.

———

BALTIMORE:

PUBLISHED BY JAMES YOUNG,

114 WEST BALTIMORE STREET.

Figure 6. Title Page, Mary L. Day, *Incidents in the Life of a Blind Girl*.

Figure 7. Mary L. Day. From *Incidents in the Life of a Blind Girl*.

actually like.[7] While the slave narrative's portrait of slavery must be deemed truthful, rather than fictionalized, in order to persuade readers of the horrors of the institution so that they will work to end it, Day's narrative has no such overtly abolitional purpose — she is not urging readers to work to end blindness. Rather, she draws implicit and explicit parallels between the plight of the slave, whose independence is expunged by that status, and the plight of blind people, whose independence is circumscribed by their "affliction." Both slaves and blind people are figured as types of "prisoners," selves who would be equal to nonslave, nonblind selves were they to be "freed" from the conditions that bind them. The slave narrative and Day's autobiography present their truthfulness as having the same direct effect on readers: through the events they present as accurate memories of what has actually occurred, both narratives ask readers to identify with the characters, particularly the first-person narrator, and to relive with the narrator the cruelties suffered as a result of their "imprisonment."

Both narratives create or demand this identification in order to produce an empathic response in readers; through the "sympathetic identification" that textual representations of suffering can produce in readers, readers themselves are asked to feel the same emotions the narrator felt. In the case of the slave narrative, or in antislavery fiction, the purpose of arousing such an empathic readerly response is to convey the full horror of slavery, and thus to inspire readers to work to end it. In the case of Day's narrative, and of other sentimental depictions of blind or disabled characters, the purpose of arousing such an empathic readerly response is to convey the trials and terrors of blindness, and thus to inspire readers to feel for the sufferings of the blind. Evoking or eliciting the empathic sensibilities of readers through blind characters, both autobiographical and fictional representations of blindness work to create individual readers who will continue to care about, and care for, blind people even when the pages of the book are closed. In so doing, these representations necessarily frame the blind character as suffering and dependent, therefore requiring the compassion the text hopes to generate. Blind characters, even when they are also the narrators of the story, thus function to ensure that the assistance and sympathy their disability requires will always be present, even in the cold, cruel world beyond the text.

Having established the position of the ideal reader as "gentle," Day begins her story by stating that she was born, to whom, and when. With the exception of the specific date, this too parallels the conventions of the slave narrative, and for similar reasons. In saying "I," the authors of slave narratives performed an essential assertion of freedom, declaring their existence as human selves through using the first person pronoun. This statement attests to the real existence of the narrator as an historical figure (rather than as a fictional creation); in slave narratives, this existential claim must appear prior to any claims of truthfulness for the narrative. The portraits, testimonials, and authenticating letters which Day's autobiography shares with slave narratives serve to reinforce the narrator's claim to existence and identity in the statement "I was born."[8]

The cultural act Day performs when she makes this statement as a blind author is not identical to that of the authors of slave narratives. In stating her existence and identity, she is challenging not sets of legal and economic institutional practices that define her as a thing, a commodity, but rather sets of cultural meanings that classify disabled people as "objects," as devices that arouse the compassion of the nondisabled. Henry Louis Gates, Jr. notes that Harriet Wilson's *Our Nig* demonstrates "the will to power as the will to write," transforming the "black-as-object" into the "black-as-subject."[9] While the status of the two types of "object" represented by the slave and the disabled person is not equivalent—no one had the right to own or sell a disabled person—their linguistic assertions of self work in similar ways to inscribe the selfhood, the unique identity, of each, and thus to challenge and reformulate the ideologies which have constructed them solely as "objects."

Having thus established, through her picture, her presence on the title page as author (and as certified blind person), her testimonials, and her opening sentence that she exists simultaneously as blind and as author, Day's narrative goes on to tell the "sad, painful story" that will evoke the sympathies of her "gentle reader." Her story reads like a classic example of a sentimental novel. A young girl is abandoned to the mercies of a cold, cruel world, and strives to find loving hearts that will respond to her dependence with compassion and care. Having borne her suffering enables her to empathize with other people's woes; finding the benevolent aid she requires encourages the development of her own empathic capacities, so that she becomes able to "do" for others who, like herself, have need of care. Born sighted, and to fond parents, Day describes her trials as beginning at age eight, with her mother's sudden death. In a description that echoes the rhetoric used by Samuel Gridley Howe in describing the death of Martha Granger, Day asserts that, though "our dear mother died among strangers," she was "not unmourned for; by her pleasant and affable manners she had gained many friends who wept with us over her grave" (Day, 10).

Unable to care for his large brood, Day's father farms his children out to neighboring families. Mary is placed with the Ruthvens, a wealthy family with an adult son and a small granddaughter in residence. When she meets Mrs. Ruthven for the first time, she was "perfectly stunned with disappointment."

I had anticipated meeting a kind motherly person, instead of which I saw a cold, stern woman. As she bent her pitiless gaze on me, I thought of my own gentle mother and burst into tears. (Day, 31)

Having already named the reader as "gentle," Day in this passage associates that reader with her deceased mother, in contrast to Mrs. Ruthven, who will provide no "kind motherly" care. The contrast is exacerbated in Day's account of Mrs. Ruthven's first words to the abandoned child: "On leaving the room I heard her exclaim in an angry tone,: 'I wonder if I am always to be bothered with other people's children!'" (Day, 31–32).

Day explains that Mrs. Ruthven's lack of motherly (or readerly) empathy comes from her status as an invalid; Day's first encounter occurs in Mrs. Ruthven's sickroom. Day connects Mrs. Ruthven's annoyance at being "bothered" with the care of a child not her own with her illness, which remains unnamed in the text. Like Marie St. Clare in *Uncle Tom's Cabin*, Mrs. Ruthven is framed as the type of invalid Diane Price Herndl describes as "a selfish, hateful, and spoiled woman whose illnesses are feigned to enable her to avoid any kind of work; she lives in luxury and thinks only of herself and her imagined ills."[10] Her illness becomes a sign of her complete self-centeredness, as it prevents her from caring for "'the weaker and more ignorant'" members of her household.[11] The dependence created by the real or imagined illness of such a figure stands in sharp contrast to the dependence created by blindness or other disability, as characters like Mrs. Ruthven and Marie St. Clare use their physical condition as an excuse for selfishness and cruelty, while disabled characters in sentimental portrayals almost unfailingly find in their physical debility the key to selflessness and compassion. The selfishness exhibited by Mrs. Ruthven leads easily to anger, which precludes empathy; when she is well enough to come downstairs and eat dinner with her husband, son, granddaughter, and Day, she speaks to Day only in "sharp, angry tones," and Day declares that this "unkind treatment almost broke my heart" (Day, 32).

Mrs. Ruthven's maltreatment of Day is not limited to cruel words; she also strikes the child when Day does not perform household tasks to her satisfaction. Mr. Ruthven treats Day with some compassion, but he does not interfere with his wife's abuse of Day. His son, George Ruthven, follows his mother's lead and regards her

as something unworthy his notice. He did not like his parents to speak one kind word to me, and although he called himself a Christian and a gentleman, he would stand by and laugh when his mother would knock me down. (Day, 32)

Day attributes George's contempt, like his mother's anger, to selfishness; concerned about inheriting "the property," he feared that Day might be included in the will if his parents felt any affection for her (Day, 33).

This last explanation, showing that monetary concerns prevented or circumscribed any possibility of compassion, demonstrates two competing definitions of "family" at work in the Ruthven household. For George, "family" is defined economically, by the inheritance of property, the transference of wealth from one generation to the next through the lines of blood kinship. Day is searching for a sentimental "family" defined by mutual affection and concern, not by blood relationship or monetary transmission. George fears that, should his parents begin to feel the latter type of affectionate familial connection to Day, they might also want to establish the former financial connection to her, so he works to keep the two definitions separate by trying "every means to increase his mother's dislike to me" (Day, 33). When the mother and son learn that Day's father has left the area in search of work and has left no clue as to his destination, they use her complete lack of defined familial connections and protection as an opportunity to treat her "with greater unkindness ever than before" (Day, 35).

The cruel Ruthvens seem to wield all the power in the household, as Mr. Ruthven is continually kind but ineffectual in altering Day's position as abused servant. The horror of Day's maltreatment is intensified by the fact that the most empathic characters, the ones most able to feel for Day's plight and to wish to help her, are also the most impotent, the least able to act on her behalf. Raising doubts about the possibility of any dependent being becoming an effective empathic agent, Day introduces another kind but powerless character in the presence of a blind gentleman who comes to board with the Ruthvens. Mr. Lee (who had become blind while studying law) has "a kind, noble heart," and shows true compassion for Day: "often has he taken me on his lap, and stroking fondly and caressingly my hair, he would say in tones I well remember: 'Poor child, I pity you'" (Day, 39). His blindness, however, prevents him from being able to turn his pity and tenderness into any kind of effective action to rescue Day from her plight. Day reports Lee declaring, "'had I my sight, you should not remain here a day longer'" (Day, 39). While his blindness, in increasing his own reliance on the care of others, fosters his empathic capacities, enabling him to feel acutely for and with Day, it also circumscribes his power to act independently; he cannot interfere with the Ruthvens' treatment of Day as long as he, too, is a dependent member of their household.

The plot of Day's story, in documenting her abuse at the hands of a woman and the ineffectiveness of the male figures to intervene, echoes Harriet Wilson's *Our Nig*, which itself combines conventions of sentimental fiction, gothic fiction, and slave narratives.[12] Like Day, Frado is left to the care of a household of selfish and unsympathetic women; like Day, the compassionate characters are powerless to help her. Structurally, both Day and Wilson separate the youthful character about whom they write from the author who is writing. This separation, in both texts, works to create a distinction between the object who evokes the readers' compassion and the subject who is working to attain (financial) independence through authorship. Both texts thus work to have it both ways: in presenting their youthful heroines as suffering and dependent, they can educate readers in the compassionate capacities necessary for them to provide support for those who need it, while presenting themselves as competent adult actors who need only to have readers purchase the volume in order to attain a desirable independence.

Mr. Lee's impotence, while raising questions about empathic agency, does offer Day her first opportunity to do something for a less fortunate being and thus develop her own empathic abilities: she becomes Lee's guide on walks. The authorial voice reminds the "gentle" reader that the child's sufferings will soon increase, noting that she did not think "then I should some day have to be led" like Mr. Lee (Day, 39). The adult author's interruption of the story of the orphaned girl serves to remind readers that their feelings for the child's sufferings are being aroused in preparation for their sympathies for worse trials; in showing how the child cares for the blind man who treats her kindly, Day not only shows how the girl will eventually become a caring adult, but also provides a model of how readers should feel toward her heroine when she becomes blind (an event of which readers are well aware, given the title of the book as well as the authorial aside). In this, Day creates the ideal empathic reader, who will respond to the text with sympathy and tears, and who thus (she hopes) will respond, when the volume is closed, to blindness, youth, and other forms of dependence with the compassion developed in the process of reading.

Day continues to encourage the reader's empathic response in detailing her further trials in the Ruthven household. Noting that she was made to stay home from church in order to cook Sunday dinner, Day emphasizes Mrs. Ruthven's hypocrisy by describing how, in the parlor, in front of ministers and other visitors, she calls her "my daughter" and asks whether she's been lonesome. In the privacy of the kitchen, however,

her whole appearance changed; her sweet motherly smile gave place to a dark, foreboding frown; her voice that had been so kind and gentle became severe and sarcastic; she caught me by my hair and beat me, first on one side of my head, and then on the other. To prevent my cries from being heard by the company in the parlor, she covered my mouth with her hand. (Day, 40–41)

As a result of this abuse, Day determines to run away, resolved to "make my own living and be happy, which would surely be preferable to living miserably, as I now did" (Day, 49).

When Day, aged ten, does run away from the Ruthvens, she finds that sympathy and compassion do exist in the world beyond familial ties. Being received inside the Palmers' farmhouse at nightfall, Day bursts into tears of relief; as she tells the Palmer family her "painful story," she sees "tears of sympathy in every eye"—incontrovertible proof that these people, unlike the Ruthvens, already have well-developed empathic sensibilities. She is unable to stay with this family for long, however, and finds in subsequent households a repetition of the financial motivations and selfishness of the Ruthvens. Dismissed from one household for staying out too late at night, Day pleads with the woman that she has no home, and no place to go. "She said: 'She did not care—it was not her look-out'" (Day, 58).

In one household—luckily, a compassionate one—Day finally is stricken blind. With the onset of this form of dependence she encounters a new form of selfishness that takes the guise of care: she becomes an object of great interest to people who propose to cure her blindness. Though Day does not explicitly explain the reasons behind this attitude, it seems likely that the motivation for attempting to cure her came not from a purely Christian compassion for her suffering but from a desire for the wealth and fame that would accrue to anyone who could claim to have cured blindness successfully. Every physician and local healer who encounters the blind girl offers a "miraculous" cure, and several times Day accompanies these people to their homes, where she is subjected to various torturous treatments. At one such household, a doctor pours a mixture of rum and alum into her inflamed eyes, which not only causes her excruciating pain but also damages her eyes further (Day, 67). In each case, when the proposed cure fails, the seemingly benevolent healer becomes disgruntled and angry with Day for continuing to be blind, and eventually expels her from the household. "[F]inding there were no hopes of my regaining my sight, [they] grew very weary of me, . . . constantly telling me how dependent I was, sometimes treating me with the greatest unkindness, and threatening to send me to the poor-house" (Day, 69).

When the poorhouse officials finally arrive to remove Day, however, they prove more compassionate than the family that was housing her; rather than relegating her to the "dark, dismal prison" of the almshouse, under the care of strangers, Mr. Cook takes her home with him. Presenting the blind girl to his wife, Mr. Cook states that, even though they already have seven children of their own, they can surely feed another, and beseeches his wife to "'be as a mother to her?'" Once again, the moral and emotional worth of this family becomes evident through their tears: Mary "could feel that [Mrs. Cook] was weeping tears of sympathy," and the children "kissed me affectionately," shared their toys with her, and "love[d] me as a sister" (Day, 71).

The result of this empathic familial treatment, as one might expect, appears in Day's efforts to do "any little thing to please my benefactress" and to help the family (Day, 73). Stating that she was never happier than when helping the Cooks, Day demonstrates that she is firmly on the path to becoming an empathic agent in her own right. Her desire to repay kindness by becoming useful to the people who have helped her comes directly from the conventions of the sentimental novel; like blind Emily Graham in *The Lamplighter*, Day shows her capacity to bear her suffering and to do for others who, like herself, have need of compassion and sympathy. But unlike Emily Graham, whose definition of selfhood ends with the ability to bear and to do, Day strives for a farther dimension of agency. Like Gerty Flint, Day, though blind, wants to find remunerative labor, a means to support herself, in her "earnest . . . desire not to be a burden to my friends." She gets a job knitting, for a dollar a week, and feels "an honest pride in providing for myself while I had health and strength" (Day, 74–75). Like a sentimental heroine, but unlike most sentimental representations of disabled people, Day strives for both economic independence and empathic responsibility; she is able, as the author of her own story, to imagine what Howe, Cummins, and other authors who spoke for disabled people could not, and to conceptualize her adult selfhood as a combination of economic self-reliance and empathic interdependence.

Day's pursuit of both types of selfhood is interrupted, however, by a letter from her long-lost sister, who is now married, living in Chicago, and trying to track down her brothers and sisters. Day embarks on a train journey to Chicago to rejoin her family, wondering whether they will still feel the ties of kinship that will prompt them to care for her dependent state, and knowing that she can rely on her own efforts, given some assistance, even among strangers. Like a sentimental heroine, Day finds the world full of kindly people, not cruel strangers; on the train, a Mr. Chamberlain looks after her as if they were related, asserting that he was "doing no more than I would wish any one to do for my sister" (Day, 83). So compassionate was Chamberlain's attitude toward Day that other passengers assumed they were brother and sister. Asked by a passenger if that man were her brother, Day replies that he is, and the passenger exclaims that she "knew it because he looks exactly like you" (Day, 84). Day's comment — "So much for family resemblance" — underscores her assertion that "family" is a construct of the heart and feelings, not of blood ties. Day reverses the usual pattern, whereby physical family resemblance provides the clue to relationship; here, instead, affectionate or empathic treatment and feelings are the primary signifier of familial relation — so powerful as to lead the observer to assume a physical resemblance on the basis of the signs of affection. In this example, the interpretation of the signs of emotional ties determines the observer's understanding of physical features, rather than seeing the resemblance first and then assuming fraternal affections.

Having reached Chicago safely, Day finds that her two brothers, her sister, and her brother-in-law combine both models for empathic conduct, welcoming her both as a family member deserving of their affection and as a blind woman requiring their compassionate assistance. Having tested the closest of family relations, Day attempts to test a more distant connection, writing to a wealthy uncle in Baltimore asking if he can help her obtain an education so that she can continue to support herself. Jacob Day writes back with a combination of familial warmth and economic shrewdness: while he and his family "deeply sympathized with me," he would not send her any money because "he was afraid of imposture" (Day, 114). Unable or unwilling to take her linguistic representation of herself as a true portrait (and unaided by the testimonials and engravings that support the authenticity of the autobiography), Jacob Day demands first-hand proof. He invites her to travel to Baltimore at her own expense; should she then prove in person to be what she claims to be, both a relative and blind, he promises to reimburse her and to assist her.

The theme of unaccompanied train travel portrayed in Day's story equates the ability to travel and move on one's own with a form of adult independence. For the blind heroine, such travel becomes a test of the availability of empathy and assistance beyond the family. "When alone and the cars were moving off, I began to realize the extent of my undertaking and the loneliness of my situation. As we whizzed past the city limits, I felt I was leaving everyone I knew on earth to seek the protection and friendship of strangers. Would they be kind to me?" (Day, 116). During this journey, unlike the previous trip, Day breaks from the expected sentimental scenario wherein other passengers unfailingly offer kind assistance; rather, as she moves toward the doubts of her uncle, which are fostered by his economic self-interest, she begins to portray a world where her disability does not automatically prompt compassion. As Day moves physically toward her uncle's house, and toward the possibility that he might fund her education and help to make her a self-supporting being, she ceases to be an effective "poster" in a sentimental framework and instead depicts herself as becoming prey to the selfishness and evil of an uncaring world of strangers.

A conductor leaves her in a station parlor, assuming that someone there will guide her to the dining room. When no one offers, Day touches "a gentleman (if such I may term him) on the arm, [and] asked him to assist me to the table. He walked away without taking any notice of my request" (Day, 118). Five or six others, including a few women, "treated me in a similar manner." Day finally asks a woman to lead her to the dining room, insisting that she will pay her for her services. Indignant at this indictment of her Christian sensibility, the woman replies that "she wanted no pay" for helping her, and consents to take her into dinner (Day, 118). Day highlights the class distinctions at work here by observing that the waiters in the dining room, unlike her genteel fellow-travelers, treated her with every kindness and attention: "'Tis not the finest broadcloth covers the most noble or manly heart" (Day, 119).

Similar incidents occur throughout her journey, as "gentlemen" refuse to get her a cup of water, help her with her bags, or help her find the correct train. The worst threat appears when the train makes an unexpected overnight stop and Day has no money to pay for lodgings. Asking the conductor for help, she is frightened "by the impertinent voice" that says "'Well, sis, what must I do for you?'" His presumption of relationship and familiarity in naming her "sis" makes her aware that she "was in the power of this man," who had "villainy in his voice." He tries to take her away from the station to stay with some "ladies" he knows, inviting her to stay with them "over night, or indeed a whole week if I liked" (Day, 129). Though Day only states that the "whole demeanor" of the "wicked conductor" was "inexplicable" to her, her language implies that he was leading her to some sort of liaison, perhaps to a house of prostitution: the ideas of familiarity, power, villainy, and impertinence all point to the idea that he has some sort of sexual intentions (Day, 133). Both blindness and femininity make her the object of the conductor's evil intentions instead of the object of his compassionate concern. While refusing to insist, in sentimental logic, that the world is unfailingly good to those who need care, Day's representation of her double vulnerability works to summon the empathic responses of readers who would save her from whatever fate the conductor has in mind for her.

Eventually Day manages to elude the conductor and make her way to the station hotel, where the sentimental worldview is reinscribed when a kind manager pays for her lodging for the night and helps her board the right train the next morning. On meeting her relatives in Baltimore, Day is once more ensconced in the bosom of a loving family. Her fears that her uncle's wife will be too grand and rich to care about a poor blind relative are answered by the fact that her aunt is in the last stages of consumption; Day portrays the invalid as one whose sufferings summon the tender feelings of others and as an empathic being who is unfailingly affectionate and gentle. At her uncle's she is reunited with her long-lost father, who does not hesitate to embrace her and weep over her, though Day herself remains reserved, remembering how he had cruelly abandoned her to the abuses of Mrs. Ruthven. Eventually, though, she does accept him and weep with him, their tears signifying the depths of emotion felt at the restitution of the broken family.

The final sections of Day's autobiography also resemble the conclusion of a slave narrative, in that both attempt to show broken families reunited and both focus on the efforts of the former "prisoners" to obtain the skills to earn their own livelihood and be no longer dependent on the kindness of the strangers who had assisted them in their escape. In Day's work, the restoration of the family occurs before her explanation of her training, whereas in many slave narratives economic independence is the necessary step to reclaiming the family. For Day, the story concludes with her residence at the Maryland Institution for the Blind, where she learns to read raised type and to write on ruled paper. The acquisition of literacy in Day's narrative, as in a slave narrative, marks a definitive step in becoming a self. Learning to write, in particular, enables Day to represent herself; in being able to write her own story, she becomes not only a speaking subject but an economically productive one, an author who can (or at least hopes to) support herself through her writings.

Day's account of her entry into the "promised land" of the school that will "liberate" by teaching her how to read and write is not entirely sentimental and positive, however. Along with the ability to write comes the ability to tell the truth about one's condition, and, like the authors of slave narratives, the ability to criticize both the conditions that kept one illiterate and the conditions under which one was freed. Day's narrative ends with her descriptions of being a student at the school for the blind, and specifically with being part of the exhibitions the school staged to show off the skills of its pupils. While Samuel Gridley Howe's descriptions of these exhibitions emphasized their potential for normalizing the blind students, by providing a framework in which the sighted observer could perceive the blind students as no different from other students, Day's description presents the other side of the story, giving voice to what it felt like to be made into an object. Visitors to the institution, Day wrote,

appeared to regard us as a race distinct from themselves. . . . There were those who seemed to consider us frightful objects, of whom they were afraid; and again, I have known persons to put their mouths to our ears and scream as though they thought we were deaf as well as blind. They would also stand close beside us and pass remarks on us, as though they had thought we were as unthinking and unfeeling as might be a breathing statue. I have known them to say aloud and immediately by our side, "We were the ugliest people they had ever seen," or "that we were pretty and interesting." These and similar comments were constantly being made in our presence as though they thought because we were blind we had also been deprived of reason, and were nothing but moving automata, walking stocks of wood or stone! (Day, 174)

Like the ex-slave author's voice that tells of first-hand experiences of objectification and oppression, both before and after the acquisition of literacy and freedom, Day's voice functions here to speak for a class previously silenced by their objectification: she is among the first disabled people to report her experiences as an inmate (and graduate) of an institution formed for her education and rehabilitation. This is the penultimate act in Day's creation of her own subjectivity, her own selfhood: refuting her status as object by "talking back" to those who have made observations about her — both the rude public and the directors of institutions who, like Howe, had anatomized her capacities and limitations in their Annual Reports — Day asserts her existence as a feeling and thinking subject, as well as a speaking and writing one. The autobiography exists as final proof of the strength of her claims. She is not only "talking back," she has written herself, and her story, into existence in the volume she hopes to sell.

Her purpose in offering the volume to the public is both to proclaim her selfhood as an author and to attempt to gain financial independence (also a mark of an adult self) through selling the book. The design of the narrative, however, following the conventions of sentimental fiction, is to produce in "gentle" readers the empathic sensibility that will ensure the continuation of care and compassion for the weak, dependent, and afflicted. The book thus frames Day as a dependent object who will elicit compassion; as an empathic agent who models for readers how they can respond to the book by working to aid unfortunate others; and as an independent adult self who writes and works to support herself. The final lines of the book, however, invoke the empathic element, not the economic element. Rather than thanking the reader for supporting her by purchasing the book, she addresses readers who "have paused to shed a tear over any line," or who have felt "any emotion of sympathy . . . [swell] your bosom in behalf of the lonely, friendless wanderer." Such "gentle readers," having responded to her "sad, painful story" with compassion, with the exercise and strengthening of their empathic capacities, "have called forth gratitude from the heart of one keenly alive to what of joy may be her portion" (Day, 206).

* * *

Mary L. Day's autobiography, drawing on the conventions of slave narratives and sentimental fictions, focuses on the development of the narrator from dependent girl to independent adult, from "poster" to author, providing a compelling plot of dangers and rescues, cruelties and kindnesses which lead to the story's happy resolution. In contrast, Mrs. S. Helen deKroyft's autobiography, *A Place in Thy Memory*, appears as a series of letters written to friends describing her various experiences of and feelings about being blind, rather than as a connected narrative with a definitive beginning and end. DeKroyft's autobiography has little in common with the novel form, but rather reads like a series of meditations or reveries, each of which could stand alone without reference to the other letters in the volume.

The letters are sometimes addressed to a specific person, who is usually identified only by a first name or an initial; more often they indicate no particular recipient, beginning with no salutation at all. This strategy of not naming the letter's audience specifically allows readers to include themselves as the person to whom the writer is speaking, rather than feeling excluded by the fact that the letter is addressed to "My Dear, Very Dear Mary" (deKroyft, 71). Readers are thus invited to identify themselves as the author's friends, on the same intimate footing with her as the named recipients; this identification also presumes that readers, like friends, will share deKroyft's world view and be able to sympathize with her feelings and perspectives. In addressing this general audience of intimate friends, deKroyft establishes a relationship between narrator and reader that assumes a communal sensibility. Unlike Day's narrative, which emphasizes the first person narrator and asks readers to observe her and to empathize with her trials, deKroyft's letters work to create a collective identity; rather than stating "I was born," and delineating the adventures that "I" goes through,

Figure 8. Mrs. S. Helen deKroyft. From deKroyft, *A Place in Thy Memory*.

deKroyft continually emphasizes what "we" think, what "we" feel, how "we" understand the world. In so doing, deKroyft creates a different notion of selfhood, one that does not rely on separation and autonomy, as does the self created in Day's story and in slave narratives. Rather, she inscribes, through her letters, a notion of a self-in-relation, a self who is always part of a community, always speaking to and with an audience of intimate friends who share the same values and concerns.

In creating this self-in-relation, deKroyft employs a number of familiar sentimental conventions. Her letters, in fact, contain many of the same elements as fictional representations of disabled people, in that deKroyft also presents herself as a dependent object needing the compassionate care of others, and as an agent able to help provide assistance for the less fortunate. Like Emily Graham, deKroyft — and her imagined community of readers — subscribe to the sentimental ideology that "we cease to live when we have no longer something to do or bear" (deKroyft, 53). She opens the volume with a preface describing the main affliction she has had to bear, which has led to the publication of these letters, which otherwise would remain private. Her betrothed, Dr. deKroyft, having been "seized with a hemorrhage of the lungs," was on his deathbed when their wedding day arrived. By his wish, "our marriage was confirmed. Soon after I saw him die." Her weeping over this tragedy resulted in an inflammation of her eyes, and she became permanently blind. "I was in one short month a bride, a widow, and blind" (deKroyft, 5).

As in many other sentimental descriptions of blindness, deKroyft's account establishes her tragic loss as the event which separates her from the care and protection of family and friends, and throws her thus on the mercy of strangers. Describing her plight to an old friend, deKroyft works to create an empathic response in her named and unnamed readers:

"Truth is often stranger than fiction," and the tale I shall tell you needs no coloring. Clara, *I am blind!* for ever shrouded in the thick darkness of an endless night. . . . Is there any sympathy in your heart? Oh then weep with me, for now, like an obstinate prisoner, I feel my spirit struggling to be free. But oh, 'tis all in vain, 'tis all over, misery's self seems stopping my breath, hope is dead, and my heart sinks in me. Clara, I am in a land of strangers too. Stranger voices sound in my ears, and stranger hands smooth my brow, and administer to my wants. (deKroyft, 93–94)

This account, focusing on her loneliness and dependence, frames deKroyft as a "poster" whose only hope of survival is to conjure compassionate feelings in others through displaying her own weakness and misery. In asking Clara to "weep with" her, she creates the possibility of an empathic identification between them, and between herself and the anonymous readers who, along with Clara, might have a similar sentimental response to deKroyft's tragic state.

Many of the earliest letters in the volume focus on deKroyft's misery in finding herself blind and widowed and alone. These letters have the dual purpose of presenting deKroyft as a object eliciting sympathy and of naming the reactions which her audience, imagined as a community of friends, should have. Amid the "[s]orrow, melancholy, blighted hope, wounded love, grief, and despair" that fell on her "silent heart and bitter fear" following her widowhood and blindness, deKroyft says she continually cried

Oh, what will become of me? Is there benevolence in this world? Must charity supply my wants? Will there be always some hand to lead me? Have the blind ever a home in any heart? Does anything ever cheer them? Are their lives always useless? Is there any thing they can do? (deKroyft, 95–96)

DeKroyft's letters document her struggle to achieve both goals: to affirm the existence of benevolence throughout the "wide wide world" and to shape the terms in which she herself can regain a sense of utility and purpose. The letters demonstrate her existence as the object of others' benevolent sensibilities and her own claim to existence as an adult empathic agent, as well as her ability to create, in writing, a community of author and readers who believe in the unfailing availability of compassion for those in need. Her laments, in the earliest letters, ask whether the empathic self that would guarantee assistance can be available outside familial ties, in a world presumably full of "strangers." Caring readers, of course, will respond to this plea by affirming that the blind widow might find a home in the hearts of those who, knowing afflictions of their own, can understand and sympathize with hers.

Indeed, deKroyft answers her own question about the availability of compassionate care beyond the ties of blood kinship in virtually every subsequent letter, as she presents a worldview firmly grounded in the sentimental assumption that the sight of need or suffering will automatically and always produce a compassionate response in others. She insists that

years have gone by since even a harsh word has fallen on my ears — since I have seen a frowning face, a look of anger or revenge. The cold, the unfeeling, whose souls are peopled with selfishness and haughty pride, never seek the friendship of the blind. . . . So you see I am necessarily always with the good; for they alone find pleasure in contributing to the happiness of one, who can make no return for their multiplied favors. (deKroyft, 59–60)

Even though blindness makes her "painfully dependent," she concludes, it also generates "the love and sympathy of friends, who everywhere hasten to do us kindness," providing for her a "well-spring of pleasure, inexhaustible as the good feelings of the human heart" (deKroyft, 76).

DeKroyft insists, with example after example, that her status will never fail to elicit the best responses of others. In letters describing her travels between the New York Institution for the Blind, where she lived as a student for three years, and the homes of friends who cared for her during this time, she emphasizes how travel made her particularly dependent on strangers to guide her; her letters assert that such guidance was always forthcoming. In one example, she recounts that a stranger asked her if she needed assistance, then "secured my baggage, gave me his arm," and led her to her destination, while the two talked "so familiarly of life, its changes, books, and places, that I forgot he was a stranger, and thought I had known him always" (deKroyft, 35). On another stage of this same trip, "Captains, railroad conductors and all, instead of presenting their bills, inquired how they could best serve me, where I would stop, &c" (deKroyft, 38). The empathic sensibility aroused by her blindness mitigated the economic imperatives of self-interest, as even those whose business it was to collect her fare felt charitable enough to pay it for her.

Rather than a world full of heartless strangers, deKroyft's letters paint a portrait of a world where all are "pitying angels" ready to assist her. "The world has bad notions of itself" deKroyft insists; "it is not a selfish, but an unselfish world — a kind, a loving, and a forgiving world" in which "men oftener love than hate, oftener do good than ill" (deKroyft, 32). Based on these experiences, deKroyft agrees with Maria Cummins in declaring that there are no such things as "strangers," if that term denotes people who feel nothing for another who bears no connection or relationship to them. Rather, the supposedly cold and heartless world is populated, in deKroyft's depiction, by people who automatically respond to her blindness with compassion and care, and who thus cannot be designated "strangers." This elimination of the category "stranger" reinforces deKroyft's efforts to create a community of sympathetic readers: if there are no strangers, but only people who will necessarily respond to the representation of need with care, then readers will respond in the same way that friends would, even when not addressed by name in the letters.

DeKroyft is, in some letters, aware that not all readers will share her sense that the world is always a kind and caring place. She acknowledges that she has painted a portrait of an ideal world, where "I give words of thanks and praise to every body who is kind, all unmindful that green-eyed prejudice is still in the world" (deKroyft, 59). But, she argues, her blindness, like other sorts of afflictions, must be part of the ordered plan of a benevolent God, who has "placed me among my fellows, and veiled my eyes, perhaps as much to try them as me" (deKroyft, 145). Her blindness exists, not to test her faith, but to create more goodness in the world, and thus to prove that "green-eyed prejudice" and unkindness must ultimately be illusory, while kindness and generous sympathy must be the reality.

Her blindness not only creates that reality, it shuts her out from perceiving any other form of reality. Because she is blind, she cannot see that those around her

may wear looks of sadness; may grow old; their teeth fall; their eyes become dim, and their locks gray; wrinkles may be on their brows, trace-marks of grief and care; but they look not so to me. The last time I saw the green earth and its inhabitants, they wore yet the sunny hues of innocence and gladness. . . . And so they seem to me now; and were I to bear a report to heaven, I should call this a charming world. (deKroyft, 60–61)

More important, however, her blindness helps her to create an ideal world because that "affliction" heightens her own empathic capacities. Echoing the assumption that blind people have a stronger need for social and affectional ties than sighted people, deKroyftroyt asserts that "we know that our feelings are more sensitive, and our attachments stronger and more lasting." In using the first-person plural here, deKroyft encourages her readers, who have already been prompted to consider themselves as compassionate beings who would offer care to a blind woman, as part of the "we" who are blind; as feeling beings, and as blind beings, she praises this community of readers for their heightened empathic sensibilities. The "we" who feel more strongly than others, deKroyft concludes, may well "doubt whether or not, when *properly* considered, it is a misfortune to be blind," because "our whole nature [is] improved, and our immortal being elevated, through this privation" (deKroyft, 172–73).

DeKroyft's ideal sentimental world is created first of all by her status as a blind widow, as a "poster" whose dependence is unfailingly met by compassionate care, and second by her own heightened ability to feel for others, which is itself produced by her blindness. This world, she insists, is shared by a collective readership, identified as "we," who, though not literally blind (else they couldn't read her volume of letters) identify with the values deKroyft creates in those letters. DeKroyft thus frames her readers, like herself, as selves-in-relation, part of an interdependent community of feeling beings, people who share "that love which makes us forget ourselves and live unto others" (deKroyft, 31).

DeKroyft's self-in-relation, marked by the pronoun "we," stands in contrast to the traditional autobiographical "I." In one particular letter, deKroyft illustrates the distinction between the two. She begins the letter, addressed to "My Dear Lizzy," by stating that "It is not pleasant to be blind," because

My *poor eyes* long to look abroad on this beautiful world, and my prisoned spirit struggles to break its darkness. I would love dearly to bonnet and shawl myself and go forth to breathe the air alone, and free as the breeze that fans my brow. (deKroyft, 21)

The "I" here longs for autonomy, the ability to be free and alone, to move independently in the world. DeKroyft follows this passage immediately with a direct address to her audience, which shifts her focus from herself as autonomous to her relation to Lizzy: "Lizzy, we must learn to bear, and blame not that which we cannot change." The shift from first person singular to first person plural creates a relationship between deKroyft and Lizzy, and, by extension, between the author and all her readers. The letter then leaves both the "I" pronoun and the hope of a liberating autonomy behind, reminding readers that

The journey of life is short. We may not stop here long, and sorrow and trial discipline the spirit, and educate the soul for a future life; and those on whom we most depend, we love most. (deKroyft, 21)

The "prison" she wishes to escape is caused not by blindness, but by God and by the circumstances of life that create "sorrow and trial"; as such, there can be no escape. Rather, the soul must teach itself to bear its imprisonment, even when that imprisonment makes one dependent on others and unable to assert an autonomous self that can be alone and free. When one accepts the necessity of imprisonment and dependence, one can respond with bonds of love, rather than with despair or regret, and thus create a community of selves who love each other in proportion to the extent that they need each other.

Blindness, for deKroyft, offers a special opportunity to understand the importance of establishing an interdependent "we" self, as it offers her both the heightened ability to feel for others and the experience of dependence which, she asserts, is part of the human condition. In other letters, she outlines how sighted people, who may not yet have experienced this dependence as adults, can learn to understand the need for a communal self-in-relation. She writes to a young friend preparing to attend boarding school that she will find there a miniature community, "in which each room answers to a dwelling, whose inhabitants we may call our neighbors." Perhaps the best lessons learned at boarding school are not those of the classroom, but those learned in the exercise of moral capacities: "here we may learn to dry away the tear of sorrow, and smooth the pillow of the sick, and pity those who suffer." Indeed, deKroyft concludes, the school may be an even better place to learn such lessons than the home, because a school more closely reproduces the wider community beyond the domestic sphere, while still providing numerous opportunities to practice empathy: "That beautiful command, that the strong should bear the infirmities of the weak, seems written almost expressly for the members of a school" (deKroyft, 40–41).

Learning how to care for others, deKroyft insists in another letter, is the most important lesson one can learn; central to this lesson is accepting one's own burdens and tribulations. Because bearing one's own trials teaches strength and submission, deKroyft tells one young friend that she would not wish her "a life free from adverse winds and storms . . . sorrow moves the feeling fountains of the heart," and prepares them to flow for others (deKroyft, 63). In a direct address to those who may not yet have experienced their own grief, she urges that they

Begin now to share another's woe, and help to bear the burden under which thy neighbor may be sinking . . . the voice of beseeching suffering calls us to it, and the cry of love and philanthropy is, "Come over and help us!" . . . And have *you* nothing to do? Shall your hands be busy only to adorn your frail body and twine garlands of flowers? Have you no energies of heart and mind to spend in the great work of self-culture, and the amelioration of mankind? (deKroyft, 98–99)

In this passage, deKroyft uses the first person plural "us" to designate both the empathic selves who can be called by "beseeching suffering" and those beings who need their assistance, who cry " 'Come over and help us!' " She thus creates the idea of an interdependent or collective self by making no distinction between the "us" who are afflicted and the "us" who respond to that affliction with care. She does, however, draw a distinction between that collective "us" self and the person who has not yet learned how to feel her own woes, or to respond to those of others; this person is addressed as "you," and admonished to relinquish selfish concerns, such as personal adornment, and join the "us" who both suffer and care. The "you" who learns "to do and to bear," by understanding her own plight and by working to ameliorate that of others, will necessarily develop the empathic self-in-relation which deKroyft's letters advocate.

While urging others to develop the ability "to do and to bear," however, deKroyft does wonder whether the burden she bears, in the form of the dependence fostered by her blindness and widowhood, will indeed allow her to find something useful to do in the world. In her earlier lament, asking "Is there benevolence in this world?" she ends her plea to find "a home in any heart" with the question of whether the blind are "always useless," whether there is "anything they can do?" (deKroyft, 96). She echoes this question in a later letter, where, expressing gratitude for the kindness and support she has received, she proclaims "how gladly would I relieve all my friends of farther anxiety . . . how gladly would I put forth my hand to meet my own wants" (deKroyft, 145). The relational self, which depends on others and offers care to others, here becomes itself a burden to bear, as deKroyft longs to be able to support herself; so powerful is her desire for this kind of autonomy, "sometimes this feeling does so possess me, that I am almost desirous of relieving the world of one so troublesome." In the next sentence, however, she banishes this suicidal wish, acknowledging that her dependent state is permanent: "never more shall I be sufficient to myself." She then reconciles herself to requiring the assistance of others, "for certainly, go where I will, I am always tasking some *hand*," and concludes that, because of her dependence, such assistance will always be available, as she will always be "sharing the generous sympathies of some heart" (deKroyft, 145; emphasis original).

Still, the idea of finding some useful work to do haunts many of deKroyft's letters. If she cannot find work which will make her self-supporting, she desires at least to find some which will allow her to exercise her empathic capacities more fully. In one letter, deKroyft speaks directly to her soul, reminding herself that she can neither escape this life nor simply wait to move on to the next one; rather, "Thy field of labor is in this life," and her soul and self must find some way to turn "what thou wouldst do for God" into something to "do for his creatures." She muses on activities which an empathic agent might be able to undertake, imagining that she might "hasten thy feet to the abodes of the distressed, set thy hand to smooth the pillow of the sick, and place cooling waters to his fevered lips" (deKroyft, 139).

There is little evidence in her letters, however, that deKroyft was ever able actually to do much of this imagined activity. Though her letters are full of words of care and concern for the welfare of her audience, on only one occasion does she describe herself as actively engaged in taking care of someone else. She mentions, without any other context, that while she has been a resident at the New York Institution for the Blind she has sometimes served as an attendant for "deaf Maggie." Somewhat surprisingly, deKroyft's account of this caretaking does not wax rapturous about the opportunities it affords for fostering and expanding an interdependent self, or for exercising her empathic capacities. Rather, her description focuses on what a trial and burden it is to tend to someone with whom she shares so little:

> To-day I engaged to entertain her, but her senseless gibberings have wearied and sickened every feeling, till my spirit cries, "How long, Oh Lord! how long?" One can play the philanthropist to the low and ignorant, and share their little thoughts, and if possible try to lift them higher, and with ready delight minister to their wants; but to be ever companioned with them, to be herded one of them, is hard to bear.[13] (deKroyft, 142)

With "deaf Maggie," whether due to her deafness, her ignorance and "lowness," or other causes, deKroyft is unable to feel any kind of bond of love. Even though they are physically part of the same community, the school (which deKroyft in another letter had named as the place that could offer such wonderful opportunities to care for others), deKroyft cannot name "deaf Maggie" as sharing her communal identity, as part of a "we" who feel and think and believe in the same things. Rather, she frames "deaf Maggie" as wholly other, as unintelligible to her, and resents being "herded" with her — even though that offers deKroyft something "to bear."

The elitism and resentment deKroyft expresses in this letter are echoed nowhere else in her autobiography; this stands as the only example of deKroyft's efforts to help a "less-fortunate" being directly, and the only example of her losing completely her placid sentimental worldview, in which affliction can only breed care and sympathy, and expressing exasperation with having to care for the needy and dependent. Other letters had raised some doubts about deKroyft's sentimental understanding of the self, questioning whether a model of an autonomous self that could be independent might not be superior, in some regards, to the empathic relational self, but in those letters deKroyft inevitably came back to championing her vision of interdependence. The lapse in the letter about "deaf Maggie" highlights the constructedness of deKroyft's sentimental worldview. The world that is always full of loving and caring people who respond unhesitatingly to suffering with sympathy is shown to be deKroyft's creation, which her letters themselves produce and affirm—except in this one incident where deKroyft is unable to sustain that view.

Her ability to create, in her writings, a world that is for the most part consistent in its sentimentality marks the third dimension of deKroyft's status as a disabled self. In addition to presenting herself as a "poster" arousing other's compassion, and thus creating a community of selves-in-relation, of "we" who can feel for, and perhaps act on behalf of, suffering others, deKroyft presents herself as an author, as a self who can speak for and represent herself. Her main achievement as an author lies in this ability consistently to create a portrait of a sentimental world. While Day used her authorial self to "talk back" to those who portrayed the institutions for the blind as wholly benevolent and caring, and to become a spokesperson for an oppressed group, deKroyft uses her authorial abilities, not to point out flaws but to create an imagined world of goodness and love. Like a sentimental novelist, deKroyft writes about the world the way it ought to be, while Day portrays it as it is; like a sentimental writer, deKroyft hopes that, by presenting an idealized world for her readers, she can make that world come into being by creating a community of readers who have learned how to feel, and who will continue to carry those feelings beyond the pages of her writing.

DeKroyft acknowledges that her blindness prevented her from seeing anything unpleasant or bad about the world; in a more positive vein, she asserts that the world she lives in, and the world she creates in her letters,

is an ideal world, and its inhabitants are beings of fancy, and of course sinless and good; their lips speak no lies, and their hands work no evil; their smiles are like the beams of the morning, and their whispers like the night breeze among the flowers, soft and healing as the breath of prayer. (deKroyft, 28)

Elaborating on the relationship between her created ideal world and the external one, deKroyft insists that what is usually called the "real" world, the world perceptible by the senses, is in fact subordinate to the reality created by the soul, the heart, and the imagination. Writing from the New York Institution for the Blind, she states that, while her residence there is a fact—"that is real, that is true"—it is not therefore something sad or painful, because reality does not exist in one's external surroundings. Reality, and the feelings we have about the world, "does not so much depend on circumstances as we think," she concludes. "Within our own hearts," where the fountain of happiness resides, we "keep alive its joyous gushings and laughing streams," whatever our outward dwelling may be (deKroyft, 64).

What the world deems "real" and "true" is, in deKroyft's writings, only the "circumstance" of our being, rather than its defining state; the merely material external world cannot dictate the reality the soul knows. As an example of this, deKroyft recounts a visit to the New York Institution by General Winfield Scott, the hero of the Mexican-American War. When the school's band played for Scott,

the General took off his hat and bowed, which they unanimously returned. The members of the Band are all blind, and how knew they when to return his bow? Were not their spirits conscious of the deference a greater spirit was paying them? (deKroyft, 65)

The bond between spirits, deKroyft insists, proved more powerful than the merely physical limitations of sight, as the band members could sense, without vision, the homage the general had paid to them. "The soul immortal has eyes independent of the body," deKroyft concludes; the eyes of the soul can perceive a world which is separate from, and superior to, the material one, and "no blindness can darken them" (deKroyft, 66–67).

Ultimately, the world perceived by the soul is more "real" than the external material world, in deKroyft's view. This platonic perspective is not limited to those who are lacking a sense, or whose perception of the material world is otherwise hampered, she proclaims; it is shared by all who identify with the "we" she names as her readership, the collective self which shares the sentimental values prizing inner emotions over outer circumstances. Even more important than the fact that "we" readers perceive this immaterial reality is the fact that "we" create this reality as well. "We are pretty much the creators of the world we live in," deKroyft writes, rejecting the determinism of the external world. Given that our imaginations, or our souls, can thus create our realities, she admonishes, "Let us see to it then, that we be good creators," and that we "people our minds" with "images of joy and gladness," rather than "those of grief and care." While outer circumstances will certainly provide incidents that cause sorrow, deKroyft writes, we can keep them as "our guests to sup and dine," but not permit them "to lodge with us" as our dwelling place (deKroyft, 73).

For deKroyft, permitting only joy and gladness to "lodge with us" is more than just sentimental optimism: she insists that "we" can indeed create a world where this condition is reality. Her letters represent that created reality; with few exceptions, the thirty-nine letters that comprise her volume present a portrait of a world where people really are unfailingly good and kind and respond to affliction with sympathy, and where whatever God has created is for the best. DeKroyft insists that the world she describes is truth, not fiction, and names as "we" the audience who shares that belief with her. Day ends her autobiography by asserting her authorial self to "talk back" to a world that had defined and limited the meaning of her blindness, but in doing so she accepts that world as real and as definitive. DeKroyft, in contrast, rejects the definitions of her blindness offered by the external world in favor of creating her own reality in her letters, and proclaims that her reality — and her act of creation — are superior to the external world. Her letters thus create, for herself and for "we" readers, a world where sentimental values, including the idea that affliction is positive, that individuals are interdependent and caring, and that one's inner created reality is more powerful than the external material world, can prevail.

8

Helen Keller

In 1889 Mrs. Bernard Whitman visited the Perkins Institution for the Blind. Her account of that visit, published in Edward Everett Hale's magazine *Lend a Hand*, described her expectation of meeting children who displayed "the helpless putting forth of hands, the uncertain walk, the sad, pathetic look which we always associate with the blind."[1] Rather than finding support for her opinion that disabled children must necessarily be dependent and melancholy, suffering objects to arouse the sympathy of others, however, Mrs. Whitman discovered a Perkins inmate who was "radiant with smiles, and full of animation, who came bounding into the parlor." Finding her preconceptions refuted, Mrs. Whitman wondered, with her readers, whether it was possible that this "could be a child so wofully [sic] afflicted!"[2]

The "woefully afflicted" child described by Mrs. Whitman was Helen Keller. Her portrayal of the "radiant" and animated eight-year-old girl bears no relation to the "wild child" depicted in *The Miracle Worker* (see Chapter 9), which was written some seventy years later. By then Keller was known throughout the United States and the world as an American "saint," a woman who, despite and because of her disabilities, had devoted her life to working for blind, deaf, and disabled people everywhere. Gibson's play, and the television and Hollywood movies made from his script, uncovered Keller's forgotten violent prelinguistic past in an attempt to break the equation between disability and sentimentality, an equation that had always been employed in public representations of Helen Keller. Mrs. Whitman's description of Keller, by contrast, inscribes her completely within that sentimental framework, naming her as the epitome of sunny childhood values associated, at the end of the nineteenth century, particularly with girl children. The two accounts of Keller's childhood frame twentieth-century definitions of the cultural meaning of disability: the first establishes Keller as the culmination of efforts to insert disabled people into conceptions of subjectivity marked by the empathic relations fostered and celebrated in sentimental representations, while the second uses Keller to indict sentimentality as a limiting factor preventing disabled people from achieving an independent and autonomous form of selfhood.

The representations of Helen Keller that appeared in countless thousands of American magazines and newspapers in the 1880s and 1890s summarized the nineteenth century's understanding of the meanings of disability. As Mrs. Whitman's article reveals, the nondisabled public still expected to treat disability as a "woeful affliction," a condition that relegated people to the status of "posters" who could elicit the benevolent care of empathic others. Her expectations were happily contradicted, however, by the example of Keller herself, who showed that her condition did not make her different from other children. In shifting the view of Keller from passive spectacle to active, happy, normal child, Whitman's account reproduces the trajectory followed in fictional and nonfictional descriptions of blind people in the nineteenth century. Subsequent accounts of Keller portray her as the triumph of fifty years of institutional concern for disabled people, noting her ability to be just like sighted and hearing people in virtually every area of achievement open to women at the end of the century.

Keller, and the popular cultural accounts of her, demonstrated her capacity to arouse others' concern, her ability to feel for others' woes in her own right, her power to act to relieve others' suffering, and her successful efforts to establish herself, through autobiographical writing, as an authorial subject. Incorporating in one person all the types of accomplishment shown by previous blind people, fictional and nonfictional, Keller's "miraculous" accession to fully human status as the equal of the nondisabled depended on her inscription in sentimental forms of discourse. In the logic of sentimental representation, the empathy Keller aroused in others and displayed as her own claim to selfhood could be celebrated and enshrined as the highest and most valuable of human characteristics. In the face of the materialism and cynicism critics feared would dominate late nineteenth-century American culture, representations of Helen Keller worked to prove that the empathic sensibility associated with disabled people still held a great deal of cultural power and significance. Indeed, because representations of Keller were "true" rather than fictional, Keller did more than any sentimental novel to foster the conception that sentimentalism accurately portrayed forces and feelings which were real and powerful in the domestic and extradomestic spheres.

As Whitman's account suggests, the earliest articles about Helen Keller stressed her position as empathic object. Florence Howe Hall, one of Samuel Gridley Howe's daughters, insisted in an article for the children's magazine *St. Nicholas* that "we all must pity her intensely for her sad deprivations."[3] In pointing out her pathetic status, however, Hall also reminded her child readers that Keller's deafness and blindness might prove a blessing in disguise. Echoing the interpretations of blindness as blessing offered by Emily Graham and Mrs. S. H. deKroyft, Hall insisted that Keller's disabilities "shield her from all unkindness, all wickedness."[4] Though the sighted children were urged to feel sorry for Keller, because "she can neither see the trees, nor the flowers, nor the bright sunshine, [and] cannot hear the birds sing," they were also told that Keller's existence was still happy and cheerful, because "she knows the best side of every human being, and only the best. She lives in a world of love, and goodness, and gentleness."[5] Indeed, Hall concluded, the disabilities that sheltered Keller from knowledge of evil and cruelty might make her state enviable; Keller's happiness implied that "she does not need our pity," rather "perhaps some of us may need hers!"[6]

Hall's description moves Keller from object of others' compassion to agent who can offer compassion to others. From the first accounts of her successful education, representations of Keller inscribed her as an empathic agent in her own right, stressing her ability to transcend her own "woeful afflictions" in order to sympathize with the suffering of other people. Keller's diary entries from 1888, after just a few months of instruction with Anne Sullivan, already provided evidence for the growth of her supposedly innate faculties of fellow-feeling. In describing how fish get caught, Keller explained that "sharp hook does stick in poor fish's mouth and hurt him much. I am very sad for the poor fish. . . . Men must not kill poor fish" (PR 1888, 115). Other diary entries for 1888 show that she urged carriage drivers not to whip the "poor horses" and that she worried about the comfort of a chained dog (PR 1888, 103).

The plights of characters in stories also aroused Keller's sympathies, as they did for the heroines depicted in sentimental fiction and Laura Bridgman. A story about a blind girl who was ill and couldn't go to school prompted Keller to feel sorry for her (PR 1888, 111). References to *Little Jakey*, a sentimental story written by Mrs. S. H. deKroyft about a poor orphaned immigrant blind boy, appear in Keller's letters to Oliver Wendell Holmes and to *St. Nicholas* in 1890.[7] In both letters she refuted Hall's assertion that she knew no sadness by stating that her blissful ignorance lasted only until she learned to read; once she read about pain and sorrow, these emotions made her feel sad. Like a sentimental heroine, however, Keller explained the necessity of such sadness by insisting that "we could never learn to be brave and patient, if there was only joy in the world" (PR 1891, 209, 211).

Describing her capacity to feel for others as the result of her reading experiences, Keller follows the trajectory inscribed in sentimental fiction. Like Gerty Flint and the readers of *The Lamplighter*, Keller becomes an empathic subject through the processes of identification and sympathetic imitation that result from the act of reading. Like Gerty Flint, Keller thus serves as a model, for those who read about her, of how that reading should affect them. The moral lessons her story illustrates are embodied in the "character" of Keller herself.

The parallels between Keller and sentimental fictional heroines were not lost on those who wrote articles proclaiming Keller's triumphs. In an 1888 account in the children's magazine *Wide Awake*, Sallie Joy White noted that "the whole story of her quick mental development reads like a fairy tale," and that "the *Arabian Nights* has nothing in it more wonderful, and certainly Hans Christian Andersen himself, in his most pathetic moods, has nothing more touching."[8] Other observers described the progress of Keller's education as "like a romance," and as "a wonderful story," just like "one of the fairy stories of our childhood" (PR 1887, 106).[9]

Some of the inspiration to compare Keller with fairy tales and romances came from the terms in which the Perkins Institution Annual Reports described her. These reports, like Samuel Gridley Howe's accounts of Laura Bridgman, were widely reprinted and serve as the basis for virtually all popular cultural representations of Keller during her association with the Institution from 1887 to 1893. The Reports that present Helen Keller as a modern miracle were written by Michael Anagnos, who succeeded Howe as the director of Perkins after Howe's death in 1876. Unlike Howe, who had built a reputation as a doctor and as a social scientist through his pioneering reform work, Anagnos's only qualifications for becoming the director of the famous school were his kind heart and the fact that he had married Howe's oldest daughter, Julia Romana Howe.[10] Operating at a disadvantage in an increasingly professionalized and credentialed field, Anagnos was eager to follow in his father-in-law's footsteps and enhance his own reputation by some feat as amazing as Howe's education of Laura Bridgman. When the Keller family wrote to him in 1886 asking if anyone at Perkins still knew the methods Howe had used with Bridgman, as they were described in Dickens's *American Notes*, Anagnos seized on the opportunity to equal or surpass Howe's successful "rescue" of a deaf-blind girl.

Anagnos's descriptions of Keller attracted the attention of the popular media, not only because the events they described seemed "miraculous,"

Figure 9. Helen Keller, 1893. From *Helen Keller Souvenir #2*, 1892–1899. Volta Bureau, Washington, D.C., 1899.

but because his accounts did not present dry statistics and cold facts, as did the scientifically oriented reports of other institutions. Rather, Anagnos's prose came directly from literary works: his distinctive style employed a plethora of literary quotations, from the Greek classics and from Shakespeare, Scott, and Wordsworth, as well as from a host of lesser-known (and largely unnamed) poets. As a disciple of Matthew Arnold's doctrine of high culture, Anagnos had reformulated the Perkins curriculum to emphasize aesthetic training for his blind students; such literary and artistic education would suit the students for adult life among the cultured white-collar class, and thus solve (in theory at least) the problem of mechanical or working-class employment for blind graduates. His descriptions of Keller echo not only the "best that has been thought and written" in literature, but also Arnold's doctrine that true culture lay in developing the highest and most ennobling human faculties, those that encouraged benevolence and compassion. In Keller, Anagnos found a subject worthy of being described in Shakespearean sonnets, one who embodied all the virtues of "sweetness and light."

Anagnos's florid accounts of Keller portray her in romantic and sentimental terms that exemplify the most florid excesses of late Victorian prose:

[S]he is a personification of goodness and happiness. She never repines, and is always so contented and gay, so bright and lively, that
"While we converse with her, we mark
No want of day, nor think it dark."
Of sin and evil, of malice and wickedness, of meanness and perverseness, she is absolutely ignorant. She is as pure as the lily of the valley, and as innocent and joyous as the birds of the air or the lambs of the field. . . . To her envy and jealousy are utterly unknown. She is in perfect harmony and on the best of terms with everyone. Her disposition,
"Like a bee in a wild of flowers,
Finds everywhere perfume."
She loves her parents, her baby sister, her teacher, her relatives and friends, her playmates and companions, her dolls, her animals, and all living creatures, with a sympathy so broad and deep that it opens her heart to the noblest inspirations. By her benevolence and good will toward all, she teaches us how to seek the highest goal,
"To earn the true success;
To live, to love, to bless." (PR 1888, 89–90)

Finding her a living example of the Arnoldian concept of human perfection, a being whose moral nature was perfectly developed on all sides, Anagnos insisted that Keller was "as perfect as a poem":

The beautiful traits of Helen's character are evenly developed in all directions. They shine from all sides of her nature like brilliant stars. Her loveliness of soul beams through her face. She is so simple and natural, so sweet and affectionate, so charming and generous, so magnanimous and unselfish, that all lovers of poetic childhood cannot help holding her dear, and counting her among the gems of humanity. (PR 1888, 92)

These examples represent only a few paragraphs of the hundreds and hundreds of pages of extravagant superlatives Anagnos used to describe Keller's perfections in his Annual Reports from 1886 through 1893.

As his own writings claimed Keller as a "miracle" whose like could only be conceived and described in the highest poetic metaphors, Anagnos spread this view to the mainstream media accounts of Keller, which largely copied his Reports as newspapers and magazines had copied verbatim Howe's accounts of Bridgman. Keller's achievements thus took on an aura of "realism," not because Anagnos could bolster his accounts with scientific data or objective proof, but because the terms in which he described Keller were already familiar to the majority of the reading public to whom these accounts were addressed. Describing Keller in the same terms as heroines of romantic or sentimental literature, Anagnos enshrined her as a living example of the values such works delineated. Rather than making readers suspect that Anagnos's reports were overblown exaggerations, his literary style helped attest to the truth of the sentimental values Keller represented. If an actual person, particularly one deaf and blind, and thus sheltered from external influences, could display the same characteristics of goodness and purity as fictional characters, then the fictions must have some element of "reality."

The "reality" of radiant happiness invoked in Anagnos's and others' descriptions of Keller was supported by the depiction of girlhood found in postbellum children's literature. As sentimental forms of representation, which had been the dominant popular cultural mode throughout the middle decades of the nineteenth century, began to wane after the Civil War and were replaced by the rise of realist forms of representation, sentimental ideals survived, and indeed flourished, in novels written for young girls. Such novels, which critic Leslie Fiedler has labeled "Good Good Girl" fiction, served as "training narratives" to instill the morality of True Womanhood in the next generation of girls.[11] Works like *Elsie Dinsmore* (1867), *What Katy Did* (1872), *The Five Little Peppers and How They Grew* (1881), *Little Lord Fauntleroy* (1886), *The Birds' Christmas Carol* (1887), *Mrs. Wiggs of the Cabbage Patch* (1901), and *Pollyanna* (1913) taught readers the importance of obedience, honesty, cheerfulness, optimism, and unselfishness.[12] They particularly emphasized the importance of suffering and misery as providing necessary instruction in empathy; as in mid-century sentimental logic, one's ability to feel for others came directly from one's own experiences of sorrow. Similarly, as in mid-century sentimental works, these "Good Good Girl" fictions represent empathy as a force powerful enough to transform both familial and economic relations.

There are two basic plots associated with this "Good Good Girl" fiction. In the first, exemplified in *The Five Little Peppers* series, *Fauntleroy*, and *Mrs. Wiggs*, a poor but industrious family, usually with no father and many small children, work happily together to make life cheerful and bright for all. Their own experience of poverty and want, instead of making them objects of pity, has strengthened their abilities to feel for others; those empathic powers eventually are employed to the benefit of a materially wealthy but spiritually impoverished person, usually an unloved and lonely older gentleman. The plot involves the reformation of the wealthy man's hardened heart, often by the inclusion of the poor but cheerful family in his household, resulting in the proper union of economic resources with tender and loving feelings.

The second type of "Good Good Girl" plot focuses on the benefits of affliction in creating the empathic subjectivity that will feel for others. In *What Katy Did*, for instance, Katy Carr's seemingly harmless disobedience results in an accident that paralyzes her, keeping her bedridden for four years. Her suffering provides her with stern moral lessons: she attends "The School of Pain," where she learns "the lesson of Patience," "the lesson of Cheerfulness," "the lesson of Making the Best of Things," "the lesson of Neatness," and "the lesson of Hopefulness."[13] She makes her sickroom a place of joy, comfort, and happiness for the rest of her family. By the end of her illness, Katy has become "The Heart of the House," gentle, womanly, tactful, and sweet, and every member of her family has changed for the better as a result of her example.[14] Similarly, in *The Birds' Christmas Carol*, Kate Douglas Wiggin presents Carol Bird, an invalid child whose sweetness and innate goodness make everyone in her family more considerate, patient, gentle, and caring. On her deathbed, Carol's final wish is to help others, to provide a Christmas celebration for the children of the poor Irish family she has watched from her bedroom window.

Representations of Helen Keller, in Anagnos's Annual Reports and in mainstream popular media accounts, described her virtues in the same terms as "Good Good Girl" fictions. Anagnos's insistence that Keller was "the personification of goodness and happiness," always sweet, loving, and sympathetic, echoed Martha Finlay's description of Elsie Dinsmore, who was "very truthful," "very diligent in her studies, respectful to superiors and kind to inferiors and equals," "gentle, sweet-tempered, patient, and forgiving" and "very sensitive and affectionate."[15] Like the Five Little Peppers, who learned to face poverty "bravely," with "a stout heart and a cheery face,"[16] and to believe that a loving family and home were all the riches they needed, Keller, though "fully aware of her great deprivations," never mourned or fretted over them; "She makes the best of her condition, and gathers up such flowers as lie along her way" (PR 1891, 289). Like Mrs. Wiggs, whose homespun philosophy focused on "keeping the dust off her rose-colored spectacles" and asserting that " 'ever'thin' in the world comes right, if we jes' wait long enough!,' "[17] Keller believed that "all things proceed from the good and end in the best."

The leading impulse and most vital feature in her character is her optimism, her firm belief that meanness cannot form a part in any of the phases of human nature. . . . This faith is the chief sentiment which gives unity to her thoughts. It is the source of the perpetual sunshine of her temperament. (PR 1891, 285)

Like Pollyanna, Keller could find "something about everything to be glad about — no matter what 'twas."[18]

Keller was familiar with most of these "Good Good Girl" fictions, either through reading them for herself in raised print, or through having them read to her. She was particularly enamored of *Little Lord Fauntleroy*, often writing in letters that she wanted to go visit him in his castle, and to pet his dog. These letters show that Keller herself took such representations as "real," and wished to meet the characters she read about. Her deafness and blindness, insofar as it limited her access both to printed texts and to more direct experiences of the lived world, helped make her the ideal reading subject, one who took the represented world of the text as an accurate depiction of reality. To Keller, who corresponded from an early age with some of the great figures in American literary history, including Holmes, Whittier, and Twain, the names she read in novels were as real to her as the names inscribed in letters from those she had never met; both existed solely in linguistic form, which she readily took as connected to a material reality.

Rather than seeing Keller's embodiment of the "Good Good Girl" virtues as a result of her reading, exacerbated by the "protection" her disabilities gave her from any other forms of representation, late nineteenth-century commentators also chose to read Keller and her fictions realistically.

They presented her as living proof that the idealistic beliefs of sentimental fiction were in fact truthful and accurate portrayals of reality. Philanthropist William Wade, one of Keller's greatest admirers, insisted that those who had "doubted whether the loving, unselfish disposition portrayed in 'Little Lord Fauntleroy' could be a real characteristic of any human being" had only to look to Helen Keller to see someone whose feelings were "superior even to the creation of Mrs. Burnett's pen, in those attributes which raise mortals to the sky" (PR 1891, 225).

Helen Keller's embodiment of the best sentimental attributes, for these late Victorian commentators, pointed toward the reality and power of such feelings, and away from the relations between reader and text that continued to construct those values as "reality." Keller delighted those who hoped to find what William Dean Howells called "a heart of ideality in . . . realism," as they took her as incontrovertible proof that what was real was also good, pure, and beautiful.[19] Howells became Keller's enthusiastic advocate, campaigning to raise funds for her education. Charles Dudley Warner, Edmund Clarence Stedman, Richard Watson Gilder, and Mark Twain similarly became fans of Keller; Twain in particular became a close friend of hers, inviting her for weekends at Stormfield for cigars and billiards.

Twain's interest in Keller came largely from her embodiment of the idealism of Victorian girlhood, the same qualities he valued in his own daughters and in his "angel fish" club. While famous for his cynicism and pessimism, especially in the last decades of his life, Twain also hungered for proof that sentimental values still existed and had power in the postbellum world. Keller provided that proof for him. Twain was under few illusions about where Keller's idealism came from; he was aware that she was the product of what she had read.[20] Nevertheless, Twain insisted, whether her view of life was "real" or "unreal," from material or fictional sources, he valued her embodiment of traits he still hoped to believe in: though her view might not be real, Twain commented, her "well put together unreality" was "hard to beat."[21]

*   *   *

The November 1886 issue of *St. Nicholas* contained a story by Louisa May Alcott entitled "The Blind Lark." Based on Michael Anagnos's accounts of the opening of the first kindergarten for the blind, Alcott's tale presented the story of blind Lizzie, a young girl who lived with her impoverished mother in a one-room Boston tenement, "condemned to lifelong helplessness, loneliness, and darkness." Lizzie's only consolation is her angelic voice, which elicits pity from neighbors who otherwise deem the child "a burden" and "a sight of trouble" for her mother.[22] Lizzie's songs eventually attract the attention of Miss Grace, a visitor from "the Flower Mission," who tells her of a "House Beautiful" where blind children could find "work and play, health and happiness, love and companionship, usefulness and independence, — all the dear rights and simple joys young creatures hunger for, and perish, soul and body, without."[23]

The kindergarten Miss Grace refers to promises to lift Lizzie from dependent object to useful worker, someone who can combine love with independence and can accede to "all the dear rights" of full selfhood, on the same terms as the sighted. Unfortunately for Lizzie, however, the school still lacks sufficient funds to open. After waiting two years to be old enough to attend the regular blind school, Lizzie is welcomed by its director, "Mr. Constantine," and feels as if she were reading "the first page of the beautiful book just opening before the eyes of her little mind — a lovely page, illustrated with flowers, kind faces, sunshine, and happy hopes."[24] After the first year of lessons, Lizzie is beloved for her "sweet temper, grateful heart, and friendly little ways"; her crowning achievement, though, is her participation in a concert given by the blind children to raise money for the kindergarten. "The Blind Lark's Song" proves wonderfully effective as a fundraiser, of course, convincing "stout old gentlemen" to "go home and write some generous checks."[25] Having done her bit to ensure the financial future of the kindergarten, Lizzie gains a sense of self-respect in the knowledge that " 'I'm not a burden any more, and I can truly help!' "[26]

Alcott's story insists that the "dear rights" of full selfhood include not only the ability to feel empathically for others, based on one's own experiences of suffering, but also to take action on their behalf, even by operating effectively in the supposedly hard-hearted economic realm. "The Blind Lark" inscribes Lizzie not only as empathic object, but as agent, someone whose selfhood is defined by her ability to "truly help" rather than be always a burden. Representations of Helen Keller followed the sentimental logic apparent in Alcott's story by asserting her capacities for empathic action; like Lizzie's, Keller's claim to full selfhood on equal terms with nondisabled people came in part from the "realistic" depictions of her efforts to assist less fortunate others.

Like depictions of characters in "Good Good Girl" fiction, these representations insisted that Keller's disabilities had sent her to "The School of Pain," enabling her to feel for others' woes rather than wallow in self-pity for her own. Keller's afflictions taught her that "the great sorrows which come into our lives, and make our hearts desolate, help us to understand and to sympathize with the sorrows of others" (PR 1892, 207).[27] Like these fictions, representations of Keller also insisted on the universal power of sympathy to sway others' emotions. Anagnos insisted that "her loving and sympathetic heart endear[ed] Helen to everybody with whom she comes in contact"; rather than observing her as a voyeuristic object, visitors who came to see Keller were moved by the "sympathetic and unselfish temper" which "render[ed] her a fairy queen who draws to herself hundreds of hearts—a kindly magician who turns all her visitors into friends and admirers" (PR 1891, 223).

Transforming visitors into friends was not the only "magic" worked, in Anagnos's sentimental celebrations, by Keller's empathic abilities; she also embodied the "reality" of the empathic subjectivity by constantly "sacrific[ing] every instinct of selfishness on the altar of generosity" and always thinking of others before herself (PR 1891, 222). Reports of Keller's unselfishness had appeared even in the earliest accounts of her progress, as Anne Sullivan participated, too, in framing Keller as the ideal sentimental heroine. During their first Christmas together, Sullivan observed that, when Keller learned of a poor girl at a church festival who had received no gifts, she "flew to her own and selected a mug, a thing which she prized most highly, and gave it to the little stranger with abundant love" (PR 1888, 100). Similarly, Sullivan recounted that, when Keller learned of a girl who had no warm cloak, she instantly took off her own new jacket, of which she was very fond, and insisted that " 'I must give it to a poor little strange girl' " (PR 1888, 101). As for Gerty Flint and Helen deKroyft, in Keller's world, as created by "Good Good Girl" fictions taken as reality, there could be no such thing as "strangers," but only suffering people whom we have not yet helped toward happiness.

Keller's "devotion to others and forgetfulness and sacrifice of self" represented her "noblest characteristics." A "born philanthropist," she delighted in "giving help and carrying relief to the suffering," and was "ever ready to assuage and solace the woes of her little brothers and sisters in misfortune."[28] The unfailing love and sympathy that had characterized her as a young child "opened to her a path to 'fair new spheres of pure activity' " as she approached adolescence, "and led her to make strenuous efforts for the accomplishment of a grand deed—the rescue of a little boy afflicted like herself" (PR 1891, 236–37). Like Gerty Flint's, Keller's accession to full adult selfhood was marked by her ability to put her feelings into concrete

action, beyond the domestic sphere (or the boundaries of the Perkins Institutional "family"), to earn money to alleviate others' woes.

Perhaps the most celebrated of Keller's accomplishments as an empathic agent was her work on behalf of Tommy Stringer, a deaf-blind boy
living in a Pennsylvania almshouse. What Samuel Gridley Howe had imagined might occur between Laura Bridgman and Oliver Caswell, but which
appeared only in an oil painting of the two, became a reality in the relation
between Keller and Stringer, as the deaf-blind girl did indeed become the
boy's champion. As soon as William Wade told Keller that the orphaned
boy "had neither a comfortable and pleasant home nor affectionate parents," she became very eager to have him brought to Boston to the Perkins
Kindergarten for the Blind (PR 1891, 237). For the next year, "Tommy became the burden of Helen's thoughts and conversation," as she resolved to
do everything in her power to call people's attention to Tommy's plight.[29]
She began her campaign by exercising her powers of self-control; her "rig-
orous course of self denial" (abstinence from soda-water and other prized
luxuries) helped her to "save money for her one great object."[30] When the
newspapers made it known that her dog had been accidentally shot, and
offers of money for a replacement came pouring in from all over, Keller
asked everyone to give their money to the fund for Tommy Stringer instead.
"In every direction Helen sent this message, always in a specially written
personal letter that was marked by the sweet simplicity and remarkable
ability of the author."[31]

Keller wrote an average of eight letters a day about Stringer, calling his
cause to the attention of editors of newspapers and to the readers of chil-
drens' magazines, and answering every donation with a personal letter of
thanks. In writing these letters, Keller also began her lifelong work of in-
scribing herself as an active empathic self, writing herself into existence and
again upholding the "reality" of sentimental fictional representations by
portraying herself in the same logic. As an empathic and authorial self,
Keller "[wrote] out the perfect law of love," not just "in verbal terms, but in
deeds that reveal[ed] all its depth and height" (PR 1891, 263).

Keller's efforts on behalf of Tommy Stringer shaped the career she
would follow for the rest of her life. She became famous, not only as the first
disabled person to become an active philanthropist, devoting her life to
fundraising and consciousness-raising on behalf of the blind, deaf, and
disabled worldwide, but as the first disabled person to document fully
her own experiences, thoughts, and feelings. Keller eventually wrote more
than fourteen volumes of autobiography, essays, biography, and poetry, of

which the best known and most widely read is her 1903 autobiography *The Story of My Life*.[32]

Keller's *Story* marks her first major effort in becoming an authorial subject as well as an empathic one. As such, the volume addresses the question of how Keller could write "the perfect law of love" in verbal terms; more important, reviewers of the work questioned whether her linguistic inscriptions of "the law of love" and herself as empathic subject could be "real." While many reviews praised the book for its unremitting idealism, optimism, and faith in human benevolence and compassion, others questioned Twain's assertion that the "unreality" of Keller's worldview, prompted by her sensory deprivations and her Arnoldian education, could indeed be preferable to harsher, more "real" views of life.

In writing *The Story of My Life*, Helen Keller wrote herself into existence as a subject on equal terms with the sighted and hearing. The work had originally been written as a series of themes for Charles T. "Copey" Copeland's composition course when Keller was a freshman at Radcliffe. "Copey" had encouraged Keller to write freely about her own experiences as a deaf-blind woman, having faith that her fluency in languages, her already-polished writing style, and her Arnoldian aesthetic education would enable her to produce what would become a masterpiece.[33] Though she had written a number of autobiographical essays for *St. Nicholas* and the *Youth's Companion* in the 1890s, Keller wrote that "it never occurred to me that it might be worthwhile to make my own observations and describe the experiences peculiarly my own."[34] "Copey"'s encouragement helped Keller to resolve "to be myself, to live my own life and write my own thoughts when I have any."[35] He thought highly enough of her freshman essays to send a sample to the *Ladies' Home Journal*, which published her autobiography in installments in 1902; Doubleday Page offered a contract and published the volume in its entirety in 1903.

Reviewers of Keller's *Story* noted with some surprise that the deaf-blind woman had a highly "idiomatic," "individual," and "rhythmical" writing style that indicated her "possession of a culture well above the level of that owned by the average college girl of her age." That "culture" consisted "not merely in knowing the usual things in literature and art, but in reaching an intelligent enthusiasm about those phenomena in her reach which appeal to her temperament."[36] So successfully had she inscribed herself as subject in her autobiography that, one reviewer noted, "one forgets to make allowances for [her] limitations . . . until a chance phrase recalls one with a start to the realization that the mind which deals so freely and so normally with the ordinary factors of human life dwells forever in silence and the dark."[37]

Able to depict "so normally" the "ordinary factors" of life, Keller's polished prose style masked or belied her disabilities. Most reviewers noted that, as they read, they forgot that the author was disabled, so vivid and precise was her imagery. Other reviewers did remind readers of Keller's status as disabled author by comparing her work to that of other blind people. In these comparisons, however, Keller again ranked as equal to the sighted. As a review in *The Independent* noted, while other blind people, "if they write at all . . . do so under such disadvantages that they write very poorly," Keller demonstrated "a literary skill unusual under any circumstances."[38] The review does not mention any specific blind authors, but seems to be referring to works like deKroyft's and Day's in noting that most blind writers discussed their emotions and the sympathetic reactions of others, and failed to present "the most vital matters, which one wishes most to know." Keller, by contrast, in focusing on her own experiences and describing her perceptions, informed the sighted and hearing public about "what we most wish to hear."[39]

Unique in placing Keller in the company of blind rather than sighted authors, this review also offered a rare criticism of Keller's work, pointing out that her writing was "woven out of two strands; the one necessarily acquired at second hand, the other distinctly original and her own." Keller's efforts to write like sighted and hearing people, to inscribe herself in the text as a "normal" subject rather than as a blind or deaf-blind one, encouraged her to use imagery of sight and sound in order that her sighted and hearing readers would not detect the differences in the author's represented sensory perceptions. The *Independent* review labeled her use of this type of language "traditional and derivative," warning that her desire to be "like other girls" would prove dangerous to her if she insisted on writing as a sighted and hearing person would. If, however, she stuck "to her own best vein," and described only those perceptions which she knew first hand, "her delicacy of sentiment, her natural sensibility, and her feeling for style" would lead her to fulfill her ambition "to do something worth while in letters."[40]

What *The Independent* mentioned gently and in the midst of praise, the reviewer for *The Nation* used as the focus of the harshest notice Keller's autobiography received. Using words descriptive of sight and sound, Keller wrote "of things beyond her power of perception with the assurance of one who has verified every word" through personal experience, while in fact "all her knowledge is hearsay knowledge, her very sensations are for the most part vicarious."[41] Keller's "unreal" autobiography, according to this review, was a prime example of "literary insincerity," as it consisted largely of borrowed knowledge and second-hand observations. Keller had violated the fundamental premise of denominational language in writing about things she could not know directly, and had violated the basic rule of autobiography by presenting as her own the linguistic expressions of others' sensory experiences. The review placed Keller firmly back in the category of "disabled" subject, removing her right to inscribe herself as a sighted and hearing subject in her textual self-representation. Reinvoking the sentimental view of disability by insisting that it seemed "cruel to criticize this unfortunate girl who has made so much of nothing," the review nonetheless insisted that, "If she were to be judged like less afflicted mortals, we should have to call a great deal of Miss Keller's autobiography unconscientious."[42]

Those who sprang to Keller's defense, including John Albert Macy, the young Harvard instructor who had helped edit the volume, refuted this claim by asserting that, had Keller not used language in ways identical to that of sighted and hearing people, her writing would have gone completely unnoticed.[43] Her education had focused on teaching her to be just like other people, rather than like the "disabled," in that she was encouraged to participate fully in all activities (including visual and auditory ones), and not to join the "separate race" of the blind Howe and others had helped to create. Rather than being "a great mistake," Macy insisted that Keller's education, especially in the language of sight and hearing, enabled her to claim full selfhood on a basis equal to that of the nondisabled. If Keller

had not tried to be like other people, if her teacher had not made her try, we should never have heard of her. . . . Only by trying to be what other people are, by trying to do what they do, by trying to use a language she has never heard, by learning of things she has never seen, and trying to grasp them as completely as she could, and write and speak about them as fully and as often as she could, only by striving to forget and deny her limitations, has she realized herself and given the lie to her afflictions.[44]

Rather than criticizing Keller for "not being herself" in writing about sights and sounds, Macy argued that she deserved praise for being "anything but herself, for herself was a mute, and her imitation is a splendid woman with speech."[45]

In this assertion, Macy summarizes for Keller the fundamental dilemma faced by disabled people attempting to claim a form of subjectivity equal to that of the nondisabled outside of sentimental frameworks. In

Figure 10. Helen Keller and Anne Sullivan, 1898. From *Helen Keller Souvenir #2,* 1892–1899. Volta Bureau, Washington, D.C., 1899.

order to write at all, Keller had to write in a "foreign" language, a language she knew only as language, and not as the names of sensory perceptions. To do so was to become a linguistic subject whose disability was not marked in her writing, but it also meant "giving the lie" to her "afflictions," denying and forgetting her status as deaf and blind. To proclaim her disabilities, as Macy noted, would be to relegate her forever to silence, or at the most to a marginalized status as an empathic object and agent; to erase them, by contrast, meant claiming her right to subjectivity in terms not circumscribed by the association of disability and sentimentality. To become a self, according to Macy's understanding, meant that Keller had to abandon "herself" and become an imitation. She thus "performed" the selfhood, the subjectivity, of a nondisabled person.

This performance of nondisabled selfhood was only possible in two media. Because Keller had no visible signs of blindness — her eyes looked "normal" — still photographs of Keller present her as no different from sighted people in appearance (Figure 10). When she spoke, of course, her speech patterns (as well as her sign language) marked her incontrovertibly as deaf, just as her movements and her need for a guide marked her physically as blind. In writing, however, as in photographs, images of Keller did not necessarily foreground her disabilities. Just as the texts she read as a girl had interpellated her into nondisabled subject positions, providing her with a "normal" subjectivity, so the texts she wrote as an adult inscribed her authorial self in nondisabled subject positions.

In analyzing a passage Keller wrote describing a landscape, a critic noted that the paragraph's visual imagery "convey[ed] the conventional meaning to the average reader"; readers could understand the meanings of Keller's words because those words referred to sensory experiences common to sighted persons.[46] Readers could not tell from the text that the author herself could not see, that her words were not expressing meaning based on direct experience. This did not mean that the visual imagery Keller employed had no meaning at all to her, but rather that words expressive of sight had subjective meanings, referring to moods or emotions instead of to "objective experience." In this sense, Keller's language use itself was "sentimental" even when the form of her writing was not: Keller's visual imagery referred, not to the material world perceptible through the operation of the physical senses, but to the emotions and feelings expressed through physical reactions. Like Mrs. deKroyft's autobiography, Keller's writings created a "reality" of their own, rather than reflecting a materially perceptible one.

The late twentieth-century observer will note that Helen Keller's writings constructed an authorial persona and an ideal reader, both of whom could see and hear. Just as sentimental readers could take linguistic descriptions of emotions as the textual equivalent of the direct perception of another's feelings, so readers of Keller's autobiographical writings took her descriptions as adequate linguistic representations of the visual and auditory experiences with which they were already familiar. Keller could employ the language of sight and sound so "realistically" and convincingly because she herself had been constructed as a sighted and hearing subject by the texts she had read, all of which supplied her with representational equivalents of sensory experiences. As a linguistic subject, Keller *could* "see" and "hear," through the textual representations that had interpellated her into the subject-positions from which she absorbed verbal descriptions of sight and sound as her own "reality." Because she could "see" and "hear" as a textually-constructed reader, she assumed that she could write from the same position, *as if* she had the same sensory experiences as the full-facultied. The text does not differentiate between readers who can confirm and verify its representations as "realistic" through independent sensory experiences and those who cannot: in the world of textual representation, all readers, and writers, are created equal, without regard to physical abilities or limitations.

Keller's autobiographical writings inscribe her as the most complete example of a disabled adult self, presenting her ability to feel for others and to act effectively on their behalf in the rational economic "wide wide world" beyond home and institution. These writings, like the thousands of articles about her, document her lifelong efforts to raise funds for and consciousness about the condition of disabled people worldwide. Keller earned her living as an independent adult through her work with organizations for disabled people; from 1924 until her retirement in the late 1950s, Keller was the paid spokesperson and fundraiser for the American Foundation for the Blind. Rather than depending on the charity of compassionate others, Keller proved in her own right that disabled people could be both empathic and economic agents. Her example has determined in large measure public attitudes and programs toward the integration of disabled people into mainstream schools and jobs throughout the twentieth century.

Her example, while it helped rewrite the Victorian cultural equations between disability and sentimentality, also reinforced certain central elements of that equation. All Keller's writings, and most of the things written about her, stress her idealism and her reliance on inner perception, on "soul" and feeling rather than on external material perception. Though framed in an Emersonian context in writings that claimed Keller as an American heroine for all to honor and emulate, these inner perceptions and feelings also aligned her with sentimental forms of representation that asserted the primacy of the unseen over the seen, the emotional over the rational.

While that sentimentality provided Keller with a framework in which her physical differences became unimportant, in relation to her emotional (and linguistic) similarities to the sighted and hearing, it also set limitations on the terms of her embodiment. Just as sexuality became the limit for sentimental representations of disability, because of the impossibility of figuring disabled bodies as simultaneously the sites of feeling and of reproductive (or pleasurable) sexual activity, so Helen Keller conceived of her subjectivity as necessarily nonsexual.[47] Representations of Keller, both biographical and autobiographical, focus on her purity, naming her an American "saint," who by analogy has transcended the merely physical.[48] In addition, Keller's own understanding of her subjectivity was premised on the erasure or marginalization of her disabilities, whether through the assertion of her empathic abilities as unimpaired by her deafness and blindness or through the assertion of her linguistic abilities as unimpaired by her missing sensory perceptions. The marginalization of her disabled body and its physical capacities enforced, for Keller, an absolute dichotomy between mind or soul and body; in order to become a self, Keller had to discard her body and its "defects" in favor of soul perception and language. Discarding her body meant necessarily discarding any notions of physical sexuality.

During a visit to Alexander Graham Bell in 1901, Bell told Keller that she should not think herself "debarred from the supreme happiness of woman" — marriage and children — because of her disabilities. Keller replied that she could not imagine a man wanting to marry her, because " 'it would seem like marrying a statue.' "[49] Her education through the sentimental values presented in "Good Good Girl" fiction, as well as the idealism inherent in her Arnoldian aesthetic education, supported this renunciation of the inferior physical and sexual self in favor of a superior spiritual and linguistic disembodied self. Keller thought of sexuality only as reproductive marital heterosexuality, just as sentimental fiction figured the only positive form of sexuality as circumscribed by those parameters. She thought of that specific sexual act as the union of two souls through the union of two bodies, but defined her body as "other" than her "self." Thus her body could never be the vehicle to reach her soul or self, and she imagined that her husband, in the physical relations of marriage, could only have intercourse with her body, a statue, a non-subject, and not with the "self" that remained always necessarily disembodied.

As the best known and most publicized example of a disabled person achieving a form of selfhood equal to that of nondisabled people, Keller has been an inspiration to twentieth-century efforts to integrate disabled people into mainstream culture. The power of her example, however, has also had its cost, namely that the ideal she upholds denies certain aspects of subjectivity to disabled people. To become a self like Helen Keller, twentieth-century disabled people have had to deny, forget, or erase the bodies that mark them as physically different. They have had to accede to forms of selfhood available through sentimental value systems, which construct them as both objects and agents of feeling and empathy, but not necessarily as capable of independent rational thought and economic autonomy. And they have had to renounce virtually all forms of physical sexuality, accepting the disabled body only as a site for feeling, rather than for production, reproduction, or pleasure. These factors, the result of more than one hundred and fifty years of sentimental representations of disability, have overdetermined the relegation of disabled people to the position of perpetual "poster children," and prevented them from becoming recognized as adults operating on the same terms, and with the same concerns and rights, as nondisabled adults.

9

Redefining Disability and Sentimentality: *The Miracle Worker*

William Gibson's *The Miracle Worker* is the most widely known portrayal of the world's most famous disabled person.[1] The play documents Helen Keller's achievements at age seven, when Anne Sullivan helped her acquire alphabetic language; though written and performed in the late 1950s, when Keller was in her seventies, the play makes no reference to the fourteen volumes of autobiography, biography, and essays Keller herself produced, nor to the two films, dozens of biographies, and thousands of newspaper and magazine articles of which she was the subject. That *The Miracle Worker* remains the most common source of knowledge about Keller's life was recently confirmed for me when, as a guest lecturer in a university colleague's senior-level seminar, I asked the students what they knew about Keller. All of them knew who she was, and almost all had read Gibson's play, generally as a required text in high school, or had seen the movie with Patty Duke and Anne Bancroft, but few knew any more than what they covered.[2]

The play currently exists as the most prevalent text defining contemporary cultural meanings of disability. Its popularity stems in part from its efforts, radical for the 1950s, to articulate a new set of meanings for disability, disrupting the frameworks that had held sway since the early nineteenth century. The play's attempt to shift the significance of disability appears most prominently in the contrast between the attitudes of Kate Keller, the deaf-blind child's mother, and her teacher, Anne Sullivan. Mrs. Keller represents the Victorian attitude toward disability, urging pity for her afflicted child and abhorring the violence that any effort to control Helen requires. Her perspective appears as decidedly middle-class and genteel, representing the "polite" mainstream understanding of the place of disabled people in the family and in American society as a whole. Sullivan, on the other hand, represents the "modern" attitude, banishing sentiment in favor of a hard-hearted insistence on requiring the disabled child to conform to norms of human social behavior.

In presenting the two different frameworks for understanding and reacting to disability embodied in Mrs. Keller and Sullivan, the play also places these attitudes in historical context: though written and produced in the late 1950s, the play is set in the mid-1880s, and it labels Mrs. Keller's stance as decidedly Victorian and sentimental, while upholding Sullivan's militantly unsentimental perspective as that of the modern twentieth-century professional. The Victorian view of disability, as illustrated in the Keller family's responses to the deaf-blind girl, unequivocally centered on conceptions of disability as a form of pathos and suffering; the reactions to that suffering vary between Captain Keller's desire to lock the child away in an asylum, in order to restore peace and gentility to his disrupted household, and Mrs. Keller's desire to pity and protect the afflicted one. Mrs. Keller's inability to discipline Helen, or to react to her with anything other than maternal sympathy, stands out as decidedly sentimental; Sullivan's non-familial perspective, by contrast, appears as objective and unemotional, as she is able to evaluate and act in the family situation precisely because she feels no attachment to the disabled child. The play emphasizes the distinction between the two attitudes in showing the necessity of removing Helen from the family home in order for Sullivan to begin her transformation of the wild child into a human subject. The maternal sentimentality that dominates the home environment, the play argues, will only suffocate and smother Helen's potential humanity, while Sullivan's professional distance will ensure that no merely emotional concerns get in the way of her disciplinary task.

The distinction between Mrs. Keller's horror at seeing her child "mistreated" and Sullivan's insistence that the child conform to social norms illustrates the distinction between the Victorian and twentieth-century understandings of the meanings of disabled bodies. For the former, disability was necessarily pitiable, providing an opportunity for the nondisabled to respond with sentimentality; this attitude framed the disabled body as a site of pain and suffering, labeling it as fundamentally "other" than the nondisabled body, hence barring disabled people, defined wholly by this understanding of the cultural meaning of their bodies, from being recognized as fully human beings. For the latter, disability is something correctable or transcendable; the differences in the disabled body, the factors that set the disabled person apart from the nondisabled, can be normalized, or at least minimized. Sullivan's attitude toward Helen Keller is that her body can be "tamed" into conformity with the normal standards of human behavior, and that the deaf-blind girl can thus become just like nondisabled people. While the sentimental Victorian ideology of disability defined disabled people entirely by the condition of their bodies, and hence confined them to being the objects of others' emotions, the "modern" ideology defined disabled people by their ability to transcend, or to marginalize, their bodily differences; the claims of disabled people to equality with the nondisabled in the latter model thus depend on their capacity for normalization. For *The Miracle Worker*, this normalization appears in Helen Keller's triumphant acquisition of alphabetic language, the factor that allows her to overcome the isolation enforced by her deaf-blind body and to claim her membership in the human family.

The Miracle Worker, in negotiating the distinctions between the Victorian sentimental attitude toward disability as pathetic and the modern attitude toward disability as something to be erased and normalized, used a popular cultural medium to attempt to redefine the existing meanings of disability. As in the nineteenth century, where popular fictional representations of disabled people worked in concert with institutional discourses on disability, Gibson's play tries to codify in dramatic form the results of more than half a century's worth of activism concerning the political, economic, and educational position of disabled people in the United States. Critical responses to the play reflected that attempt, as they addressed not only the play's intrinsic dramatic qualities but also the new meanings of disability the work articulates. Most of those who reviewed the play's first appearance on Broadway in 1959 expected the play to depict Keller's disability as a form of suffering and affliction, and hence to employ sentimental tropes. While some were delighted that Gibson avoided the sentimental conventions in refiguring disability, others were shocked that he chose to make a spectacle out of what should have been a sight too painful and personal to watch.[3] All critics agreed that, for good or ill, what disrupted the expected Victorian portrayal of disability as a pitiable affliction was the play's insistence on foregrounding Helen Keller's physicality, the wildness of her untamed deaf-blind body. Their discussions of the play's presentation of Keller's body and the meanings it attached to that body centered on analyzing two crucial scenes: the fight scene in the second act, which most graphically shows the violence of Sullivan's struggles with Keller, and the final scene, which presents Keller's "miraculous" acquisition of language.

In the fight scene, Anne Sullivan (portrayed by Anne Bancroft) battles to get the ferocious Keller (portrayed by Patty Duke) to sit properly at the dinner table, to eat with a spoon, and to fold her napkin when finished. This scene opens with the Keller family at breakfast, trying to hold a normal conversation while Helen wildly grabs handfuls of food from whatever plate she can reach as she dashes around the table. Sullivan, increasingly upset by the Kellers' refusal to force Helen to behave, tries to discipline the child. She argues with the Kellers until they agree to leave her alone with Helen. A silent but all-out ten-minute battle ensues between the stubborn teacher and the equally stubborn child: Helen flings food in Sullivan's face; Sullivan forces spoon after spoon into the raging child's hands, only to have them thrown back at her. They wrestle over sitting in a chair, exchange pinches and pull hair over using a napkin, and come to blows over folding the napkin properly on the table at the meal's end.

Many critics found the violence of this scene profoundly disturbing; one declared that it verged on "emotional obscenity," and appeared as "a grotesque lark, like visiting at Bedlam."[4] The reference to Bedlam points to the critic's assumption that the public display of disability must necessarily be the display of a form of suffering, and the fear that such display can only result in the callous mockery of an audience, rather than by eliciting their sympathy. Putting the wild body of the deaf-blind girl on center stage was a form of voyeurism to these critics; the "obscenity" lay in the play's unrelenting focus on showing that disabled body in its full physicality, complete with its uncomprehending violence as well as its pitiable gropings. That the body on display was that of a girl, especially one who could not return the audience's scrutiny, increased the critics' feeling that the fight scene was offering something "obscene."

For other critics, the obscenity of the play lay not in its portrayal of violence, but simply in the exhibition of disabled bodies themselves. Noting that the play cast blind children in the roles of the students of the Perkins School for the Blind, Sullivan's alma mater, Kenneth Tynan declared that this lent the play a "faint aura of exploitation." While Sullivan's efforts on Keller's behalf were praiseworthy in themselves, Tynan concluded, they were "too delicate to be submitted to Broadway tailoring," and offered for public viewing.[5] His use of the word "delicate" echoes the Victorian equation of disability with obscenity, naming the disabled body as something that should be kept private, hidden from public scrutiny. Even when not shown in fits of horrifying violence, a disabled body, to these critics, was in itself too disturbing to be placed on center stage.

In the opinion of several critics, however, it was precisely this voyeuristic display of Keller's disabled body that undercut any possibility of sentimentality in the play. Brooks Atkinson, for example, found the violence the play's saving grace, the element that kept the story of Keller and Sullivan from being the expected tribute to noble self-sacrifice, "a tale of virtuous social service between ladies."[6] As a "ferocious little beast" tamed by Sullivan's "stubbornness and . . . callousness," Duke's enactment of Keller was "altogether superb—a plain, sullen, explosive, miniature monster whose destructive behavior makes sympathy for her afflictions impossible, but whose independence and vitality are nevertheless admirable."[7]

Defined in sentimental representations as "posters," as beings whose bodies were signs and sites of suffering and affliction, disabled people were primarily framed as the objects of others' compassion. As Atkinson points out, *The Miracle Worker*, in defining Keller's disabled body as violent, as a spectacle, as fierce and feral, provides an alternative model for understanding the selfhood of disabled people. Rather than being solely the objects of others' sympathetic emotions, disabled people like Keller can become independent and autonomous beings, conforming to notions of nondisabled selfhood, and can be represented in more realistic modes that do not rely on producing a sentimental emotional response. By foregrounding Keller's body, the source of the limitations that would usually evoke pity, the play inscribes that body as fiercely independent, despite its limitations. Its gropings and collisions as the deaf-blind child flings herself across the stage cease being the source of pathos and become assertions of Keller's will to maintain her autonomy at all costs. The violence some critics found so disturbing is in fact the marker of the emergence of a new notion of disabled selfhood, the inscription of a disabled body into an unsentimental framework based on the assumption of independence rather than the assumption of dependence.

In reformulating the disabled body as the site of independence rather than of suffering and pathos, the play posits sentimentalism as quintessentially Victorian, family-oriented, and feminine; it also argues that that sentimentality is directly harmful to the disabled person. The play's enthusiasm for Sullivan's hardhearted discipline, according to one critic, presented a challenge "to all parents who under the impulse of love and pity settle for less than the maximum development of their children's capacities for independence and contact with the glories of living."[8] The message was clear, for parents of handicapped and nonhandicapped children alike: family sentiment, particularly as embodied in maternal affection, was dangerous, smothering; unemotional involvement alone could foster the "independence" which was part of "the glories of living."

Anne Sullivan was able to provide this unemotional antidote to mater-

nal smothering because she was decidedly not a product of a traditional
middle-class family. Through devices such as the loudspeaker voice of Sullivan's tubercular brother Jimmy, who recalls their childhood in the Tewks-
bury almshouse, and the chorus of blind girls who, in bidding goodbye to
Sullivan as she leaves for Alabama, remind the audience that Sullivan too
has been a resident of the Perkins School for the Blind, Gibson's play takes
great pains to establish Sullivan's exclusion from the sentiments of middle-
class family life epitomized by the Kellers. Because she was a poorhouse
orphan, who presumably never knew the sheltering tenderness of maternal
love, Sullivan can provide the objectivity needed to tame the wild Keller.
But, the play insists, because she cared for her tubercular brother, and
because she herself had been cured of blindness, Sullivan can also identify
with Keller's situation. And because she is, after all, a woman, Sullivan must
come to feel some love for her pupil. The play thus presents Sullivan's
detachment as balanced by her empathy; when her toughminded discipline
has succeeded in taming Keller, in the final scene, she gives way to her
feelings in the declarations of eternal love that (re)integrate both Keller and
Sullivan into the circle of middle-class sentimental familial relations. Gibson presents Sullivan's love, which dominates the final scene of the play, as
different from maternal love because it is balanced with a disinterested
objectivity; it emerges only after she has "liberated" Keller from the confines of her body, through the acquisition of language, and hence is not as
confining as Mrs. Keller's protective maternal affections.

     The threat of maternal overprotection was doubly dangerous for hand-
icapped children because their perceived dependence made mothers even
more reluctant to allow them to separate and become autonomous; as Mrs.
Keller illustrates, such Victorian mothers were unwilling to force their children to live up to the rules and expectations required of nondisabled children.[9] Such smothering mother-love was dangerous even to handicapped
adults, as Dore Schary's play *Sunrise at Campobello* (1959) demonstrated.
The play shows Franklin Roosevelt learning humility and dependence
through his paralysis, traits that countered his Brahmin-born elitism and
made him able to identify with a democratically-inspired ideal of the "common man." While this play emphasizes the necessity for a privileged male
leader to learn empathy through his own suffering, thus showing the political benefits of FDR's "feminizing" disability, it shares with *The Miracle
Worker* a mistrust of maternal affection as overly-protective. In one of the
play's climactic scenes, as FDR tries to relearn how to walk, with braces and
crutches, in order to resume his political career, his mother urges him not to

try and hopes that he will be content to remain a wealthy private gentleman, living a sheltered life on the family estate, rather than expose himself to physical injury and possible humiliation. In *Sunrise at Campobello*, Eleanor Roosevelt performs a function similar to that of Sullivan in Gibson's play, providing uncritical support for FDR's determination to become as physically independent as possible. Where his mother cringes at the sight of him crawling on the floor and up the stairs, Eleanor offers no assistance, but rather gives encouragement. Like Sullivan, whose womanly emotions emerge once the battle is over, Eleanor Roosevelt weeps over the pathetic spectacle FDR presented, but only when out of his sight and hearing.

These two plays tie representations of disability firmly to ideas of the importance of developing and maintaining an autonomous, independent self, which is directly threatened by maternal affection and by the sentimentality associated with that affection. Such motherly feeling, while still posited in both plays as the necessary basis for family life, must be countered with an unemotional, objective assessment of the hard realities of discipline and struggle necessary for the shaping of truly autonomous adults. By choosing to explore the dynamics of familial relations through disabled characters, these two plays point out that dependence, seemingly an inherent component of the selfhood of children and of disabled people of all ages, inevitably provokes a mother's desire to protect her offspring — a response that is figured as negative and destructive, or at the very least as ineffective. The solution each proposes is to refigure the cultural images of the type of selfhood available to children and to disabled people, so that that self is no longer defined as dependent. By demonstrating that children and disabled people can become autonomous selves if rampant maternal love is checked by a more objective and realistic force, both plays encourage the integration of the disabled into mainstream definitions of healthy selfhood, while denouncing the maternal sentimentality that is credited with keeping them dependent.

* * *

Of course, the Helen Keller portrayed in Gibson's play, unlike Schary's FDR, is not an ideal model of an autonomous self. Throughout most of *The Miracle Worker* she is an untamed monster, with the freedom to do what she wants when she wants but with absolutely no sense of familial relations or obligations. This is powerfully demonstrated in the first act, when the wild Keller tries to tip her infant sister Mildred out of her cradle. Keller's isolation, enforced by the sensory limitations of her body, prevents her from knowing or responding to any sense of emotional relation to anyone or anything. The task of the plot, and of Sullivan, is thus not just to prevent Keller from being smothered by an excess of maternal affection, but to tame her wild autonomy by bringing her into relationship with others, especially her family. As one reviewer noted, the play follows E. M. Forster's dictum in *Howard's End* to "only connect."[10]

In establishing this emotional connection, Sullivan must be careful not to extinguish Keller's fierce autonomy, the core of what the play promises will be Keller's healthy self; she must be equally careful, however, not to let that autonomy prevent Keller from becoming a member of the human community. The mediating term in this equation of selfhood, between a smothering emotionality and a destructive autonomy, is, as Sullivan discovers, obedience: Keller must be tamed into acceptable selfhood through Sullivan's strict discipline, which forces her to conform to norms of human social behavior, before any emotional connection or intellectual comprehension can be forged. This struggle for obedience is exemplified in the fight scene in the second act, as Sullivan adamantly insists that Keller fold her napkin at the end of the meal. Sullivan's elation at this victory strikes the Kellers, as well as the audience, as ironic, given the wartorn state of the dining room; to Sullivan, however, Keller's acquiescence in this small rule of etiquette marks the beginnings of obedience, a foundation necessary to a healthy selfhood because it ensures a balance between autonomy and connectedness.

Gibson based his play on his reading of Sullivan's letters, written to Perkins director Michael Anagnos during her stay with the Keller family; for Sullivan herself, the real "miracle" of Keller's struggle for selfhood was not the marvelous moment when she connected signifier and signified, but the moment when Keller obeyed Sullivan for the first time. According to Sullivan, "obedience is the gateway through which knowledge, yes, and love, too enter the mind of a child."[11] Less than a month after Sullivan's arrival at the Keller homestead, she wrote to Anagnos that

A miracle has happened! The light of understanding has shown on my little pupil's mind, and behold, all things are changed! The wild creature of two weeks ago has been transformed into a gentle child. . . . The great step — the step that counts — has been taken. The little savage has learned her first lesson in obedience, and finds the yoke easy.[12]

It was two weeks after Sullivan's "miracle" of obedience that the more recognized "miracle" at the water pump occurred.

The difference between the two miracles and their relative importance in shaping selfhood lies in the relation each has to the body in which the self presumably resides. For Sullivan, the miracle of obedience represented the acquiescence of the unreasoning and unemotional physical body to regulation, the first condition of membership in human society. The miracle of language, by contrast, represented the transcendence of the merely physical body into realms of abstraction, into thought which could exist independently from physical perception.

The new meaning of disability created in the play's foregrounding of Keller's fierce physicality reframes the disabled body, not as woefully afflicted and suffering but as a source of violence. As illustrated in both the scene where Keller tips her sister from her cradle and the second act fight scene, the disabled body is labeled specifically as *disobedient*, needing to be subjected to discipline and forced into conformity with forms of human behavior that mark normal ablebodied selfhood.

For Sullivan — both as characterized in Gibson's play and as revealed in her own letters — the most important step in claiming Keller as a fully human being lay in taming her unreachable and disobedient body and in controlling the animate physicality that recognized no means of persuasion other than the violence of physical force. In order to escape the familial sentimentality which, in framing Keller's body as pitiful and suffering, precluded the use of force to subdue that body, Sullivan insisted on removing herself and her charge to a separate cottage. There, Sullivan reasoned, the untamed child would learn that Sullivan was her only source of satisfying material or physical needs, such as hunger, thirst, or warmth. In the absence of the maternal affection that would anticipate and fulfill the child's every need, Sullivan theorized, Keller would begin to grasp, on the most basic level, that her physical comfort depended on Sullivan's will, not on her own. Thus, as both Gibson's play and Sullivan's letters document, while living in the cottage Keller did not eat until she obeyed Sullivan and used a spoon; she did not dress until she obeyed Sullivan and buttoned her clothes correctly.

In Sullivan's pedagogy, the first step in creating a human self from an animalistic physical body was to subdue that body's sense of independence; by making Keller dependent on her for her material welfare, Sullivan created in Keller her first awareness of the necessity of connection to others, the necessity of human relationship and interdependence. Having established that connection, transforming the disobedient disabled creature into a docile body, Sullivan could work toward the next step, which was to connect the child's obedient body to a form of signification that would expand her awareness of social rules and relationships.

The culmination of taming the disobedient disabled body, then, occurs in the play's final scene, when Keller reconnects the signifier and the signified. Drunk on language, the child reels about the stage frantically touching everything in reach, and asking Sullivan to supply its name. After mastering concrete nouns, including "water," she learns the words "mother," "father," and "teacher" as the labels for the people around her, and is fervently embraced by them as she spells their titles in the manual alphabet. The scene, and the Broadway play, end with Sullivan spelling into Keller's hand that she loves her "for ever and ever," and with the child leading her teacher to rejoin the Keller family inside the house.[13] This dramatic climax, which reviewers either praised or lamented as a reinscription of sentimentality, frames the "miracle" of obedience, and its consequence, the "miracle" of language, as enabling Keller to understand the basic denominational principle of language — that every object has a name — and the most basic aspect of human relatedness — that every person has a position, a title, which designates a relation to oneself. Thus the final scene promises that, with the acquisition of language, Keller has acquired a recognizably human form of selfhood; in substituting obedience for sentimentality, this selfhood will allow her emotional connections that do not compromise her autonomy, just as it allows her an autonomy that does not threaten her emotional connections.

But in order to acquire this language which marks her membership in the human community, Keller must first surrender her own form of language. In addition to the physical conformity to norms of behavior, Sullivan's discipline insists that Keller learn the normative version of alphabetic language in order to communicate. When Sullivan commenced her lessons, according to both the play and the biographical account, Keller already had a vocabulary of some sixty gestural signs. Having become deaf and blind at the age of eighteen months, when she was just beginning to speak her first words (including a baby version of "water"), the basic structures of language in Keller's brain had already been activated; in the period between her illness in 1882 and Sullivan's arrival in 1887, when Keller was seven years old, these basic structures held together the relation between Keller's gestures and the objects she wanted, but otherwise lay dormant. As Keller's needs grew more complex, her sign system proved increasingly inadequate, and her rage and frustration at her inability to make her needs and desires known grew to the point where she represented a positive danger to her family. This is the point at which Gibson's play begins, after a brief prologue showing Mrs. Keller's reactions to discovering Helen's afflictions. Throughout the play Helen attempts to use her gestural language to obtain desired objects, but Sullivan frames that language as another form of disobedience and refuses to respond to anything but the manual alphabet she is trying to teach Helen. Among the play's more poignant moments is the scene where the child, alone with the tyrannical Sullivan in the cottage, repeatedly and forlornly strokes her cheek with her hand, the gesture that signifies her mother.[14]

Sullivan, while subduing Keller's body into dependence and obedience, is constantly spelling the letters of the manual alphabet into Keller's hand, trying desperately to get the child to understand the connection between the motions of her fingers and the objects Keller desires. To accomplish this, she has simultaneously to build on the association between signifier and signified already existing in Keller's own gestural system and to break the associations Keller herself has created between objects and gestures. In other words, Sullivan has to maintain the fundamental structure of association between object and sign while breaking apart and discarding the system in which Keller already operated. The historical rationale behind this effort to discipline Keller's language along with her disobedient body came from Sullivan's understanding of the nature of language itself, an understanding she had garnered from reading Samuel Gridley Howe's 1840s reports of the education of deaf-blind Laura Bridgman. Howe believed that gestural or "natural" language, such as the sign language employed by deaf people (which was widely taught at schools for the deaf before the oralist movement began in the postbellum era) was a universal but primitive form of communication, one characteristic of, and suited only to, savage societies.[15] In contrast, arbitrary or alphabetic language was the language of civilization, the only form recognized as fully human.

The basis for Howe's distinction lay in his characterization of gestural language as the language of objects and emotions, while arbitrary language was the language of abstractions. Gestures, Howe argued, could only denote material objects, things whose traits could be signified through imitation, such as making the motion of drinking to signify thirst; gestures could also denote emotional states, as facial expressions were a clear material sign of the emotions occurring internally. The communicative needs of primitive societies could be met through such natural language, Howe argued, but more advanced communities needed a more advanced language, one that would enable people to think and talk abstractly, about qualities and ideas that had no material analogue.[16] The only fully human language, in

Howe's view and thus in Sullivan's view, was arbitrary language, the form that seemed the least reliant on the physical world, and on the sensory perception of that world, for its structures of meaning.

In systems of natural language, according to Howe, communication depended on the similarity between the gesture used to signify an object or trait and the thing signified. In arbitrary alphabetic language, in contrast, communication depended only on a society's initial agreement about the meaning of words; once that agreement had been reached, the physical basis of meaning could and did disappear as insignificant. Howe's insistence that arbitrary language was the only properly human form enforced a separation between the system of thought and communication and the physical or bodily perceptions that had originally formed the connections between signifier and signified.[17] As the marker of fully human subjectivity, the acquisition of arbitrary language that allowed for this abstraction was another means of erasing the physicality of selfhood. Arbitrary language users did not need to be embodied, as their language use depended neither on their physical perception of objects as the source of meaning, nor on their bodies as the source of gestural signification.

Anne Sullivan's insistence that Helen Keller discard her own gestural system and adopt the normative alphabetic system was the final step in transforming the disobedient disabled body into a docile, and disembodied, human subject, defined not by her physical limitations but by her linguistic potential. The triumph of *The Miracle Worker*'s final scene lies in Keller's ability to transcend the limits of her deaf-blind body through the acquisition of alphabetic language.

Because Gibson ends his play with Keller learning the word "love," an abstract concept with no palpable referent, he reinforces the notion that language is Keller's key to transcending or escaping the merely material world, and the key to her liberation from her body and its cultural meanings as either afflicted or disobedient. With the word "love," Gibson reinscribes Keller firmly in the sentimental framework of affectionate family relationships his play had initially found so inadequate to the task of molding a human subject from a wild deaf-blind body. The "reward" or result of Sullivan's harsh discipline, forcing Keller's physical and linguistic conformity to nondisabled norms, is thus the celebration of sentimental connections, stripped of their dangerous tendency to smother through the play's redefinition of the meaning of Keller's disabled body. Defined as once disobedient but now docile, rather than as a place of suffering and compassion, the disabled body in the final scene summons a sentimental response, but the emotion it generates is that of joyful reunion, rather than pity and sympathy. The acquisition of language, and its ultimate result, the understanding of "love," frame Keller's human selfhood as fundamentally disembodied; the triumph of language is shown to be the triumph of taming the wild body that had taken center stage through most of the play, in order to liberate the human self "imprisoned" in that body.

But while celebrating Keller's transcendence of her physical limitations, the play also highlights her bodily configuration; the sentimentality of the ending indicated in the importance of the word "love" and in Keller's reinscription in familial relations focuses attention back on Keller's body, this time as the vehicle for language and human connection, rather than as the object of pity and compassion. Though the play's construction of language insists that arbitrary language is the means through which the body can be minimized or marginalized, the portrayal of Helen Keller's acquisition of that language necessarily shows her as an embodied linguistic subject, one whose language depends directly and explicitly on her sensory perception of the motions of another's hand in hers. Relying on her ability to connect the physical feeling of water running over her hand with the physical feeling of Sullivan spelling letters into her other hand, Keller's acquisition of language adds a new dimension to her embodiment; rather than being the obstacle that defines her as irredeemably "other," her body becomes the vehicle for her participation in a normative linguistic community.

The disabled body the play places on center stage ultimately cannot be erased, though its cultural meanings can be shifted; while Sullivan's insistence on obedience and on arbitrary language work to normalize Keller's body, that body continues, even in the final scene, to refuse its own marginalization. For all that arbitrary language, the sign of Keller's inclusion into definitions of normal human selfhood, points away from the body and its physical perceptions, Keller's use of arbitrary language also points back to her body. Samuel Gridley Howe's account of the immateriality of arbitrary language obscures the fact that arbitrary language, too, has a physical component: though words may have no perceptible connection to their referents — words do not necessarily sound like, or look like, the things they represent — the communication of arbitrary language requires the embodiment of the subject, who must have a mouth with which to speak, or ears to hear, or hands to write or spell letters manually. Helen Keller's necessarily physical acquisition of language works to remind the nondisabled audience that, while we celebrate Keller's normalization, her ability to function just like us, we too rely on our bodies for our language. And therein may lie the play's most powerful message: the events of *The Miracle Worker*, while ostensibly insisting that Keller's acquisition of human subjectivity depends on the control, if not the erasure, of her body, work to reverse that equation, and to remind nondisabled audiences that all of our forms of subjectivity are indeed dependent on our bodies.

Perhaps the final irony of Gibson's play lies precisely in the vehicle he uses to explore the relations between subjectivity and bodily configuration: by highlighting the body of a deaf-blind girl, particularly in that most physical of media, the theater, the play continually reminds us of the inescapability of embodiment while it works to erase or transcend the specifics of that embodiment. What the play does demonstrate, through depicting Helen Keller, is that disability is an obstacle to the acquisition of normative forms of subjectivity. While nondisabled people acquire their sense of self unconsciously, through regular developmental stages, disabled people, as represented by Helen Keller, must work consciously to become fully human. This work encounters three types of problems that circumscribe the forms of subjectivity available. The first is the problem of the disabled body itself, the problem of incorporating a radically "different" body into models of selfhood based on normative ideas of physicality; this is the problem "solved," in Gibson's play, by Sullivan's insistence on obedience. The second involves the nature of subjectivity itself and the tension between an autonomous selfhood, which recognizes little or no connection to others in its insistence on independence, and the relational or connected selfhood, which has emotional ties to others but may never achieve a desirable level of autonomy. While holding out the possibility that the ideal subject finds a balance between the two, the play ultimately solves this problem by favoring the relational model celebrated in the final scene; despite the dangers of reinscribing sentimentality, Gibson's work emphasizes that relationality is the most appropriate form of selfhood for someone who is both disabled and female. In positing Keller's disabled body as the source of her ferocious independence and as the barrier to her acquisition of subjectivity, *The Miracle Worker* seems to insist on the subordination of that body to the demands of human relationships and affectional ties. These ties are forged through the play's solution to the third problem of human subjectivity, the acquisition of language, and the relation between the form of language and the configuration of the human body.

While seeming to insist on the transcendence and hence normalization of the disabled body through the acquisition of arbitrary language that leads to the understanding of immaterial concepts like "love" and "family," the play redefines the cultural meaning of the disabled body. Initially rejecting the sentimental portrayal of that body as a site of suffering and as an object of compassion for the nondisabled, the play ends up reinvoking a sentimental framework that simultaneously highlights and masks the determinism of disabled physicality. Showing Keller's connection to others through "love," the play focuses on Keller's emotions, her inner self, which had been "imprisoned" by the limitations of her body; by making language the vehicle for that relational self to emerge, however, the play necessarily points back to Keller's embodiment as the means by which she communicates. Like the sentimental Victorian constructions of disability that foregrounded the inescapable differences of the disabled body, *The Miracle Worker* ultimately retains the focus on the body itself as the basis for the cultural meanings of disability, while succeeding only in shifting the terms in which that body is problematized and normalized.

Though Gibson's play tries to create new meanings, new cultural understandings of disability, it falls back on existing frameworks of sentimentality, physicality, and selfhood. The continued popularity of *The Miracle Worker* as the best-known popular cultural representation of disability may stem from precisely that inability to create new meanings; the play reinforces traditional understandings of disability, ones so deeply rooted in Western cultural conceptions of the meaning of different and normal bodies as to be virtually unshakable.

Notes

Introduction

1. The word "apartheid" to describe the system of segregation of disabled people is used particularly by Susan Hannaford, in *Living Outside Inside: A Disabled Woman's Experience. Towards a Social and Political Perspective* (Berkeley, Calif: Canterbury Press, 1985); see especially "The Charity Business," pp. 24–27, and "Sisters Speak Out," pp. 127–28. My own reading has centered largely on questions of gender and disability; the following books on women with disabilities contain useful sources on disability rights, including extensive bibliographies of books and periodicals, covering the personal, political, and professional (medical-legal-educational) aspects of disability: Michelle Fine and Adrienne Asch, eds., *Women with Disabilities: Essays in Psychology, Culture, and Politics* (Philadelphia: Temple University Press, 1988); Susan E. Browne, Debra Connors, and Nanci Stern, eds., *With the Power of Each Breath: A Disabled Women's Anthology* (Pittsburgh: Cleis Press, 1985); Gwyneth Ferguson Matthews, *Voices from the Shadows: Women with Disabilities Speak Out* (Toronto: Women's Educational Press, 1983); Mary Willmuth and Lillian Holcomb, eds., *Women with Disabilities: Found Voices* (New York: Haworth, 1993). For specific information about lesbians with disabilities, see *Sinister Wisdom* 39, "On Disability" (Winter 1989–90).

2. Laura Hershey, "False Advertising: Let's Stop Pity Campaigns for People with Disabilities," *Ms.* 5, 5 (March/April 1995): 96.

3. See in particular Joanna K. Weinberg, "Autonomy as a Different Voice: Women, Disabilities, and Decisions," in Fine and Asch, eds., pp. 269–96. This essay focuses on the rights of women with mental disabilities, including retardation and mental illness, to make decisions about their own lives, and extends the argument to all forms of physical and mental disability. On the various aspects of civil rights activism in the disability rights movement, see Marian Blackwell-Stratton, Mary Lou Breslin, Arlene Byrnne Mayerson, and Susan Bailey, "Smashing Icons: Disabled Women and the Disability and Women's Movements," in Fine and Asch, eds., pp. 306–32; Debra Connors, "Disability, Sexism, and the Social Order," in Browne, Connors, and Stern, eds., pp. 92–107; Anne Finger, "Claiming All of Our Bodies: Reproductive Rights and Disability," in Browne, Connors, and Stern, eds., pp. 292–307.

4. Hershey, p. 96.

5. One of the leading figures in educating the disabled, Samuel Gridley Howe, the founder of the first U.S. schools for the blind and for the mentally retarded, was also very active in Boston abolitionist circles and in prison reform; his

wife, Julia Ward Howe, was an active feminist as well, and his best friend, Horace Mann, is known for his advocacy of educational reform in the Massachusetts public school system.

6. My sister Sally chooses to refer to herself as mentally retarded or disabled. She does like to call her disability "Up Syndrome" to remove some of the negative connotations of its official title.

7. See Diane Price Herndl, *Invalid Women: Figuring Feminine Illness in American Fiction and Culture, 1840–1940* (Chapel Hill: University of North Carolina Press, 1993).

8. See Karen Sánchez-Eppler, *Touching Liberty: Abolition, Feminism, and the Politics of the Body* (Berkeley: University of California Press, 1993); Sánchez-Eppler, "Bodily Bonds: The Intersecting Rhetorics of Feminism and Abolition," in Shirley Samuels, ed., *The Culture of Sentiment: Race, Gender, and Sentimentality in Nineteenth-Century America* (New York: Oxford University Press, 1992), pp. 92–114; Laura Wexler, "Tender Violence: Literary Eavesdropping, Domestic Fiction, and Educational Reform," in Samuels, ed., pp. 9–38; Shirley Samuels, "The Identity of Slavery," in Samuels, ed., pp. 157–71; Joy Kasson, "Narratives of the Female Body: *The Greek Slave*," in Samuels, ed., pp. 172–90.

9. Samuels, "The Identity of Slavery," p. 160.

10. Gillian Brown, *Domestic Individualism: Imagining Self in Nineteenth-Century America* (Berkeley: University of California Press, 1990).

Chapter 1: The Semiotics of Disability

1. On explanations of disability as a kind of marking in premodern European culture, see Harry Best, *Blindness and the Blind in the United States* (New York: Macmillan, 1934); Merle E. Frampton and Hugh Grant Rowell, *Education of the Handicapped*, vol. 1, *History* (Yonkers-on-Hudson, N.Y.: World Book Co., 1938); Berthold Lowenfeld, *The Changing Status of the Blind: From Separation to Integration* (Springfield, Ill.: Charles C. Thomas, 1975).

2. On blindness as worse than death, see Sophocles, *Oedipus at Colonus*; Jacob Twersky, *Blindness in Literature: Examples of Depictions and Attitudes*, Research Series 3 (New York: American Foundation for the Blind Publications, 1955), pp. 15–17.

3. Old Testament references to the special treatment of the blind and deaf, linking their status to that of widows and orphans, appear in Exodus 22:21–24; Deuteronomy 24:17–18, 27:18; Leviticus 19:9–11, 23:22.

4. On Christ's treatment of the blind in particular, see Matthew 9:27–29, 20:30–34; Mark 8:22–25.

5. See Frampton and Rowell, pp. 14–15.

6. See Margret A. Winzer, *The History of Special Education: From Isolation to Integration* (Washington, D.C.: Gallaudet University Press, 1993), p. 58; Best, *Blindness* p. 303; Lowenfeld, p. 68; Frampton and Rowell. Haüy's account appears in his *Essai sur l'éducation des aveugles*, first published in Paris in 1786.

7. By far the best collection of essays on "freaks" is Rosemarie Garland Thomson, ed., *Freakery: Cultural Spectacles of the Extraordinary Body* (New York: New York

University Press, 1996). On the history of "freak shows" and other exhibitions of bodily exotics, see Leslie Fiedler, *Freaks: Myths and Images of the Secret Self* (New York: Simon and Schuster, 1978); Robert Bogdan, *Freak Show: Presenting Human Oddities for Amusement and Profit* (Chicago: University of Chicago Press, 1988). For a more theoretical approach to the meanings of bodily exoticism, see Susan Stewart, *On Longing: Narratives of the Miniature, the Gigantic, the Souvenir, the Collection* (Durham, N.C.: Duke University Press, 1994), esp. Chap. Four.

8. Robert Bogdan's concluding chapter, on the relation between freaks and contemporary notions of disability, asserts that the freaks existed as exhibits, as signs, within the particular signifying system of the carnival, wherein their signification produced income. Outside this context/system, these people were not freaks but existed merely as humans, not as exhibits to be consumed by audiences. In Bogdan's explanation, what was largely absent in both contexts or systems was the attitude of pity or pathos; the freak as sign did not signify suffering or misery, and the human offstage was not an object of sympathy. While Bogdan does not delve particularly into the relation between disability and pity, he does insist that the loss of status as freak and the reassignment of bodily variation to the category of disabled involved a loss of autonomy and self-respect. It is only with the invention of the "poster child" and the rhetoric of sentimentality and pity that surrounds it, Bogdan argues, that the freak show is seen as dehumanizing and repulsive.

9. Bogdan, p. 267.

10. See Winzer, p. 43; Frampton and Rowell, p. 25; Gabriel Farrell, *The Story of Blindness* (Cambridge, Mass: Harvard University Press, 1956), pp. 13–14; William R. Paulson, *Enlightenment, Romanticism, and the Blind in France* (Princeton, N.J.: Princeton University Press, 1987), pp. 10–12, 28–30.

11. *Diderot's Early Philosophical Works*, ed. and trans. Margaret Jourdain (London: Open Court Press, 1916), pp. 89–104.

12. Dugald Stewart, *Elements of the Philosophy of the Human Mind*, vol. 3 in *The Collected Works of Dugald Stewart*, ed. Sir William Hamilton (Edinburgh: Thomas Constable, 1854), p. 315.

13. Stewart, p. 320.

14. Stewart, p. 353.

15. Paulson, p. 30.

16. Paulson, p. 30.

17. Diderot, p. 147.

18. Diderot, p. 152.

19. Thomas Reid, *Essays on the Active Powers of the Human Mind* (1788), ed. Baruch Brody (Cambridge, Mass: MIT Press, 1969), p. 160.

20. Reid, p. 161.

21. In Reid's explanation, God had given every creature, including animals, the capacity to generate and comprehend these emotional signs. As with any capacity, according to Common Sense philosophy, proper training was necessary to develop the ability fully, and lack of such training would cause the capacity to atrophy and disappear. Hence Reid's "unlucky boy" failed to read the bird's signs because he had not been given enough practice at home.

22. Reid, p. 151.

23. See Reid, pp. 118–99.

24. The word "empathy," from the same Greek root as "sympathy," is a translation of the German word "einfühlung," coined in 1858 by philosopher Rudolf Lotze in his *Mikrokosmus* and defined as "the power of projecting one's personality into (and so fully comprehending) the object of contemplation." The word was first used in English in 1904. See the *Oxford English Dictionary*; Ernest Klein, *A Comprehensive Etymological Dictionary of the English Language* (New York: Elsevier, 1966), 1: 515; Eric Partridge, *Origins: A Short Etymological Dictionary of Modern English* (London: Routledge and Kegan Paul, 1958), pp. 181, 575.

25. Judith V. Jordan, "Empathy and the Mother-Daughter Relationship," in Jordan, Alexandra G. Kaplan, Jean Baker Miller, Irene P. Stiver, and Janet L. Surrey, eds., *Women's Growth in Connection: Writings from the Stone Center* (New York: Guilford Press, 1991), p. 28.

26. Many philosophers and theorists debated the extent of the connection between arbitrary language and bodily or physical experiences; the crux of these debates was the conception of the relation between sensory perception of objects and the words used to signify those objects. Rousseau's speculations about the origins of language represent an important part of these debates; for more on how the physicality of arbitrary language was articulated in practice in the education of the blind and deaf, see Chapter 6.

27. David Hume, *A Treatise of Human Nature* (1739–40), ed. L.A. Selby-Bigge and P. H. Nidditch (Oxford: Clarendon Press, 1978), p. 370.

28. Diderot, pp. 80, 81.

29. Diderot, p. 81.

30. He also extends this argument to the deaf, asking "How different would [the morality] of a deaf man likewise be from [that of a blind man]?" Diderot, p. 82.

31. Diderot, p. 82.

32. Diderot, pp. 147–148.

33. Stewart, p. 239.

34. Irving Lukoff and Martin Whiteman, "Attitudes and Blindness: Components, Correlates, and Effects," Vocational Rehabilitation Administration, U.S. Department of Health, Education, and Welfare, Grant No. 835s, 1963, quoted in Michael E. Monbeck, *The Meaning of Blindness: Attitudes Toward Blindness and Blind People* (Bloomington: Indiana University Press, 1973), p. 18.

35. Paulson, pp. 52–53.

Chapter 2: Institutional Meanings for Blind Bodies

1. See Harry Best, *Blindness and the Blind in the United States* (New York: Macmillan, 1934), pp. 216–318, esp. p. 306 and n.

2. The New England Asylum was renamed The Perkins Institution and Massachusetts Asylum for the Blind in 1840, in recognition of the funding granted by the state of Massachusetts and of the donation of his mansion by Col. Thomas H. Perkins. The word "Asylum" was replaced with "School" in 1876. I refer to the institution hereafter as the Perkins Institution.

3. Howe, initially assigned as a surgeon to field hospitals, eventually took over the distribution of relief to Greek refugees, building hospitals, schools, and towns and reorganizing agricultural production to support more people. He also served as a foreign correspondent for a Boston newspaper, describing the Greek war for a sympathetic American audience, which brought him to public attention. See Harold Schwartz, *Samuel Gridley Howe: Social Reformer, 1801–1876* (Cambridge, Mass.: Harvard University Press, 1956), pp. 7–38.

4. *Address of the Trustees of the New England Institution for the Education of the Blind* (Boston, 1833, reprinted 1873), p. 6.

5. Annual Report of the New England Asylum for the Blind, 1833, p. 7. Future references to the Annual Reports of the Perkins Institution, abbreviated as PR and year, will appear parenthetically in the text.

6. See Schwartz; Laura E. Richards, *Samuel Gridley Howe* (New York: Appleton-Century, 1935); S.G. Howe, *The Letters and Journals of Samuel Gridley Howe*, vol. 2, *The Servant of Humanity*, ed. Laura E. Richards (Boston: Dana Estes, 1909); Julia Ward Howe, *Memoir of Dr. Howe* (Boston: Albert J. Wright, 1876); *Proceedings at the Celebration of the One Hundredth Anniversary of the Birth of Dr. Samuel Gridley Howe, Nov. 11, 1901* (Boston: Wright and Potter Printing Co., 1902). Whittier's poem was entitled "The Hero"; Holmes's poem, written on the occasion of Howe's death, was "A Memorial Tribute."

7. See Herbert Stroup, *Social Welfare Pioneers* (Chicago: Nelson-Hall Publishers, 1986), pp. 147–72; Ronald G. Walters, *American Reformers, 1815–1860* (New York: Hill and Wang, 1978), p. 204; Schwartz, pp. 93–138, 147–238. Howe worked with Dorothea Dix in insane asylum reform, with close friend Horace Mann in education reform, and with Charles Sumner and Theodore Parker in abolition. He was one of the "secret six" who funded John Brown's raid on Harper's Ferry. He served on the U.S. Sanitary Commission during the Civil War and after the war was instrumental in organizing the American Social Science Association, the American Association of Instructors of the Blind, and the Massachusetts Board of State Charity. Like many reformers, Howe believed in hydropathy, phrenology, and diet reforms, and put these beliefs into practice in his schools and his family.

8. John L. Thomas, "Romantic Reform in America, 1815–1865," in David Brion Davis, ed., *Ante-Bellum Reform* (New York: Harper and Row, 1967), pp. 162–63.

9. See Thomas, pp. 153–76; Stroup, pp. 147–72.

10. Samuel Gridley Howe, "The Education of the Blind," *New England Magazine*, March 1833, p. 1.

11. Howe, "Education," p. 1.

12. It is worth noting that Howe's plan for integrating the blind into mainstream society according to their ability to perform intellectual or manual labor anticipates the debates between W.E.B. DuBois and Booker T. Washington about the proper means for integrating freed slaves into mainstream white-dominated culture. Like any disenfranchised group, the blind would need to prove that the majority were capable of self-support at a basic level, while an elite few proved themselves capable of competing with the most talented in the dominant culture.

13. The gendered pronoun here and below indicates Howe's dilemma over

what to do with his female blind students. He trained them in domestic skills as well as in intellectual pursuits, but he expected that all female graduates of his institution would be able to return to family or friends, and would no more have to work for their livings than the average sighted middle-class white woman. As the number of working-class and especially immigrant (Irish) blind female students grew throughout the 1840s and '50s, Howe repeatedly tried to find ways to train blind women in gender-appropriate tasks through which they could support themselves; in addition to knitting, sewing, cleaning, and cooking, Howe's curriculum attempted to train girls to work as domestic servants or in laundries. His efforts here met with no more success than his efforts to train blind men to support themselves through manufacturing, and he continued to have to rely on family and charity networks for assistance for his blind women graduates.

14. See Chapter 1. For more on antebellum theories of language, see Michael P. Kramer, "The Study of Language and the American Renaissance: An Essay in Literary Historiography," Part One, *Emerson Society Quarterly* 34, 3 (1988): 207–27; Part Two, 34, 4 (1988): 282–307. My thanks to Marty Bickman for pointing this article out to me.

15. Howe's theories of language were articulated in most detail in his Reports of the education of deaf-blind Laura Bridgman, which are addressed in Chapter 6. Because deafness was figured as primarily a linguistic problem, the most extensive accounts of the relations between disability and language use can be found in the Reports of institutions and schools for the deaf, such as the American Asylum for the Deaf.

16. See, for example, Karen Sánchez-Eppler, "Bodily Bonds: The Intersecting Rhetorics of Feminism and Abolition," in Shirley Samuels, ed., *The Culture of Sentiment* (New York: Oxford University Press, 1992), pp. 92–114.

17. The idea that all intellectual, moral, and emotional processes had their roots in some physical organ in the brain comes from the pseudo-science of phrenology, which was widely popular in the United States at the time. Howe, like Horace Mann and many other reformers, was a staunch devotee of phrenology, having learned about it as a physician in the period before phrenology became part of popular culture and was marketed by the enterprising Fowler Brothers and others. All Howe's views on reform, and particularly his ideas about the education of the blind, were based on phrenological principles. On phrenology in general, see John Dudley Davies, *Phrenology: Fad and Science; A 19th-Century American Crusade* (New Haven, Conn.: Yale University Press, 1955); on phrenology in Boston, see Anthony A. Walsh, "Phrenology and the Boston Medical Community in the 1830s," *Bulletin of the History of Medicine* 50, 2 (1976): 261–73 and Robert E. Riegel, "The Introduction of Phrenology to the United States," *American Historical Review* 39 (1933–34): 73–78. On Howe and phrenology, see Harold Schwartz, "Samuel Gridley Howe as Phrenologist," *American Historical Review* 57 (1951–52): 644–51.

18. Howe is recognized as the pioneer in developing the cottage system of institutional life, which had become the predominant mode of institutional organization by the beginning of the twentieth century. Planned in the 1850s but not implemented until the 1870s, the system was meant to rectify the many ills of congregate living by providing blind students (and, by extension, the inhabitants of

any large institution, educational or not) with a substitute for family life. Rather than having large numbers of students in dormitories, governed by strict rules and surveillance, Howe and the Perkins Trustees agreed that cottages, where students would live in small numbers with a matron, would provide a more effective means to separate the sexes, eliminate vice, and classify and group students according to ability. The rhetoric in the Annual Reports detailing the desirability of establishing the cottage system, however, focuses on portraying the cottages as a reproduction of family life — presumably because the matron would serve as "mother." This model, of course, assumes an absent father, framing domestic life as purely the concern of women and children. Accounts of the cottage plan can be found in the Annual Reports from 1850 on; the most extensive descriptions are in the Reports for 1866, 1868, 1869, and 1870.

Chapter 3: Sentimental Posters

1. Charles Dickens, *Barnaby Rudge* (New York: Penguin Books, 1980), p. 421. Cited hereafter in the text as *BR*.

2. Charles Dickens, "A Christmas Carol," in *The Christmas Books*, vol. 1 (New York: Penguin Books, 1971). Cited hereafter in the text as *CC*.

3. I use the gendered pronoun purposefully here, as the characters who are shown undergoing this transformation — or needing to undergo this transformation — are usually male in sentimental fiction. Women, as bearers of womanly, and usually maternal, sensibilities, usually need no such (re)education in the powers of empathy.

4. Dinah Mulock Craik, *John Halifax, Gentleman* (New York: E. P. Dutton & Co., 1906, rpt. Of 1856 edition). Cited hereafter in the text as *JH*. I am using the definitions of "best seller" provided in James D. Hart's *The Popular Book: A History of America's Literary Tastes* (Berkeley: University of California Press, 1950) and Frank Luther Mott's *Golden Multitudes* (New York: Macmillan, 1947). Mott lists *John Halifax, Gentleman* as an overall best seller, representing sales to more than 1 percent of the total U.S. population in its year of publication. Mott ranks Craik with Susan Warner, Maria Cummins, Harriet Beecher Stowe, E.D.E.N. Southworth, Charles Dickens, and T. S. Arthur as among the most popular authors in mid-century U.S. culture. He notes that (due to the laxity of international copyright laws) mid-century readers could choose from over a dozen different editions, the cheapest of which cost a dime. "Despite its English setting, readers on this side of the Atlantic thought it highly American in its insistence on the importance of middle-class ideas and on the success theme" (Mott, p. 133).

5. See Cathy Davidson, *Revolution and the Word: The Rise of the Novel in America* (New York: Oxford University Press, 1986), pp. 110–50.

6. Davidson, pp. 137–39.

7. Edward Bulwer-Lytton's novel *The Last Days of Pompeii* (1834; reprint New York: Dodd, Mead, 1946) offers a different inscription of the relation between disability and female sexuality by shifting, in mid-novel, his characterization of Nydia, a blind slave girl, from that of sentimental girl heroine, who functions as

"poster," to that of sexually desiring female who functions as a threat to existing social relations.

As a slave, Nydia is the opposite of the sentimental blind heroine: described as angry and passionate, she is "erring, unwomanly, frenzied," and governed by "un-controlled, unmodified passion" (p. 231). As Bulwer-Lytton details the depths of Nydia's slave-based passions, directed toward her master Glaucus (and in hatred against Glaucus's love, Ione), he also shifts the meaning of her blindness. Rather than making others feel for her affliction, her blindness, coupled with her un-womanly passions, estranges her from sighted others. As Nydia plays a love song, the narrator describes her eyes as incomprehensible and alien:

you could never familiarize yourself to their aspect: so strange did it seem that those dark wild orbs were ignorant of the day, and either so fixed was their deep mysterious gaze, or so restless and perturbed their glance, that you felt, when you encountered them, that same vague, and chilling, and half-preternatural impression, which comes over you in the presence of the insane, — of those who, having a life outwardly like your own, have a life in life — dissimilar — unsearchable — unguessed! (p. 135)

This portrayal of Nydia as other, as alien, due to her blindness, prevents readers from any kind of empathic identification with her; that this portrayal appears at precisely the point where readers are told of Nydia's passionate love for Glaucus reinforces Bulwer-Lytton's portrait of her as an anti-sentimental character, marked by both strangeness (rather than similarity) and sexual desire (rather than self-sacrifice). When the threat of Nydia becoming a fully sexual being becomes the center of the narrative, her blindness is reinscribed as alienating, and readers are thus encouraged to distance themselves further from her dangerous passions.

8. Charles Dickens, "The Cricket on the Hearth," in *The Christmas Books*, vol. 2 (New York: Penguin Books, 1971), pp. 9–120.

Chapter 4: The Angel in the Text

1. Maria Susanna Cummins, *The Lamplighter* (New Brunswick, N. J.: Rutgers University Press, 1988; reprint of 1854 edition). Cited hereafter in the text as *TL*.

2. Howe articulates these views about language frequently in his discussions of teaching blind and deaf-blind children to read; he makes his arguments about the civilized status of arbitrary language most forcefully in his writings about deaf-mutes, where he advocates teaching them oral speech rather than sign language. On arbitrary language in the education of the blind and deaf-blind, see PR 1842, 19–22; PR 1843, 25–28; PR 1847, 11–12, 24–25, 34–36; PR 1850, 47–48, 69–77. On gestural versus arbitrary language for deaf-mutes, see Howe, "Remarks Upon the Education of Deaf Mutes" (Boston, 1866).

3. Howe's work with deaf-blind Laura Bridgman will be discussed in more detail in Chapter 6.

4. See also Karen Sánchez-Eppler's discussion of the physicality of reading sentimental fiction in "Bodily Bonds: The Intersecting Rhetorics of Feminism and

Abolition," in Shirley Samuels, ed., *The Culture of Sentiment: Race, Gender, and Sentimentality in Nineteenth-Century America* (New York: Oxford University Press, 1992), p. 99; also Sánchez-Eppler, *Touching Liberty: Abolition, Feminism, and the Politics of the Body* (Berkeley: University of California Press, 1993).

5. Nina Baym cites *The Lamplighter* in particular as having all the characteristics that typify the genre of sentimental fiction. Baym takes Susan Warner's *The Wide Wide World*, however, as the archetypal sentimental novel, and thus reads Cummins's work as a rewriting, or misreading, of Warner. See Nina Baym, *Woman's Fiction: A Guide to Novels By and About Women in America, 1820–1870* (Ithaca, N.Y.: Cornell University Press, 1978).

6. See Carol Zosowitz Stearns and Peter N. Stearns, *Anger: The Struggle for Emotional Control in America's History* (Chicago: University of Chicago Press, 1986), pp. 36–37.

7. His grandfather, by contrast, is described as having "a want of sympathy" for others' cares — a sure sign, in sentimental logic, that his character is flawed (*TL*, 38).

8. This explanation offers a rebuttal to Philip Fisher's assertion, in *Hard Facts*, that tears are the sign of helplessness and powerlessness, marking readers' inability to affect action in the text. In sentimental logic, "feeling right" was a form of action, the basis of all action, as Jane Tompkins points out in *Sensational Designs*, rather than the inability to act. See Fisher, *Hard Facts: Setting and Form in the American Novel* (New York: Oxford University Press, 1985), p. 105; Tompkins, *Sensational Designs: The Cultural Work of American Fiction, 1790–1860* (New York: Oxford University Press, 1985), p. 133.

9. Cummins does raise these questions at the very end of the novel, when Emily's long-lost suitor, who had wanted to marry her before her blindness, returns and proposes to her. Unlike other sentimental novelists, Cummins does not kill off her blind heroine when she is faced with the problem of sexual reproduction; rather, Cummins allows the two to marry, but ends the novel before the question of children can arise to complicate her nonmaternal model of empathic adulthood.

10. See Raymond Williams, *The Country and the City* (New York: Oxford University Press, 1973); Fred Kaplan, *Sacred Tears: Sentimentality in Victorian Literature* (Princeton, N. J.: Princeton University Press, 1987); Janet Todd, *Sensibility: An Introduction* (London and New York: Methuen, 1986).

11. With, of course, the exception of Nan Grant.

Chapter 5: Institutional Sentimentalism

1. After the mid-1850s, Howe became less involved in the daily operations of the Perkins Institution for the Blind, as he turned his attention toward exploring the education of the mentally retarded and, increasingly, toward questions concerning abolition. The Annual Reports from 1853 through the end of Howe's tenure as director at his death in 1876 are perfunctory accounts of financial and curricular arrangements; the voluminous "Director's Reports," which had contained both the statistical analyses and the sentimental portrayals of the students, disappeared.

2. The question of consciousness must arise in this characterization of Howe's

use of sentimental tropes: to what degree might Howe have employed sentimental rhetoric consciously, being aware of the effect it would have on his audience? Given that his letters and journals frequently expressed a dislike for sentimentalism, and that he worked actively to prevent his wife, Julia Ward Howe, from the public display of emotions the publication of her poetry would provide, it is likely that Howe would have been appalled to realize how much sentimentalism pervades his Reports. In my opinion, Howe's use of sentimental tropes testifies to the pervasiveness of sentimentalism in all aspects of mid-nineteenth-century American middle-class culture. Consciously or unconsciously, Howe used the assumptions, language, and scenarios available in the culture at large to express and represent Christian beliefs, domestic feelings, and the "tender" emotions in general. Sentimental rhetoric formed virtually the only vocabulary in which such topics could be articulated, and Howe, like most other writers addressing the general public of that time, automatically employed the tropes most readily at hand, which the greatest number of readers would find familiar.

3. See Julia Ward Howe, *Memoir of Dr. Samuel Gridley Howe* (Boston: Albert J. Wright, 1876), pp. 19–21.

4. Howe to Mann, 27 March 1842, cited in Harold Schwartz, *Samuel Gridley Howe: Social Reformer, 1801–1876* (Cambridge, Mass: Harvard University Press, 1956), p. 65; emphasis original.

5. For examples of Howe's diatribes against the dangers of maternal over-protectiveness, see PR 1841, 5–6, 8–9; 1847, 5.

6. See PR 1834, 16; 1837, 12; 1846, 48.

7. See Larzer Ziff, *Writing in the New Nation: Prose, Print, and Politics in the Early United States* (New Haven, Conn.: Yale University Press, 1991), and Thomas Haskell, *The Emergence of Professional Social Science: The American Social Science Association and the Nineteenth-Century Crisis of Authority* (Urbana: University of Illinois Press, 1977).

8. Harry Best, *Blindness and the Blind in the United States* (New York: Macmillan, 1934), p. 313.

9. There is, of course, a poststructuralist irony involved in contrasting Howe's written accounts of the workings of the school with the live exhibitions he staged, and that is the fact that the descriptions of the exhibitions appear in the written accounts themselves. One hundred and fifty years later, we have only Howe's portrayals and those of other visitors from the time who recorded their observations of the blind students to reconstruct the actual exhibitions. Thus the distinction between the exhibitions as experiential events and as (re)produced in written accounts is perhaps moot. However, there is no reason to doubt that the exhibitions did in fact occur, as corroborating evidence from visitors confirms; the question at hand is not whether there is a concrete historical referent to which the written descriptions refer, but rather how those written descriptions gave shape and meaning to the live events. We cannot know how audience members responded to the exhibitions apart from the feelings they recorded, or from Howe's admonishments to his readership as to how they ought to respond to the "spectacle" he presented. What is under examination here is Howe's narrative, in which he imagined an audience with a certain set of expected responses, and which he used to rewrite those responses, prompting his imagined audience to "read" the exhibitions differently.

10. Elizabeth Palmer Peabody, letter to Julia Ward Howe, cited in J. W. Howe, *Memoir of Dr. Howe*, p. 18.

Chapter 6: Laura Bridgman

1. One of the first educators of the blind in the eighteenth century, the Abbé de l'Épee, had suggested a potential course of education that would reach a person both deaf and blind, but had not found a subject on whom to test his theories. Scottish Common Sense philosopher Dugald Stewart had observed and written about deaf-blind James Mitchell at the end of the eighteenth century; he reported on his gestural language and his mental characteristics and suggested a possible course of education for the boy, but did not undertake the task. The first recorded attempt to educate a deaf-blind person came in 1825, when Julia Brace entered the Hartford Asylum for the Deaf and Dumb at age eighteen. Teachers there expanded on Brace's existing system of gestural signs, but did not make any attempt to teach her arbitrary (alphabetic) language via the manual alphabet, vocal speech, or writing. Given the emphasis placed in the latter half of the nineteenth century on teaching deaf people to use "normal" arbitrary language rather than gestural signs, Brace's education was not counted a "success" in the annals of the education of deaf and deaf-blind people.

The term "deaf-blind," widely used to designate people who are both deaf and blind, emphasizes blindness as the primary condition, with deafness as the qualifier; this usage stems largely from the fact that institutions for the blind, particularly the Perkins Institution, were the recognized pioneers in educating blind and deaf people. Thus Laura Bridgman and later Helen Keller were designated as "deaf-blind," except in some publications of institutions for the deaf, where they were called "blind-deaf."

2. There are two main sources of information on Laura Bridgman. The most extensive and detailed accounts appear in the Annual Reports of the Perkins Institution from 1838 through 1850, when Howe worked most closely with Bridgman; summaries of these accounts also appeared in Howe's last Annual Report, in 1874, and in the Annual Report for 1889, the year of Bridgman's death. The 1889 Report, written by Michael Anagnos, who succeeded Howe as director of Perkins, was reprinted in 1893 with the title *The Education of Laura D. Bridgman*; further references to this volume will appear in the text as *ELB*. The original Perkins Annual Reports and their reprints form the basis for virtually all other accounts of Bridgman's life and education, including *Laura Bridgman: Dr. Howe's Famous Pupil and What He Taught Her* (Boston: Little, Brown, 1904), the biography of Bridgman written by Howe's daughters, Maud Howe and Florence Howe Hall.

The second main source is *The Life and Education of Laura Dewey Bridgman: The Deaf, Dumb, and Blind Girl* (Boston: Houghton, 1878), written by her former teacher, Mary Swift Lamson, and published two years after Howe's death. Lamson's account differs significantly from Howe's, as Lamson and Howe disagreed over many aspects of Bridgman's education, particularly regarding her religious training. Howe eventually dismissed Lamson as Bridgman's primary teacher and caregiver as a result of these disagreements. Not willing to challenge directly the words of the world-renowned pioneer in the education of the blind and deaf-blind, Lamson waited until after Howe's death to publish her version, which was based on her journals and her recollections of her work with Bridgman. Lamson worked with Bridgman day in and day out, implementing the theories Howe originated; her accounts of Bridgman's education focus on their painstaking daily routine rather than on the triumphant moments, as do Howe's descriptions.

My argument here focuses almost exclusively on Howe's accounts as the more widely read and influential of the two; I concentrate on the ways Howe's reports shaped cultural beliefs and assumptions about disability rather than on the accuracy or veracity of either account of Bridgman's education.

3. Howe and Hall, p. 38.

4. Julia Ward Howe, introduction to *ELB*, p. 4.

5. Howe and Hall, p. 56.

6. Lamson, pp. 46–47.

7. Sumner and Longfellow were close friends of Howe. During this visit to the Perkins Institution, they introduced Julia Ward to Howe; the two were married two years later, in April 1843.

8. Charles Dickens, *American Notes and Pictures from Italy* (New York: Oxford University Press, 1957, rpt. 1987), pp. 31–32.

9. Dickens, *American Notes*, p. 32, 40.

10. Dickens, *American Notes*, pp. 40–41.

11. Dickens, *American Notes*, p. 32.

12. Dickens, *American Notes*, p. 32.

13. As a proper Victorian residential school, the Perkins Institution was sex-segregated; the boys and male teachers lived in one part of the school and the girls and female teachers in another. Classes on intellectual matters were for the most part coeducational; classes on manual skills, deemed gender-specific, were segregated. Bridgman, who worked only with her private teachers and with Howe, lived exclusively in the female wing of the institution; though she had contact with male teachers and students, the vast majority of her social interactions came with the female residents of the school.

14. Nellie Bly, "Deaf, Dumb, and Blind," *New York World*, 17 February 1889, n. pag. (Perkins Archives).

15. Caswell never attracted the national and international attention Bridgman did, in part because Bridgman's education came first and represented the pioneering innovation and triumph, while Caswell's was just a repetition of a method proven successful. Because he commenced his education later than Bridgman, and perhaps because of gender differences in language acquisition and usage, he never became as fluent in arbitrary language as Bridgman did; Howe describes Caswell as being altogether of a more stolid and less lively temperament than Bridgman as well. Similarly, as a boy, Caswell's plight as doubly "imprisoned" was less pathetic than Bridgman's, whose status as sentimental heroine was overdetermined by her disabilities, her gender, her age, and her prettiness, and thus he did not attract the media attention Bridgman did.

16. I have not yet been able satisfactorily to trace the origin of this picture or the painter; a reproduction of it appears in the 1889 Annual Report and in the reprinted version.

17. Laura E. Richards, *Samuel Gridley Howe* (New York: Appleton-Century, 1935), p. 104.

18. Richards, pp. 104–5.

19. *Letters and Journals of Samuel Gridley Howe*, vol. 2, *The Servant of Humanity*, ed. Laura E. Richards (Boston: Dana Estes & Co., 1909), p. 126. See also Julia Ward Howe, *Reminiscences, 1819–1899* (Boston: Houghton, 1899); Richards, *Samuel Gridley Howe*.

20. See David Marshall, *The Surprising Effects of Sympathy: Marivaux, Diderot, Rousseau, and Mary Shelley* (Chicago: University of Chicago Press, 1988) for a discussion of how the interaction between spectator and spectacle operates in sentimental theatrical conventions.

21. Dickens, *American Notes*, p.42.

22. Letter from Howe to Dickens, 18 May 1868, Perkins Archives.

23. Elizabeth Gitter, "Laura Bridgman and Little Nell," *Dickens Quarterly* 8, 2 (June 1991): 76.

24. Gitter, p. 77.

25. Laura Mulvey, "Visual Pleasure and Narrative Cinema," *Screen* 16, 3 (1975): 7; see also Gitter, p. 77.

26. For a more detailed account of Howe's problems with Bridgman's religious education, see Klages, " 'More Wonderful Than Any Fiction': The Representation of Helen Keller", Ph.D. dissertation, Stanford University, 1989, pp. 292–311.

27. For Howe's own extensive commentary on the nature of language and the problems faced by blind people in becoming competent language users, see PR 1842, 20–22; 1843, 32–33; 1847, 11–13, 35–37;1850, 68–77. For how this view of language affected Bridgman directly, see Klages, pp. 272–81.

28. More extensive excerpts from Bridgman's diaries can be found in Lamson.

29. Excerpts from this autobiography appear in Lamson.

Chapter 7: Can the Blind Girl Speak?

1. My own collection of nineteenth-century American writings by blind people currently includes four autobiographical volumes: Mrs. S. Helen deKroyft, *A Place in Thy Memory* (1849; reprint New York: John F. Trow, 1864; cited hereafter in the text as deKroyft), Mary L. Day, *Incidents in the Life of a Blind Girl* (Baltimore: James Young, 1859; cited hereafter in the text as Day), J. M. Dixon, *The Valley and the Shadow: Comprising the Experiences of a Blind Ex-Editor* (New York: Russell Brothers Publishers, 1868), and William Artman and L. V. Hall, *The Beauties and Achievements of the Blind* (Auburn, N.Y.: Miller, Orton, and Mulligan, 1854). The last-named volume contains several biographies of blind people, as well as references to other publications, including poetry, autobiography, and essays by blind authors.

2. There is, of course, a strong connection between sentimental representations and slave narratives; see Philip Fisher, *Hard Facts: Setting and Form in the American Novel* (New York: Oxford University Press, 1985); Karen Sánchez-Eppler, "Bodily Bonds: The Intersecting Rhetorics of Feminism and Abolition," in Shirley Samuels, ed., *The Culture of Sentiment: Race, Gender, and Sentimental-*

ity in Nineteenth-Century America (New York: Oxford University Press, 1992), pp. 92–114; Shirley Samuels, "The Identity of Slavery," in Samuels, ed., pp. 157–71; and Harryette Mullen, "Runaway Tongue: Resistant Orality in *Uncle Tom's Cabin, Our Nig, Incidents in the Life of a Slave Girl,* and *Beloved*," in Samuels, ed., pp. 244–64.

3. The examples of autobiographical writings I have found are all from people who lost their sight due to accident or illness as adolescents or adults, and who thus were already "native speakers" when they became blind. They thus cannot confirm or refute Samuel Gridley Howe's doubts about whether a person born blind could ever become an effective writer or use language on an equal basis with a sighted person.

4. Harriet Wilson, *Our Nig; or, Sketches from the Life of a Free Black, in a Two-Story House, North, Showing That Slavery's Shadows Fall Even There* (1859; reprint New York: Vintage, 1983).

5. Harriet Jacobs, *Incidents in the Life of a Slave Girl: Written by Herself,* ed. Jean Fagan Yellin (Cambridge, Mass.: Harvard University Press, 1987). The title "Incidents in the Life of . . ." was in fairly common use during the nineteenth century for all manner of autobiographical accounts. A quick search by title through the Library of Congress online catalog uncovered some 97 volumes published between 1800 and 1890. These included the "Incidents in the Life of" a pastor, a sailor, a soldier, an Italian, Jenny Lind, Our Savior, Timothy Dwight, and William Henry Harrison, in addition to Jacobs's better-known work. Day's autobiography, to judge from this list, appeared in several editions, under the name Mary L. Day and under her married name, Mary L. Arms. The first edition was published in 1859; a fifth edition is dated 1860.

6. See James Olney, "'I Was Born': Slave Narratives, Their Status as Autobiography and as Literature" in Charles T. Davis and Henry Louis Gates, Jr., eds., *The Slave's Narrative* (Oxford: Oxford University Press, 1985), pp. 152–53.

7. See Olney, p. 150.

8. Olney, p. 155.

9. Henry Louis Gates, Jr., introduction to Wilson, *Our Nig.*

10. Diane Price Herndl, *Invalid Women: Figuring Feminine Illness in American Fiction and Culture, 1840–1940* (Chapel Hill: University of North Carolina Press, 1993), p. 51.

11. Herndl, 53.

12. On the Gothic elements of Wilson's novel, see Julia Stern, "Excavating Genre in *Our Nig*," *American Literature* 67, 3 (September, 1995): 439–59. On the novel's relation to sentimental fiction and to slave narratives, see in particular Gates; Hazel Carby, *Reconstructing Womanhood: The Emergence of the Afro-American Woman Novelist* (New York: Oxford University Press, 1987), pp. 43–45; Kari J. Winter, *Subjects of Slavery, Agents of Change: Women and Power in Gothic Novels and Slave Narratives, 1790–1865* (Athens: University of Georgia Press, 1992).

13. Without further explanation, it is impossible to know anything about who "deaf Maggie" was, but, given that she seems to have been in residence at the school for the blind, it is possible that she was both blind and deaf, which would explain some of deKroyft's frustrations with her "senseless gibberings."

Chapter 8: Helen Keller

1. Mrs. Bernard Whitman, "Helen Keller," *Lend a Hand Magazine*, April 1889: 289.

2. Whitman, 289.

3. Florence Howe Hall, "Helen Keller," *St. Nicholas*, September 1889: 838.

4. Hall, 838.

5. Hall, 838.

6. Hall, 838.

7. See Mrs. S. Helen deKroyft, *Little Jakey* (New York: Hurd and Houghton, 1872).

8. Sallie Joy White, "The Story of Helen Keller," *Wide Awake*, July 1888: 79–80.

9. "Miracles of Today," *Lend a Hand Magazine*, May 1893: 358.

10. At his death, Howe was respected as the foremost social scientist in the United States. In addition to his work with the blind, deaf-blind, and idiotic, his prison reform work, and his abolitionist efforts, Howe had founded and presided over the first professional organization for people who worked with disabled populations, the American Association of Instructors of the Blind. During the Civil War he had headed a branch of the U.S. Sanitary Commission; after the war he had served as the chair of the Massachusetts Board of State Charities, and had been influential in the formation of the American Social Science Association. See Harold Schwartz, *Samuel Gridley Howe: Social Reformer, 1801–1876* (Cambridge, Mass.: Harvard University Press, 1956), pp. 254–76. Anagnos, by contrast, had a degree in classical Greek literature; he began to work as a teacher at Perkins after marrying Julia and became Howe's successor more or less by default, as Howe's other activities drew his attention away from the daily routines of Perkins.

11. See Leslie Fiedler, *Love and Death in the American Novel* (New York: Dell, 1966).

12. Martha Finlay, *Elsie Dinsmore* (1867; reprint New York: Dodd, Mead & Co., 1893); Sarah Chauncey Woolsey (Susan Coolidge), *What Katy Did* (1872; reprint London: Andrew Dakers, Ltd., n.d.); Margaret Sidney, *The Five Little Peppers and How They Grew* (1881; reprint Boston: Lothrop, Lee, and Shepard, 1909); Frances Hodgson Burnett, *Little Lord Fauntleroy* (1886; reprint New York: Charles Scribners' Sons, 1890); Kate Douglas Wiggin, *The Birds' Christmas Carol* (1887; reprint Boston: Houghton Mifflin, 1914); Alice Hegan Rice, *Mrs. Wiggs of the Cabbage Patch* (1901; reprint Racine, Wis.: Whitman, 1962); Eleanor Porter, *Pollyanna* (1913; reprint New York: Dell, 1986).

13. Coolidge, pp. 128–29.

14. Coolidge, pp. 198–99.

15. Finlay, pp. 36–37.

16. Sidney, pp. 12, 20.

17. Rice, p. 138.

18. Porter, p. 38.

19. See John E. Bassett, *"A Heart of Ideality in My Realism" and Other Essays on Howells and Twain* (West Cornwall, Conn.: Locust Hill Press, 1991), esp. p. 20. The reference comes from a letter from Howells to Edmund Clarence Stedman in 1878.

20. This is apparent in Twain's reaction to Keller's 1891 "trial" for plagiarism while at Perkins. Keller had written a story, "The Frost King," thinking it was original, and Anagnos had published it as such. The story turned out to be a copy of a work that had been read to Keller. Anagnos defended his wounded authority by holding a mock "trial" of Keller, complete with a jury of 6 sighted and 6 blind Perkins residents. Twain's comments on this trial, and the trauma and doubt it created for Keller, point out that everything one writes or says is borrowed from somewhere else. See Joseph Lash, *Helen and Teacher: The Story of Helen Keller and Anne Sullivan Macy* (New York: Delta Books, 1980), pp. 154–55.

21. Lash, 321.

22. Louisa May Alcott, "The Blind Lark," *St. Nicholas*, November 1886: 12.

23. Alcott, 14.

24. Alcott, 17.

25. Alcott, 19.

26. Alcott, 19.

27. Anagnos raises no doubts or questions about Keller's capacity for genuine empathic action, unlike Samuel Gridley Howe's suspicions about Laura Bridgman. Anagnos's certainty must be attributed in large part to the reinforcement offered by "good good girl fiction," as these stories left no room for questioning the efficacy of pain and sorrow as routes to selflessness; it may also be due to the thoroughness with which Keller embodied and modeled the empathic traits she had learned in reading such stories.

28. "Miracles of Today," 359.

29. William T. Ellis, "Helen Keller and Tommy Stringer," *St. Nicholas*, October 1897: 997.

30. Ellis, 997.

31. Ellis, 997.

32. It is worth noting that Keller limited herself to "factual" genres of writing, particularly autobiography and essays, because of the doubts that had been raised about her language usage during the "Frost King" plagiarism trial. This incident, and the uproar it produced about the truthfulness of Anagnos's accounts and about Keller's linguistic abilities, are fully described in both Keller's *The Story of My Life* (1903; reprint New York: Dell, 1974) and Joseph Lash's biography *Helen and Teacher* (New York: Delta, 1980). The incident shattered Keller's faith in her own ability to write about the world in her own terms, without using language supplied by books she had read. After this incident, Keller never wrote another piece of fiction; she confined herself to writing about what she could know directly, through her own experiences, and even then worried constantly that her words had come from sources she had read but forgotten. Her choice to write only "factual" prose illustrates once again the conflict between the denominational view of language, in which one can use words authoritatively only when one has a direct experience of the things the words represent, and the poststructuralist view of language, which recognizes that words derive meaning from being part of a system of language. In the former view, Keller, who could not know most objects or experiences directly, due to her sensory deprivations, is an illegitimate language user, one who could only

steal others' words for sensory experiences. In the latter view, Keller uses language like everyone else, as a member of a linguistic community who does not need to verify the meaning of a word through individual experience.

33. On Keller's Arnoldian aesthetic education, see Klages, "'More Wonderful Than Any Fiction': The Representation of Helen Keller," Ph.D. dissertation, Stanford University, 1989, pp. 61–138.

34. Lash, p. 278.

35. Lash, p. 278.

36. "Helen Keller's *Story of My Life*," *Atlantic Monthly*, June 1903: 842–43.

37. "Helen Keller's *Story of My Life*," 842.

38. "Miss Keller's Autobiography," *The Independent*, 30 April 1903: 1033–34.

39. "Miss Keller's Autobiography": 1034.

40. "Miss Keller's Autobiography": 1034.

41. Nella Braddy, *Anne Sullivan Macy: The Story Behind Helen Keller* (New York: Doubleday, 1933), p. 201.

42. Braddy, pp. 201–2.

43. John Macy eventually married Keller's companion Anne Sullivan; their stormy marriage lasted some fourteen years. For details, see Lash. Macy became a noted literary critic in the 1920s.

44. John Albert Macy, "Helen Keller's Critics," *Boston Transcript*, 27 May 1903: n.pag. Perkins Archives.

45. Macy, "Critics."

46. Thomas Cutsforth, *The Blind in School and Society: A Psychological Study* (1933; reprint New York: American Foundation for the Blind, 1951), p. 52.

47. For a dissenting view on Keller's sexuality, see Dorothy Herrmann, *Helen Keller: A Life* (New York: Knopf, 1998).

48. For a discussion of Keller's cultural significance as "saint," see Klages, "'More Wonderful Than Any Fiction,'" pp. 232–38.

49. Helen Keller, *Midstream: My Later Life* (New York: Doubleday, 1929), p. 134.

Chapter 9: Redefining Disability and Sentimentality

1. William Gibson, *The Miracle Worker* (New York: Knopf, 1957). Gibson's work was first produced on television's *Playhouse 90* in 1957; it opened as a Broadway play in 1959, and appeared as an Academy-Award-winning film in 1961.

2. The movie follows the script of the play with some minor variations; for ease of citation, I will refer primarily to the playscript published in 1957.

3. Critics who approved of the play's lack of sentimentality included Brooks Atkinson, in "'Miracle Worker': Two Strong Minds and Two Strong Players," *New York Times*, 1 November 1959, Sec. II: 1 and "Theatre: Giver of Light," *New York Times*, 18 October 1959, Sec. II: 1; Kenneth Tynan, "Ireland Unvanquished," *New Yorker*, 35, 31 October 1959: 133; and Robert Brustein, "Two for the Miracle," *New Republic*, 9 November 1959: 28. Critics who were shocked by the play's unsentimen-

tal attitude included Richard Hayes, "Images," *Commonweal* 71, 4 December 1959: 289; and Henry Hewes, "The Miracle of Work," *Saturday Review*, 7 November 1959: 28. Virtually all reviews discussed the question of sentimentality in depicting disability; see also Nan Robertson, "Broadway Slugging Match," *New York Times*, 20 December 1959, Sec. II: 5; "A Hit at 10," *Newsweek*, 2 November 1959: 97; "Who Is Stanislavsky?" *Time*, 21 December 1959: 47; "New Plays on Broadway," *Time*, 2 November 1959: 30.

4. Hayes, p. 289.

5. Tynan, p. 134.

6. Atkinson, "Theatre," p. 1.

7. Atkinson, "Theatre," p. 1.

8. Hewes, p. 28.

9. Such warnings about the dangers of maternal love to handicapped children were not new to the twentieth century; from his earliest public reports on the education of blind children Samuel Gridley Howe urged parents, especially mothers, to treat their blind children exactly as they did their sighted offspring, allowing them to explore their world freely.

10. "New Plays on Broadway," *Time*, 2 November 1959: 30.

11. Joseph Lash, *Helen and Teacher: The Story of Helen Keller and Anne Sullivan Macy* (New York: Delta Books, 1980), p. 56.

12. Lash, p. 56.

13. William Gibson, *The Miracle Worker and Monday After the Miracle* (Garden City, N.Y.: Doubleday, 1983), pp. 113–14. The *Playhouse 90* version, unlike the Broadway production and the movie, contains a final scene in which Sullivan and Keller sit on a porch swing and discuss the meaning of "love."

14. The play's insistence that the "disobedience" of disability includes a wayward form of language is reworked in Mark Medoff's play *Children of a Lesser God* (1980). In that play (and film), the deaf character battles to retain her right to use sign language, which she claims as her own, rather than having to learn and use oral speech, which is the normative form of communication of the nondisabled. The drama of the play consists in part in the tension surrounding her stubbornness and whether her teachers (and lover) will persuade her, or discipline her, into using the "obedient" normalized form of language instead of her chosen form.

15. See Howe's Annual Reports from 1842 to 1846. Howe commented that natural language was so universal that any American Indian, of any tribe, could walk into any school for the deaf and instantly understand what the residents were saying. On the sign language versus oral speech controversy in schools for the deaf in the nineteenth century, see particularly Douglas C. Baynton, "'A Silent Exile on this Earth': The Metaphorical Construction of Deafness in the Nineteenth Century," *American Quarterly* 44, 2 (June 1992): 216–43; Jack R. Gannon, *Deaf Heritage: A Narrative History of Deaf America* (Silver Springs, Md.: National Association for the Deaf, 1981), 1–92; Harlan Lane, *When the Mind Hears: A History of the Deaf* (New York: Vintage Books, 1989); Margret A. Winzer, *The History of Special Education: From Isolation to Integration* (Washington, D.C.: Gallaudet University Press, 1993).

16. These discussions of the benefits of arbitrary language pervade Howe's Annual Reports on Laura Bridgman from 1841 to 1846.

17. Howe's writings about this aspect of arbitrary language, especially in his discussions of Laura Bridgman's linguistic education, reflect his uneasiness about this separation. Adhering ultimately to the denominational view of language, Howe was reluctant to sever completely any connection between words and things, even while he insisted that arbitrary language alone could convey abstract words that did not depend on physical perception or material objects to generate meaning.

Bibliography

Address of the Trustees of the New England Institution for the Education of the Blind. Boston, 1833. Reprint 1873.

Alcott, Louisa May. "The Blind Lark." *St. Nicholas*, November 1886: 12–19.

——. *Little Women*. 1868. Garden City, New York: Literary Guild, 1950.

"The American Girl Who Won the Greatest Victory in All History." *New York American*, 21 October 1904: n. pag. Perkins Archives.

Anagnos, Michael, ed. *The Education of Laura D. Bridgman*. 1889. Boston, 1893.

Arnold, Matthew. *Culture and Anarchy*. 1869. New York: Chelsea House, 1983.

Artman, William and L. V. Hall, eds. *Beauties and Achievements of the Blind*. Auburn, N.Y.: Miller, Orton, and Mulligan, Stereotypers and Printers, 1854.

Atkinson, Brooks. "'Miracle Worker': Two Strong Minds and Two Strong Players." Review of *The Miracle Worker* by William Gibson. *New York Times*, 1 November 1959, Sec. II: 1.

——. "Theatre: Giver of Light." Review of *The Miracle Worker* by William Gibson. *New York Times*, 18 October 1959, Sec. II: 1.

Bassett, John E. *"A Heart of Ideality in My Realism" and Other Essays on Howells and Twain*. West Cornwall, Conn.: Locust Hill Press, 1991.

Baym, Nina. *Woman's Fiction: A Guide to Novels By and About Women in America, 1820–1870*. Ithaca, N.Y.: Cornell University Press, 1978.

Baynton, Douglas C. "'A Silent Exile on This Earth': The Metaphorical Construction of Deafness in the Nineteenth Century." *American Quarterly* 44, 2 (June 1992): 216–43.

Best, Harry. *Blindness and the Blind in the United States*. New York: Macmillan, 1934.

——. *Deafness and the Deaf in the United States*. New York: Macmillan, 1943.

Blackwell-Stratton, Marian, Mary Lou Breslin, Arlene Byrnne Mayerson, and Susan Bailey. "Smashing Icons: Disabled Women and the Disability and Women's Movements." In *Women with Disabilities*, ed. Michelle Fine and Adrienne Asch, 306–32. Philadelphia: Temple University Press, 1988.

Bly, Nellie. "Deaf, Dumb, and Blind." *New York World*, 17 February 1889: n. pag. Perkins Archives.

Bogdan, Robert. *Freak Show: Presenting Human Oddities for Amusement and Profit*. Chicago: University of Chicago Press, 1988.

Bower, Eli M. , ed. *The Handicapped in Literature: A Psychosocial Perspective*. Denver and London: Love Publishing Co., 1980.

Braddy, Nella. *Anne Sullivan Macy: The Story Behind Helen Keller*. New York: Doubleday, 1933.

Brooks, Van Wyck. *Helen Keller: Sketch for a Portrait*. New York: Dutton, 1956.

Brown, Gillian. *Domestic Individualism: Imagining Self in Nineteenth-Century America*. Berkeley: University of California Press, 1990.

Browne, Susan E., Debra Connors, and Nanci Stern, eds. *With the Power of Each Breath: A Disabled Women's Anthology*. Pittsburgh: Cleis Press, 1985.

Brustein, Robert. "Two for the Miracle." Review of *The Miracle Worker* by William Gibson. *New Republic*, 9 November 1959: 28–29.

Bulwer-Lytton, Edward. *The Last Days of Pompeii*. 1834. Reprint New York: Dodd, Mead, 1946.

Burnett, Frances Hodgson. *Little Lord Fauntleroy*. New York: Scribner's, 1886.

Carby, Hazel. *Reconstructing Womanhood: The Emergence of the Afro-American Woman Novelist*. New York: Oxford University Press, 1987.

Coates, Florence Earle. "Helen Keller with a Rose." *Century Magazine*, August 1905: 397.

Combe, George. *Education: Its Principles and Practice*. London: Macmillan and Co., 1879.

——. *Notes on the United States of North America During a Phrenological Visit in 1838–9-40*. Philadelphia: Carey and Hart, 1841.

Connors, Debra. "Disability, Sexism, and the Social Order." In *With the Power of Each Breath*, ed. Susan E. Browne, Debra Connors, and Nanci Stern, 92–107. Pittsburgh: Cleis Press, 1985.

Craik, Dinah Mulock. *John Halifax, Gentleman*. 1856. Reprint New York: E.P. Dutton and Co., 1906.

Cummins, Maria S. *The Lamplighter*. 1854. Reprint New Brunswick, N.J.: Rutgers University Press, 1988.

Cutsforth, Thomas D. *The Blind in School and Society: A Psychological Study*. 1933. Reprint New York: American Foundation for the Blind, 1951.

Davidson, Cathy. *Revolution and the Word: The Rise of the Novel in America*. New York: Oxford University Press, 1986.

Davies, John Dudley. *Phrenology: Fad and Science; A 19th-Century American Crusade*. New Haven, Conn.: Yale University Press, 1955.

Davis, Charles T. and Henry Louis Gates, Jr., eds. *The Slave's Narrative*. New York: Oxford University Press, 1985.

Davis, David Brion, ed. *Ante-Bellum Reform*. New York: Harper and Row, 1967.

Davis, Fannie Stearns. "Of Helen Keller." *Good Housekeeping*, June 1910: 746.

Davis, Lennard J. *The Disability Studies Reader*. New York: Routledge, 1996.

Day, Mary L. *Incidents in the Life of a Blind Girl*. Baltimore: James Young, 1859.

DeKroyft, Mrs. S. Helen. *Little Jakey*. New York: Hurd and Houghton, 1872.

——. *A Place in Thy Memory*. 1849. Reprint New York: John F. Trow, Printer and Stereotyper, 1864.

"Deliverance." *The Outlook*, 17 September 1919: 83.

Dickens, Charles. *American Notes and Pictures from Italy*. 1842. The Oxford Illustrated Dickens. New York: Oxford University Press, 1957; reprint 1987.

——. *Barnaby Rudge*. 1841. Reprint New York: Penguin Books, 1980.

——. "A Christmas Carol." 1843. *The Christmas Books*, vol. 1. New York: Penguin Books, 1971.

——. "The Cricket on the Hearth." 1846. *The Christmas Books*, vol. 2. New York: Penguin Books, 1971.

Diderot, Denis. *Lettre sur les aveugles*. In *Diderot's Early Philosophical Works*, ed. Margaret Jourdain, 89–104. London: Open Court Publishing, 1916.

"A Distinguished Lady." *Newsweek*, 26 March 1956: 104.

Dixon, J. M. *The Valley and the Shadow: Comprising the Experiences of a Blind Ex-Editor*. New York: Russell Brothers Publishing, 1868.

Elbert, Sarah. *A Hunger for Home: Louisa May Alcott's Place in American Culture*. New Brunswick, N.J.: Rutgers University Press, 1987.

Ellis, William T. "Helen Keller and Tommy Stringer." *St. Nicholas*, October 1897: 996–1000.

Farrell, Gabriel. *The Story of Blindness*. Cambridge, Mass.: Harvard University Press, 1956.

Fay, Edward Allen. "How Helen Keller Acquired Language." *American Annals of the Deaf* (April 1892): 138–59.

Fiedler, Leslie. *Freaks: Myths and Images of the Secret Self*. New York: Simon and Schuster, 1978.

——. *Love and Death in the American Novel*. New York: Dell, 1966.

Fine, Michelle and Adrienne Asch, eds. *Women with Disabilities: Essays in Psychology, Culture, and Politics*. Philadelphia: Temple University Press, 1988.

Finger, Anne. "Claiming All of Our Bodies: Reproductive Rights and Disability." In *With the Power of Each Breath*, ed. Susan E. Browne, Debra Connors, and Nanci Stern: 292–307. Philadelphia: Cleis Press, 1985.

Finlay, Martha. *Elsie Dinsmore*. 1867. Reprint New York: Dodd, Mead and Co., 1893.

Fisher, Philip. *Hard Facts: Setting and Form in the American Novel*. New York: Oxford University Press, 1985.

Frampton, Merle E. and Hugh Grant Rowell. *Education of the Handicapped*. Vol. 1, *History*. Yonkers-on-Hudson, N.Y.: World Book Co., 1938.

Gannon, Jack R. *Deaf Heritage: A Narrative History of Deaf America*. Silver Springs, Md: National Association for the Deaf, 1981.

Gates, Henry Louis Jr. Introduction to *Our Nig*, by Harriet Wilson. New York: Vintage Books, 1983.

Gibson, William. *The Miracle Worker*. New York: Knopf, 1957.

——. *The Miracle Worker and Monday After the Miracle*. Garden City, N.Y.: Doubleday, 1983.

Gilder, Richard Watson. "Of One Who Neither Sees Nor Hears (Helen Keller)." In *The Poems of Richard Watson Gilder*, 178–79. Boston: Houghton, 1908.

Gilman, Arthur. "Helen Keller at Cambridge." *Century Magazine*, January 1897: 473–75.

Gitter, Elizabeth. "Laura Bridgman and Little Nell." *Dickens Quarterly* 8, 2 (June 1991): 75–79.

Groce, Nora. *Everyone Here Spoke Sign Language: Hereditary Deafness on Martha's Vineyard*. Cambridge, Mass.: Harvard University Press, 1985.

Hale, Edward Everett. "Helen Keller." *The Outlook*, 6 December 1902: 830–31.

——. "Helen Keller's Life." *The Outlook*, 22 June 1907: 379–83.

Hall, Florence Howe. "Helen Keller." *St. Nicholas*, September 1889: 834–43.

Hannaford, Susan. *Living Outside Inside: A Disabled Woman's Experience: Towards a Social and Political Perspective*. Berkeley, Calif.: Canterbury Press, 1985.

Hart, James D. *The Popular Book: A History of America's Literary Taste.* Berkeley: University of California Press, 1950.

Haskell, Thomas L. "Capitalism and the Origins of the Humanitarian Sensibility, Part One." *American History Review* 90, 2 (April 1985): 339–61.

——. "Capitalism and the Origins of the Humanitarian Sensibility, Part Two." *American History Review* 90, 3 (June 1985): 547–66.

——. *The Emergence of Professional Social Science: The American Social Science Association and the Nineteenth-Century Crisis of Authority.* Urbana: University of Illinois Press, 1977.

Haüy, Valentin. *Essai sur l'éducation des aveugles.* Paris, 1786.

Hayes, Richard. "Images." Review of *The Miracle Worker* by William Gibson. *Commonweal*, 4 December 1959: 289.

"Helen Keller." *Lend a Hand Magazine*, March 1888: 137–46.

"Helen Keller Explains How She Unknowingly Plagiarized." *New York Herald*, 29 March 1903: n. pag. Perkins Archives.

"Helen Keller in Cambridge." *The Critic*, 14 November 1896: 303.

"Helen Keller's *Story of My Life.*" *Atlantic Monthly* (June 1903): 842–43.

Herndl, Diane Price. *Invalid Women: Figuring Feminine Illness in American Fiction and Culture, 1840–1940.* Chapel Hill: University of North Carolina Press, 1993.

Herrmann, Dorothy. *Helen Keller: A Life.* New York: Knopf, 1998.

Hershey, Laura. "False Advertising: Let's Stop Pity Campaigns for People with Disabilities." *Ms.* 5, 5 (March/April 1995): 96–97.

Hevey, David. *The Creatures Time Forgot: Photography and Disability Imagery.* London: Routledge, 1992.

Hewes, Henry. "The Miracle of Work." Review of *The Miracle Worker* by William Gibson. *Saturday Review*, 7 November 1959: 28.

Hillyer, Barbara. *Feminism and Disability.* Norman: University of Oklahoma Press, 1993.

"A Hit at Ten." Review of *The Miracle Worker* by William Gibson. *Newsweek*, 2 November 1959: 97.

Holmes, Oliver Wendell. "Over the Teacups." *Atlantic Monthly* (May 1890): 691–93.

Howe, Julia Ward. *Memoir of Dr. Howe.* Boston: Albert J. Wright, 1876.

——. *Reminiscences, 1819–1899.* Boston: Houghton, 1899.

Howe, Maud and Florence Howe Hall. *Laura Bridgman: Dr. Howe's Famous Pupil and What He Taught Her.* Boston: Little, Brown and Co., 1904.

Howe, Samuel Gridley. "The Education of the Blind." *New England Magazine*, March 1833.

——. Letter to Charles Dickens, 18 May 1868. Perkins Archives.

——. *The Letters and Journals of Samuel Gridley Howe.* Ed. Laura E. Richards. 2 vols. Boston: Dana Estes and Co., 1909.

——. *Remarks Upon the Education of Deaf Mutes.* Boston: Walker, Fuller and Co., 1866.

——. *Thoughts on Language: A Lecture Delivered Before the American Institute of Instruction.* Boston: William D. Ticknor, 1842.

Hume, David. *A Treatise of Human Nature.* Ed. L. A. Selby-Bigge and P. H. Nidditch. Oxford: Clarendon Press, 1978.

"In a Silent World." *Current Literature* (April 1903): 406.

"In Regard to Helen Keller." *The Critic*, 17 April 1897: 277.

Jacobs, Harriet. *Incidents in the Life of a Slave Girl*. 1861. Reprint Cambridge, Mass.: Harvard University Press, 1987.

Jastrow, Joseph. "Psychological Notes on Helen Kellar [sic]." *Psychological Review* 1 (1894): 356–62.

———. "The Story of Helen Keller." *The Dial*, 16 April 1903: 1–5.

Jordan, Judith V. "Empathy and the Mother-Daughter Relationship." In *Women's Growth in Connection: Writings from the Stone Center*, ed. Judith V. Jordan, Alexandra G. Kaplan, Jean Baker Miller, Irene P. Stiver, and Janet L. Surrey. New York: Guilford Press, 1991.

Jordan, Judith V., Alexandra G. Kaplan, Jean Baker Miller, Irene P. Stiver, and Janet L. Surrey, eds. *Women's Growth in Connection: Writings from the Stone Center.* New York: Guilford Press, 1991.

Kaplan, Fred. *Sacred Tears: Sentimentality in Victorian Literature.* Princeton, N.J.: Princeton University Press, 1987.

Kasson, Joy. "Narratives of the Female Body: *The Greek Slave.*" In *The Culture of Sentiment: Race, Gender, and Sentimentality in Nineteenth-Century America*, ed. Shirley Samuels, 172–90. New York: Oxford University Press, 1992.

Keith, Merton S. "Final Preparation for College." *Helen Keller Souvenir No.2, 1892–1899.* Washington D.C.: Volta Bureau, 1899: 34–59.

Keller, Helen. *Midstream: My Later Life.* New York: Doubleday, 1929.

———. *My Key of Life.* London: Isbister and Co., 1904.

———. *My Religion.* 1927. Reprint New York: Citadel Press, 1963.

———. *Out of the Dark: Essays, Letters, and Addresses on Physical and Social Vision.* New York: Doubleday, Page and Co., 1914.

———. "Sense and Sensibility." *Century Magazine*, February 1908: 566–77; March 1908: 773–83.

———. "Sister Mabel." *St. Nicholas*, August 1890: 892.

———. *The Story of My Life.* 1903. Reprint New York: Dell, 1974.

———. *Teacher: Anne Sullivan Macy.* Garden City, N.Y.: Doubleday, 1956.

———. *The World I Live In.* New York: Century Co., 1914.

Kent, Deborah. "In Search of a Heroine: Images of Women with Disabilities in Fiction and Drama." In *Women with Disabilities*, ed. Michelle Fine and Adrienne Asch, 90–110. Philadelphia: Temple University Press, 1988.

Klages, Mary. " 'More Wonderful Than Any Fiction': The Representation of Helen Keller." Ph.D. dissertation, Stanford University, 1989.

Kramer, Michael P. "The Study of Language and the American Renaissance: An Essay in Literary Historiography, Part One." *Emerson Society Quarterly* 34, 3 (1988): 207–27.

———. "The Study of Language and the American Renaissance: An Essay in Literary Historiography, Part Two." *Emerson Society Quarterly* 34, 4 (1988): 282–307.

Lamson, Mary Swift. *The Life and Education of Laura Dewey Bridgman: The Deaf, Dumb, and Blind Girl.* Boston: Houghton, 1878.

Lane, Harlan. *The Mask of Benevolence: Disabling the Deaf Community.* New York: Vintage Books, 1992.

——. *When the Mind Hears: A History of the Deaf.* New York: Vintage Books, 1989.

Langworthy, Jessica L. "Blindness in Fiction: A Study of the Attitude of Authors Toward Their Blind Characters." *Journal of Applied Psychology* 14, 3 (June 1930): 269–86.

Lash, Joseph P. *Helen and Teacher: The Story of Helen Keller and Anne Sullivan Macy.* New York: Delta/Seymour Lawrence, 1980.

"Laura Bridgman." *The Christian Observatory*, March 1847: 130–39.

"Laura Bridgman, the Deaf, Dumb, and Blind Child." *North American Review* (April 1841): 467–86.

"Laura Bridgman Teaching Oliver Caswell to Read." *Phrenological and Physiological Almanac*, 40–41. New York: Fowler and Wells Phrenological Cabinet, 1849.

"A Life of Joy." *Time*, 7 June 1968: 30.

"The Lounger." *The Critic* (June 1903): 494–95.

Lowenfeld, Berthold. *The Changing Status of the Blind: From Separation to Integration.* Springfield, Ill.: Charles C. Thomas, 1975.

Lukoff, Irving and Martha Whiteman. "Attitudes and Blindness: Components, Correlates, and Effects." Vocational Rehabilitation Administration, U.S. Department Of Health, Education, and Welfare Grant no. 835s, 1963. Quoted in Michael Monbeck, *The Meaning of Blindness: Attitudes Toward Blindness and Blind People*, 18. Bloomington: Indiana University Press, 1973.

Macy, John Albert. "Helen Keller's Critics." *Boston Transcript*, 27 May 1903: n. pag. Perkins Archives.

——. *The Spirit of American Literature.* New York: Doubleday, Page and Co., 1913.

Marshall, David. *The Surprising Effects of Sympathy: Marivaux, Diderot, Rousseau, and Mary Shelley.* Chicago: University of Chicago Press, 1988.

Matthews, Gwyneth Ferguson. *Voices from the Shadows: Women with Disabilities Speak Out.* Toronto: Women's Education Press, 1983.

Medoff, Mark. *Children of a Lesser God.* Clifton, N.J.: J. T. White, 1980.

"Miracles of Today." *Lend a Hand Magazine*, May 1893: 357–68.

"Miss Helen Keller on How Women Should Dress." *Boston Morning Post*, 23 February 1913: n. pag. Perkins Archives.

"Miss Keller's Autobiography." *The Independent*, 30 April 1903:1033–34.

Monbeck, Michael E. *The Meaning of Blindness: Attitudes Toward Blindness and Blind People* . Bloomington: Indiana University Press, 1973.

Mott, Frank Luther. *Golden Multitudes: The Story of Best Sellers in the United States.* New York: Macmillan, 1947.

Mullen, Harryette. "Runaway Tongue: Resistant Orality in *Uncle Tom's Cabin, Our Nig, Incidents in the Life of a Slave Girl*, and *Beloved.*" In *The Culture of Sentiment*, ed. Shirley Samuels, 244–64. New York: Oxford University Press, 1992.

Mulvey, Laura. "Visual Pleasure and Narrative Cinema." *Screen* 16, 3 (1975): 6–18.

"The New Pictures." *Time*, 12 July 1954: 90–92.

"New Plays on Broadway." Review of *The Miracle Worker* by William Gibson. *Time*, 2 November 1959: 30.

Olney, James. "'I Was Born': Slave Narratives, Their Status as Autobiography and as Literature." In *The Slave's Narrative*, ed. Charles T. Davis and Henry Louis Gates, Jr., 148–75. New York: Oxford University Press, 1985.

Paterson, Janet G. "The Blind in Fiction." Paper read at teachers' meeting of the Pennsylvania Institution for the Blind, 27 November 1905. Typescript, Perkins Archives.

Paulson, William R. *Enlightenment, Romanticism, and the Blind in France*. Princeton, N.J.: Princeton University Press, 1987.

Perry, Adeline G. "A Visit from Helen Keller." *St. Nicholas*, June 1892: 573–77.

Porter, Eleanor. *Pollyanna*. 1913. Reprint New York: Dell, 1986.

Proceedings at the Celebration of the One Hundredth Anniversary of the Birth of Dr. Samuel Gridley Howe, Nov. 11, 1901. Boston: Wright and Potter Printing Co., 1902.

"A Question Between Training and Genius." *The Mentor*, June 1899: n. pag. Perkins Archives.

Quimby, Neal F. *A Study of the Curriculum for Residential Schools for the Blind*. Collegeville, Pa.: The Independent Press, 1939.

Reid, Thomas. *Essays on the Active Powers of the Human Mind*. 1788. Reprint, ed. Baruch Brody. Cambridge, Mass.: MIT Press, 1969.

"The Religion of Helen Keller." *Current Literature* (December 1908): 645–48.

Rice, Alice Hegan. *Mrs. Wiggs of the Cabbage Patch*. 1901. Reprint Racine, Wis.: Whitman Publishing, 1962.

Richards, Laura E. *Samuel Gridley Howe*. New York: Appleton-Century, 1935.

Riegel, Robert E. "The Introduction of Phrenology to the United States." *American Historical Review*, 39 (1933–34): 73–78.

Robertson, Nan. "Broadway Slugging Match." Review of *The Miracle Worker* by William Gibson. *New York Times*, 20 December 1959, Sec.II: 5.

Rogow, Lee. "Miss Keller for Posterity." *Saturday Review*, 12 June 1954: 26.

Ross, Isabel. "The Extraordinary Story of Helen Keller." *Reader's Digest*, July 1950: 161–68.

Rothman, David. J. *The Discovery of the Asylum: Social Order and Disorder in the New Republic*. Boston: Little, Brown and Co., 1971.

Sacks, Oliver. *Seeing Voices: A Journey into the World of the Deaf*. Berkeley: University of California Press, 1989.

———. "To See and Not See." *New Yorker*, 10 May 1993: 59–73.

Samuels, Shirley, ed. *The Culture of Sentiment: Race, Gender, and Sentimentality in Nineteenth-Century America*. New York: Oxford University Press, 1992.

———. "The Identity of Slavery." In *The Culture of Sentiment*, ed. Samuels, 157–71. New York: Oxford University Press, 1992.

Sánchez-Eppler, Karen. "Bodily Bonds: The Intersecting Rhetorics of Feminism and Abolition." In *The Culture of Sentiment*, ed. Shirley Samuels, 92–114. New York: Oxford University Press, 1992.

———. *Touching Liberty: Abolition, Feminism, and the Politics of the Body*. Berkeley: University of California Press, 1993.

Schlossberg, Hattie. "Helen Keller: An Appreciation." *New York Call*, 4 May 1913: 15.

Schwartz, Harold. "Samuel Gridley Howe as Phrenologist." *American Historical Review* 57 (1951–52): 644–51.

———. *Samuel Gridley Howe: Social Reformer, 1801–1876*. Cambridge, Mass.: Harvard University Press, 1956.

Sidney, Margaret. *The Five Little Peppers and How They Grew*. 1881. Reprint Boston: Lathrop, Lee, and Shepard Co., 1909.

Sinister Wisdom 39 (Winter 1989–90).

Stearns, Carol Zosowitz and Peter N. Stearns. *Anger: The Struggle for Emotional Control in America's History*. Chicago: University of Chicago Press, 1986.

Stedman, Edmund Clarence. "Helen Keller." *The Poems of Edmund Clarence Stedman*, 450–51. Boston: Houghton, 1908.

Stern, Julia. "Excavating Genre in *Our Nig*." *American Literature* 67, 3 (September 1995): 439–59.

Stewart, Dugald. *Elements of the Philosophy of the Human Mind*. Vol. 3 of *The Collected Works of Dugald Stewart*, ed. Sir William Hamilton. Edinburgh: Thomas Constable, 1854.

Stewart, Susan. *On Longing: Narratives of the Miniature, the Gigantic, the Souvenir, the Collection*. Durham, N.C.: Duke University Press, 1994.

Stroup, Herbert. *Social Welfare Pioneers*. Chicago: Nelson-Hall, 1986.

Sutton, Estella V. "Helen Keller, the Deaf and Blind Phenomenon." *Education*, February 1894: 341–50.

Thomas, John L. "Romantic Reform in America, 1815–1865." In *Ante-Bellum Reform*, ed. David Brion Davis, 153–76. New York: Harper and Row, 1967.

Thomson, Rosemarie Garland. *Extraordinary Bodies: Figuring Physical Disability in American Culture and Literature*. New York: Columbia University Press, 1997.

——, ed. *Freakery: Cultural Spectacles of the Extraordinary Body*. New York: New York University Press, 1996.

——. "Redrawing the Boundaries of Feminist Disability Studies." *Feminist Studies* 20 (Fall 1994): 583–95.

Todd, Janet. *Sensibility: An Introduction*. London and New York: Methuen, 1986.

Tompkins, Jane. *Sensational Designs: The Cultural Work of American Fiction, 1790–1860*. New York: Oxford University Press, 1985.

Tomsich, John. *A Genteel Endeavor: American Culture and Politics in the Gilded Age*. Stanford, Calif: Stanford University Press, 1971.

Townsend, John Rowe. *Written for Children*. Harmondsworth, Middlesex: Penguin, 1983.

Trustees of the Perkins Institution and Massachusetts Asylum for the Blind. *Annual Reports*. 62 volumes. Boston, 1832–1893. Cited in the text as PR.

Twersky, Jacob. *Blindness in Literature: Examples of Depictions and Attitudes*. Research Series 3, New York: American Foundation for the Blind Publications, 1955.

Tynan, Kenneth. "Ireland Unvanquished." Review of *The Miracle Worker* by William Gibson. *New Yorker*, 31 October 1959: 132–34.

Van Cleve, John, and Barry Crouch. *A Place of Their Own: Creating the Deaf Community in America*. Washington, D.C.: Gallaudet University Press, 1989.

Walsh, Anthony A. "Phrenology and the Boston Medical Community in the 1830s." *Bulletin of the History of Medicine*, 50, 2 (1976): 261–73.

Walters, Ronald G. *American Reformers, 1815–1860*. New York: Hill and Wang, 1978.

Warner, Charles Dudley. "Editor's Study." *Harper's New Monthly Magazine*, May 1896: 962–64.

Weinberg, Joanna K. "Autonomy as a Different Voice: Women, Disability, and

Decisions." In *Women with Disabilities*, ed. Michelle Fine and Adrienne Asch, 269–96. Philadelphia: Temple University Press, 1988.

Wexler, Laura. "Tender Violence: Literary Eavesdropping, Domestic Fiction, and Educational Reform." In *The Culture of Sentiment*, ed. Shirley Samuels, 9–38. New York: Oxford University Press, 1992.

White, Barbara A. *Growing Up Female: Adolescent Girlhood in American Fiction*. Westport, Conn.: Greenwood Press, 1985.

White, Sallie Joy. "The Story of Helen Keller." *Wide Awake*, July 1888: 77–85.

Whitman, Mrs. Bernard. "Helen Keller." *Lend a Hand Magazine*, April 1889: 289–303.

"Who Is Stanislavsky?" Review of *The Miracle Worker* by William Gibson. *Time*, 21 December 1959: 46–8.

Wiggin, Kate Douglas. *The Birds' Christmas Carol*. 1887. Reprint Boston: Houghton Mifflin, 1914.

Williams, Raymond. *The Country and the City*. New York: Oxford University Press, 1973.

Willmuth, Mary and Lillian Holcomb, eds. *Women with Disabilities: Found Voices*. New York: Haworth Press, 1993.

Wilson, George S. "The Blind in Literature." In *Proceedings of the Eighteenth and Nineteenth Biennial Convention of the American Association of Instructors of the Blind, 1906–1908*, 7–16.

Wilson, Harriet. *Our Nig; or, Sketches from the Life of a Free Black, In a Two-Story White House, North: Showing That Slavery's Shadows Fall Even There*. 1859. Ed. Henry Louis Gates, Jr. New York: Vintage Books, 1983.

Winter, Kari J. *Subjects of Slavery, Agents of Change: Women and Power in Gothic Novels and Slave Narratives, 1790–1865*. Athens: University of Georgia Press, 1992.

Winzer, Margret A. *The History of Special Education: From Isolation to Integration*. Washington, D.C.: Gallaudet University Press, 1993.

Woolsey, Sarah Chauncey (Susan Coolidge, pseud.). *What Katy Did*. 1872. Reprint London: Andrew Dakers Ltd., n.d.

Wright, David. *Deafness: An Autobiography*. New York: HarperCollins, 1994.

Ziff, Larzer. *Writing in the New Nation: Prose, Print, and Politics in the Early United States*. New Haven, Conn.: Yale University Press, 1991.

Index

Acknowledgments

This book would not have been possible without the unstinting support of a host of people at several institutions. The project first blossomed, in a Stanford University doctoral dissertation, with the nurturing attention of Diane Wood Middlebrook, Barbara Charlesworth Gelpi, and David Halliburton, and with the invaluable assistance of the staff of the Rare Book Room in Green Library. Kenneth Stuckey, research librarian for the Perkins Institution for the Blind in Watertown, Massachusetts, provided unreserved access to extensive primary source materials. At the University of Colorado, the staff of the interlibrary loan program and Skip Hamilton, reference librarian for English and American literature, helped me track down other needed volumes. A Junior Faculty Development Award provided time for rewriting, and an Elizabeth Colwell Wiegers partial fellowship paid expenses for duplication and office equipment.

The editors of the University of Pennsylvania Press have been unfailingly patient and helpful. Jerome Singerman never lost enthusiasm for the project, though he waited long to see it finished, and Alison Anderson provided helpful suggestions in editing the final version. I'm also grateful to Jeffrey Robinson and Beth Robertson, my colleagues in the English Department at CU, for eagerly pitching the manuscript, in its very early stages, to Jerry Singerman.

Among other colleagues, John Stevenson and Marty Bickman provided moral as well as intellectual support for the project, as did the CU Women's Studies Work-in-Progress Group. The book has benefited greatly from the efforts of Suzanne Juhasz, my mentor and friend, who has supported me through all phases of my work with dedication, humor, and love.

Kelly Hurley, squid lover and bowler extraordinaire, traded my chapters for hers, ate burgers, and provided boundless affectionate encouragement and constructive criticism. Without her incisive comments, witty remarks, and loving friendship, this book would not exist. Lee Krauth, a.k.a. "The Great God Lee," also knows the value of a good swap. He got me through the final phases, under the pressures of a tenure deadline, by devoting an entire summer to helping me revise the manuscript, chapter by chapter, and by never failing to tell me his honest opinion. To these two generous and dear friends I owe more than I can say or repay.

My family, too, has contributed enormously to this project. My mother did not live to see its completion, but she saw its beginnings and read early drafts; she is the lay reader who became my ideal audience and who prevents me even now from falling into overly-academic jargon. I miss her intelligence and wit every day. My father and older sister, both authors themselves, have provided patient support, and have not asked too often when the book would finally be finished. My younger sister, Sally, has shown me that disability need not be a handicap to achievement; she remains the inspiration for my interest in disability studies. I'm happy to thank my daughter, Spencer, who considerately lost the race to see whether book or baby would be finished first. And with wonder and gratitude I thank my life partner, Tasha, whose unfailing love and unending belief in me have made everything possible.